AF394421

HOW TO THINK LIKE
AN ARTIST

For Emily and Joe

HOW TO THINK LIKE AN ARTIST

Painters and Sculptors Who Have Changed The Way We See The World

CATHERINE DAUNT

BLOOMSBURY CONTINUUM

LONDON · OXFORD · NEW YORK · NEW DELHI · SYDNEY

BLOOMSBURY CONTINUUM
Bloomsbury Publishing Plc
50 Bedford Square, London, WC1B 3DP, UK
Bloomsbury Publishing Ireland Limited
29 Earlsfort Terrace, Dublin 2, D02 AY28, Ireland

BLOOMSBURY, BLOOMSBURY CONTINUUM and the Diana logo
are trademarks of Bloomsbury Publishing Plc

First published in Great Britain 2026

A catalogue record for this book is available from the British Library

Library of Congress Cataloguing-in-Publication data has been applied for

ISBN: HB: 978-1-3994-2292-5; TPB: 978-1-3994-2293-2; eBook: 978-1-3994-2291-8;
ePDF: 978-1-3994-2288-8

2 4 6 8 10 9 7 5 3 1

Typeset by Lumina Datamatics Ltd
Printed and bound in Great Britain by Clays Ltd, Elcograf S.p.A

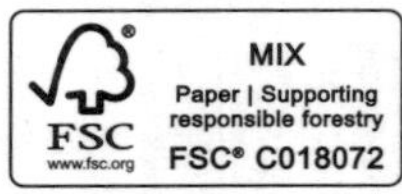

To find out more about our authors and books visit www.bloomsbury.com
and sign up for our newsletters
For product safety related questions contact productsafety@bloomsbury.com

CONTENTS

INTRODUCTION

This book is about art, about what used to be called Fine
Art, and is often referred to as the Visual Arts, although
not everything we define as art today can be described as
visual. It is about meaning and understanding, and the
ways in which art is essentially a medium of communication from one human to another, encompassing a human
interaction that can transcend temporal and geographical barriers. Art can be experienced in many ways but to
participate in this human interaction and to 'understand'
art, it helps to know what the artist was thinking. As an art
historian and curator, I am frequently faced with the question: *What does it mean?* It is a question that I often ask
myself when I look at art and a question I seek to answer
when I write a display label or give a talk. The answer is
never simple. First of all, what is meant by 'meaning'?
When faced with a painting on a wall or a sculpture on
a plinth, viewers often look for an explicit message. This
might be a story, a depiction of a specific event or thing, a
political argument, a metaphor or a moral lesson. In some
cases, that message will be there – although extra information may be required to understand it – but at other times
a single, explicit meaning cannot be derived, at least not
with any certainty. Examples of this might include abstract
art that is not intended to represent something tangible or
art that is made instinctively in an unpremeditated way so
that even the artist is surprised by the outcome. This kind

of art can still be understood, however, and meaning can still be found within it, although this is likely to require a deeper engagement with the context in which it was made, which includes knowledge of the artist's motivations. Of course, art *can* be experienced quite legitimately without this knowledge. Viewers can find pleasure, stimulation and personal meaning in a work of art without knowing anything about the artist or the circumstances in which it was made. We can project our own ideas onto art, draw our own conclusions and allow a work's beauty, humour, horror (delete as appropriate) to resonate in whatever way feels relevant and meaningful to us. As the contemporary Kenyan artist Wangechi Mutu expressed in an interview in 2008: 'You don't have to know everything that's going on in my mind to enjoy the work'.[1] But the frequency with which the question is asked – *What does it mean?* – suggests that for most people, there *is* a desire to understand an artist's intention and to gain an insight into what *was* in their mind when they produced the work.

All art involves the expression of an idea or set of ideas: a thought, a tale, an emotion, a view, an observation, a comment, a reflection, a concept. In my view, it is this central idea and the creative impulse of an artist to explore, realize and communicate it in some way, that truly defines art. Without this, it is just another thing. Nice to look at, perhaps, but hollow, without substance. As such, I believe that art relies on the human interaction that is inherent within. Art is intended to be seen or experienced, the ideas within it passed from person to person as part of a creative conversation about the world. And in order to fully participate in this conversation, it is necessary to reach beyond the physical object to its maker and the world in which they existed. It is this inherent communicative nature of art – its capacity to hold and transmit an idea – that to my mind not only defines something as art and gives it meaning but empowers art with the capacity to change the world. The American painter Mark Rothko understood this. In a lecture given in 1958, he described art as 'a communication about the world to someone else' and went on to suggest that 'After the world is convinced about this communication it changes. The world was never the same after Picasso or Miró. Theirs was a view of the world which transformed our vision of things.'[2] I agree that art can transform our vision of things, but in order to be convinced by what an artist is communicating, I believe we must try to understand what they are saying.

In this book I have attempted to provide some insights into how artists think and how their thoughts are expressed and communicated in their work. I have selected 30 artists as case studies, travelling the centuries and continents from ancient Greece to contemporary New York with stops in Renaissance Italy, Edo-period Japan and post-Revolution Mexico along the way. The idea is that learning about the lives of these artists, the circumstances in which they worked, and the way they approached their art, can help us to understand not only their specific output, but collectively can help us to understand the various ways that artists think. It goes without saying that no two artists think exactly alike; all are shaped and motivated by personal and external factors and no two sets of circumstances are the same. But there are some common threads to be found, not least a seemingly innate disposition to want to explore, reflect and comment upon the world. As a non-artist myself, my insight into how artists think comes primarily from their work, but also from their writings, their interviews, conversations with living artists and the work of many, many art historians and curators who have provided context and suggested ways of seeing and understanding in the form of books and exhibitions. Reflecting my own knowledge and training, the selection I have made skews towards Europe and North America and with one exception – the ancient Greek, Apelles – comprises artists who have been alive in the last 800 years. But I have attempted to be diverse in my choices with the aim of considering a broad range of experiences and approaches, and different ways of thinking. It has been my aim to highlight the varied and sometimes contradictory ways in which artists think and work, as well as the common threads and similarities.

The artists that I have chosen are well-known and celebrated; most are household names. To return to Rothko's comments, they are artists whose views of the world have in some ways 'transformed our vision of things'. Although organized chronologically, this book is not intended to be a history of art. The selection is more idiosyncratic, I hope, than simply a timeline of important artists and art movements. Beside which, as is being increasingly acknowledged, the history of art is more complicated than a single line along which one moves from artist to artist to find an unbroken progression of developments and new ideas, especially if it is to be understood in a global context. But of course, artists have always been influenced by what has come before, as well as the work of their contemporaries, in both positive and negative ways. Connections will therefore be made between the artists that I have selected, which will sometimes suggest a sense of progression as one artist learns from another and builds upon their ideas.

Finally, not all of the artists have been chosen because they are inspirational in the way that they think. All have, I believe, proven themselves to be important artists who have produced impactful works of art, but their characters, ideas and motivations, while important to understand, are not necessarily to be admired.

1

Apelles: The G.O.A.T.

The fact that the first artist I have chosen is an ancient Greek is something of a red herring. My decision to include Apelles is less about what we know about *his* art and how *he* thought and more about how he was viewed in later centuries when his fame set a template for what it meant to be an artist. During the Renaissance, when artists, writers and thinkers rediscovered and revered ancient Greek and Roman art and literature, the name Apelles became synonymous with great art. Although none of his works were known to survive, the Greek painter, who lived in the fourth century BCE, had become famous through the circulation of ancient texts that lauded his achievements, primarily Pliny the Elder's *Natural History* (77–79 CE). The Roman author's 37-volume encyclopaedia included several chapters on painting as part of an exploration of the uses of various minerals and metals, in which Apelles was described as having 'surpassed all the painters that preceded and all who were to come after him'.[3] This superlative assessment, which Pliny illustrated through numerous anecdotes as well as descriptions of Apelles' works, was supported by other ancient writers and became accepted by the educated elite in Europe from the fourteenth century. Writing on art from this point onward is riddled with references to Apelles, made by writers who had never seen his work. And many of the leading artists in Europe of this period and beyond, including Giotto, Albrecht Dürer, Titian and Goya, were compared to their ancient Greek predecessor, whose reputation was so high that it became the ultimate compliment to describe a painter as 'even greater than Apelles'.

Today, Pliny remains our richest source for details about Apelles' life and art. It is probable that Pliny's text, written nearly 400 years after Apelles died and reliant on earlier Greek histories, contains inaccuracies or at least embellishments, but it nevertheless provides us with an idea of who Apelles was and how he approached his art, and more importantly for my purposes here, the view that later artists had of him. Apelles was born in Colophon, Ionia (modern day Türkiye), probably in the first half of the fourth century BCE. He trained first in the ancient Ionian city of Ephesus and then in Sicyon, southern Greece, with the famous painter Pamphilus. Pamphilus was known for his academic approach to art, incorporating the study of arithmetic and geometry, which Apelles put into practice to achieve compositional balance in his paintings. After making his name as the best artist of the Sicyon school, Apelles went on to become court painter to both Philip II of Macedon (382–336 BCE) and Philip's son, Alexander the Great (356–323 BCE), a position that would have been reserved for a highly skilled artist. It is said by Pliny that Alexander, with whom Apelles developed a close relationship, would only be painted by Apelles. In addition to portraits of kings, members of their court and at least one self-portrait, Apelles painted allegorical and mythical subjects, including the work considered to be his masterpiece *Aphrodite Anadyomene*, which depicted the goddess Aphrodite (known to the Romans as Venus) rising from the sea and wringing water from her hair. This painting was taken to Rome for display where it was placed by the Emperor Augustus in the Temple dedicated to Julius Caesar. When the lower part of the picture became damaged, no artist could be found with the required skill to repair it.

Apelles' most celebrated qualities as an artist were his ability to replicate a subject in an extremely lifelike way, his ability to depict phenomena that most artists could not successfully capture in paint, such as thunder and lightning, and the ability to infuse his paintings with 'grace' or just the right degree of beauty. Apelles always knew, Pliny tells us, 'when to take his hand away from a picture'.[4] Almost all of Pliny's anecdotes about Apelles stress his skill in portraying a subject in such a realistic way that it was almost impossible to distinguish between his painting and the real thing. To illustrate this point, Pliny relates a story of a painting competition in which Apelles was involved, which required each artist to paint a horse. Fearing that the judging was not fair, Apelles suggested that horses be brought along to view the paintings. When this was done, the horses neighed only at Apelles' painting, believing they were looking at the real thing. Apelles' portraits of people were also considered to be incredibly lifelike, to the extent, it was said, that physiognomists could accurately depict a person's future or glean information about their past from his images alone. Perhaps his greatest skill, however, was not his ability to reproduce the tangible, but his ability to paint 'things that cannot be represented in pictures'.[5] In a famous portrait of Alexander the Great, the king is shown holding a thunderbolt, which Apelles painted in such a way to give the impression that the king's fingers and the thunderbolt were protruding from the space. Apelles' knowledge of perspective no doubt helped him to pull off this visual trick, but it is also likely that he used highlights and even darkened Alexander's complexion to make the thunderbolt stand out.

Apelles worked hard, practising every day, and striving to improve. To this end, he is said to have placed new paintings on display in a covered area at the front of his house and then watched the reactions of the passing public from a hidden spot. One time, a shoemaker passed and pointed out a problem with a sandal, which was missing a loop. Apelles took the criticism on board and corrected the image, although when the same man criticized his figure's leg the following day, he decided the feedback had gone too far and revealed himself in order to tell his cobbling critic to stick to the shoes. Nevertheless, it seems that Apelles was always willing to learn, including from other artists, whose skills he was happy to acknowledge and publicly praise. Pliny tells us that Apelles admired the artist Melanthius, for example, for his arrangement of figures, and Ascelpiodorus, an Athenian painter who he praised for his 'nicety of measurement'.[6] He was also a supporter of Protogenes, a painter based in Rhodes whose stalling career he invigorated by buying a number of his paintings and spreading the word that he intended to claim he had painted them himself. This lofty endorsement was enough to create a demand for Protogenes's paintings and raise his profile.

The relationship between Apelles and Protogenes became legendary, not because of Apelles' support for the lesser-known artist but because of the story behind their first meeting. According to Pliny, Apelles had heard about Protogenes's talents and so sailed to Rhodes to see his work. Finding Protogenes to be out when he arrived at his studio, he noticed a panel on an easel, blank but primed for painting. Asked by Protogenes's servant, an old woman, who she should say had called, Apelles took a brush and painted a single fine line across the panel. He told the woman to 'say it was this person', gesturing towards the line. When Protogenes returned and saw the panel, he knew that only Apelles could have painted such a fine line and in response, took a different colour and painted a finer line through the first. He then asked his servant to tell Apelles, should he return, that he had found the man he was looking for. Apelles did come back and, taking a third colour, painted an even finer line, which he knew couldn't be surpassed. When Protogenes saw what he had done, he reached the same conclusion and went to find Apelles to admit defeat. This story has been interpreted in many different ways; some understand it to mean that each line was divided vertically by the next until this was no longer possible, thus demonstrating the ability of each artist to paint an extremely thin line. It has also been suggested that Apelles' third line added a highlight, making the composition appear three dimensional, or that the two artists were in some way grappling with the problem of perspective. Whatever the meaning, the story indicates that Protogenes was almost as skilled as Apelles and that Apelles recognized and admired this. Their joint creation was clearly a thing of wonder, as the panel was afterwards put on public display where this simple, abstract but exquisite composition was 'more esteemed than any masterpiece'.[7]

We are led to understand by Pliny and others that Apelles was technically as well as creatively inventive. He innovated, for example, the use of a thin dark layer over his paintings, probably a kind of varnish, which protected them from dust and softened their colours. He was also inventive in finding creative solutions to technical problems. For example, he is said to have innovated the three-quarter profile position for a portrait of Antigonus Monophthalmos, Alexander's general, to hide his subject's missing eye. Apelles' ability to make portraits that showed his sitters at their strongest and most attractive no doubt contributed to the friendship that developed between himself and Alexander, who often visited Apelles in his studio. On one occasion, Pliny tells us, when Alexander was talking inexpertly about art in a loud voice, Apelles felt bold enough to ask the powerful ruler to be quiet because it was distracting his young assistants, who were finding it funny. It is possible that this story, like others that Pliny relates, is apocryphal, but even if this is the case, its telling indicates a mutual respect between the two men, providing a template of an ideal relationship between artist and patron. On another occasion, Alexander gave Apelles his favourite concubine, Campaspe, after he realized that the painter had fallen in love with her while painting her picture, a potentially dangerous situation in a royal court. But Apelles served his master well, fulfilling the role of the court artist by creating pictures that amplified the power of the ruler. In addition to his portrait of Alexander holding a thunderbolt, he produced allegorical images that presented him as triumphant and formidable.

Apelles died in Cos, probably in the early years of the third century BCE, while working on a second version of his painting of Aphrodite. His achievements as an artist live on not only in the written descriptions of his life and art, but in the great art that they inspired. By at least the end of the fifteenth century, artists were not only hoping to be compared to the Greek painter but were attempting to recreate his paintings. The *Calumny of Apelles*, in particular, caught the creative imagination. This allegorical work warning of the dangers of calumny, or slander, was known chiefly through a description written by the ancient Greek author Lucian of Samosata in the second century BCE. In his work *Slander*, Lucian claimed that Apelles had been accused of betraying Ptolemy, who intended to have him executed until someone came forth with the truth. Apelles created a painting in response, in which the personification of Calumny drags a half-naked man before a king amid a cast of characters that includes personifications of Ignorance, Suspicion, Treachery, Deceit and Truth. Lucian's description circulated widely in translations during the Renaissance and inspired numerous versions of the scene. The most famous example is a painting from about 1495 by Sandro Botticelli (Uffizi Museum, Florence), but the subject was also depicted by Andrea Mantegna, Raphael, Dürer, Pieter Bruegel the Elder and, in the seventeenth century, by Rembrandt. Scenes of Apelles' life also inspired artists including the eighteenth-century Italian Giovanni Battista Tiepolo, who painted *Alexander the Great and Campaspe in the Studio of Apelles* in around 1740. Stories about Apelles captured the artistic imagination. From the fourteenth century to the eighteenth, when the livelihood of artists still relied on royal courts and powerful patrons, artists strove to achieve the fame and stature of Apelles. But beyond that, they sought to think like him: to be creatively and technically brilliant, to create works of art that made viewers gasp and that surpassed all others, but to be humble and always willing to work hard and to learn, never becoming complacent, forever experimenting and innovating. What we know of Apelles tells us much about the aspirations and ambitions of many artists who followed him.

2

Giotto: Painting the Human Experience

There are some artists whose achievements are considered to be so great that apocryphal stories develop around them and their careers provide historical markers defining an era or marking a new direction in art. The fourteenth-century Florentine artist Giotto is one, just as Apelles, to whom Giotto was frequently compared, was another. Like Apelles, Giotto was celebrated for his ability to paint in an incredibly lifelike way, a skill that became a yardstick by which to measure greatness throughout the Renaissance. Yet my decision to include Giotto here is less to do with his capacity for tricking the eye and more to do with his ability to communicate human emotion and the influence that this had on Western art. I first understood this about Giotto when I visited Padua as a student. There, in around 1305, Giotto completed a fresco cycle in a newly built private chapel belonging to Enrico Scrovegni, a banker who had purchased some land on the site of an ancient Roman arena, where he had built a family palazzo. The adjoining chapel not only provided a private place of worship but was intended by Scrovegni as an attempt to atone for the sins of his father, Reginaldo, a notorious money lender who had been condemned by the Church. Hugely wealthy, in part due to his father's ill-gotten gains as well as his own money-lending activities, Scrovegni wanted to build something magnificent and to that end, hired Giotto to design and execute the painted decoration that was to cover the walls and ceiling of the interior. The frescoes survive and today are visited by many tourists, eager to experience this remarkable, all-encompassing painted scheme. As a student I marvelled at the vivid colours and attention to detail, but what caught my eye above all else, and what made the strongest impression on my memory, were the faces in the scenes depicting the life of Christ, particularly the mourners at the Crucifixion and lamentation, and the mothers protecting their children from King Herod's soldiers during the Massacre of the Innocents. Despite the stylized nature of the images to my contemporary eyes, the emotion on those faces – fear, grief and profound pain – seemed so real and human that the centuries between myself and the artist seemed to melt away.

The Scrovegni chapel was an important commission for Giotto, and today the cycle is one of the few surviving works of art known definitively to be by him. The paintings, which Giotto probably worked on for around two years with the aid of assistants, comprise a didactic yet spectacular series of scenes from the life of Christ, the Virgin Mary (to whom the chapel was dedicated) and Mary's parents Joachim and Anne. On the triumphal arch, which divides the main body of the church from the altar, God the Father instructs the Archangel Gabriel to give the news to Mary that she is to conceive, while at the opposite end of the chapel, a huge fresco of the Last Judgement fills the west wall. Roundels containing images of Christ, the Virgin, the four Evangelists and the prophets float on the ceiling above, against a deep blue that twinkles with gold stars. The experience of viewing the frescoes – both for fourteenth-century worshippers and the many tourists who visit today – is physically immersive, designed to encourage viewers to imagine themselves within the action and empathize with the figures portrayed. In addition to the relative realism of the images, helped by the clever use of perspective and illusionary techniques such as *trompe l'oeil* architectural elements, there is a profound humanity to the scenes due to Giotto's ability to depict dramatic tension and human feeling. Few who have experienced grief could fail to relate to the deep pain on the faces of the figures mourning Christ, while the horrors of the Last Judgement are likely to make anyone want to examine their behaviour on Earth. The cycle exemplifies Giotto's style and achievements as a painter who moved medieval art into a more lifelike and emotionally expressive phase, opening up the path to the Renaissance.

Giotto di Bondone was born in around 1267 in the village of Colle di Vespignano in the Mugello countryside near Florence, the son of a peasant farmer. His birthdate, like many details of his life, is uncertain, but there is evidence that he was around 70 when he died in 1337. During Giotto's life, Italy had yet to become a unified country and was divided into numerous regions and city-states that were governed independently, although each recognized the authority of Rome. Artists were usually part of a workshop and relied on commissions from the Church and other elite patrons to produce portraits or art for religious settings. Giotto was in his thirties when he painted the frescoes in Scrovegni's chapel and may have been working on high-profile commissions since the 1290s. According to the biographer Giorgio

Vasari, whose *Lives of the Most Excellent Painters, Sculptors, and Architects* was first published in 1550, Giotto demonstrated a talent for drawing as a child, which he practised by drawing the sheep that his father asked him to watch. In what is sadly almost certainly an apocryphal tale, Vasari describes how on one such occasion, Cimabue – the leading Florentine painter at the time – passed by and witnessed the ten-year-old Giotto sketching the animals with a pointed rock on a smooth, polished stone. Cimabue was astounded by the lifelike nature of the drawings and invited Giotto to join his workshop in Florence, subject to his father's approval.[8] Whatever the origins of their meeting, Giotto does seem to have trained with Cimabue – who must have become aware in some way of the younger artist's prodigious talents – and within a few decades Giotto had surpassed his master's achievements. As the poet Dante Alighieri put it in the *Divine Comedy*, probably written between 1308 and 1321: 'In painting Cimabue thought he held the field, and now it's Giotto they acclaim – the former only keeps a shadowed fame.'[9]

Giotto's output is subject to debate, but it is possible that one of his first projects was to contribute areas of the frescoes in the Basilica of St Francis in the Umbrian town of Assisi. Probably painted in the 1290s, the decoration in the Basilica was partly painted by Cimabue and his workshop, and partly by artists from elsewhere, including Rome. Some of the paintings bear similarities to Giotto's known works, including the frescoes in Padua, but his involvement remains uncertain. It is known, however, that in addition to working in both Florence and Padua, Giotto undertook commissions in Rome and Naples, producing both frescoes and paintings in tempera on wood.

It is likely that he was in Rome working for the papal court in around 1300, when Pope Boniface VIII proclaimed the first jubilee of the Roman Catholic Church (a holy year), suggesting that his skills were highly prized by this point. Later, from around 1328 to 1333, he was employed by King Robert I of Anjou at his court in Naples, where he occupied a powerful position and earned a large salary. The city of Florence then lured him back with what was probably an even larger sum of money, and in April 1334 appointed him chief surveyor and architect for the city. His duties in this role included working with the sculptor Andrea Pisano to design decorations for the bell tower of the city's cathedral. Few works survive that are firmly accepted as being by Giotto, but those that do include the *Ognissanti Maestà* (Uffizi Museum, Florence), a panel painting of the Virgin and Child produced for the Ognissanti (All Saints) church in Florence, probably in around 1300–05. It is also widely accepted that he painted partially surviving frescoes in the Basilica of Santa Croce in Florence before moving to Naples. Other works by Giotto and his workshop, mainly sections from altarpieces, survive in museums around the world including the National Gallery, London, the Louvre in Paris and the North Carolina Museum of Art in the USA.

Giotto's skills as an artist went far beyond his ability to draw sheep in a naturalistic way, although his ability to replicate the real world convincingly was certainly something for which he was highly celebrated. In a story that echoes that of Apelles and the horses, Vasari makes this point in another anecdote about his time with Cimabue, in which Giotto paints a fly on the nose of a figure painted by Cimabue, which 'looked so natural that when his master returned to continue his work, he tried more than once to drive the fly away with his hand, convinced that it was real.'[10] Giotto was born at the end of the Middle Ages, when the predominant style in European art was somewhat flat and rigid. His use of modelling to give the illusion of three dimensions was a radical approach. The bodies of his figures in the chapel in Padua, for example, which are shown from many different perspectives, can be clearly made out beneath their clothes, their contours seemingly causing the painted fabrics to stretch and crease as fabric truly does. Faces are individualized and framed with hair that curls and hangs and tufts. Water and veils appear transparent and translucent, while the bones and muscles can be made out beneath the skins of the sheep and cattle. Giotto's scenes in Padua are set in realistic environments with recognizable rocks and trees and contemporary-style buildings that give a real sense of space.

Throughout the Scrovegni series, as I have noted, there are profound moments of emotional connection and expression. In addition to the pain of the mourners at the Crucifixion, these include more tender moments, such as a touching kiss between Joachim and Anne, and the Virgin Mary's gentle settling of her newborn child. Beneath the human drama of these scenes, which were intended to reflect the real world, Giotto painted an allegorical series of Vices and Virtues, which runs around the lower section of the chapel. The Vices include Desperation in the form of a hanged woman, and Wrath, represented by a woman tearing her clothes from her chest in rage. The calmer, more aspirational Virtues include an angelic Hope and a benevolent Charity. Giotto painted these figures in *grisaille* (grey) against dark backgrounds to give the illusion that they were sculpted from stone. They were not only there to warn their viewers against the dangers of sin, but to demonstrate the artist's innovative and virtuosic abilities with a brush. Meanwhile, on the west wall, rivers of fire flush the naked damned into hell, while Christ sits serenely above with the souls he has saved arranged neatly to his right. All kinds of horrific punishments are meted out: money lenders are hanged by the strings of their purses, others are tortured by demons, while some are devoured by the devil himself. Hoping to avoid such a fate, Enrico Scrovegni had himself pictured to Christ's right, presenting a model of the chapel to the Virgin. The believability of Giotto's art no doubt helped his viewers to better understand and relate to the Christian stories and lessons contained within, while at the same time reminding them of the status and wealth of Scrovegni, the patron who had the means to commission the greatest artist of his day.

Giotto's own reputation could not have been higher when he died on 8 January 1337. He was given a lavish state funeral in Florence in recognition of his achievements. Less than two decades later, the poet Giovanni Boccaccio wrote in the *Decameron* that Giotto had 'brought back to light that art which had for many ages lain buried beneath the blunders of those who painted rather to delight the eyes of the ignorant than to satisfy the intelligence of the wise.'[11] The implication was that Giotto produced art that was closer to that of the ancient Greeks and Romans than it was to that of their medieval successors. This view – that Giotto had freed European art from the stiffness of the Middle Ages – has been echoed in writing about art ever since, including that of Leonardo da Vinci, who argued that art had stagnated before Giotto because painters had got into the habit of copying each other rather than innovating and taking the time to look at the world around them.[12] It was Giotto's drive to do something new, Leonardo argued, his inventiveness and his reconnection with the real world, that allowed him to move forward. Leonardo revered Giotto, and many other artists have cited him as a profound influence. Vincent van Gogh, for example, an artist predisposed to deep emotion, found himself deeply moved by Giotto, whom he described as '*always suffering* and always full of kindness and ardour as if he were already living in a world other than this.'[13] Henri Matisse described his visit to the Scrovegni Chapel in 1907 as a defining moment in his development as an artist, seeing in Giotto's frescoes the Italian artist's genius for communicating emotional expression. 'When I see the Giotto frescoes at Padua', he wrote in 1908, 'I do not trouble myself to recognize which scene of the life of Christ I have before me, but I immediately understand the feeling that emerges from it, for it is in the lines, the composition, the colour.'[14] Giotto's ability to portray the human experience not only resonated deeply with his contemporaries, but continues to resonate seven centuries on.

3

Hieronymus Bosch: (Poor) People are Terrible

While Giotto sought to communicate the Christian messages that he had been commissioned to depict by encouraging his viewers to empathize with the characters in his realistic scenes, Hieronymus Bosch (c.1450–1516) took a different tack. In his paintings, the Netherlandish artist used humour and fantasy to draw his viewers into a bizarre and tempting, yet dangerous, world, before admonishing them for viewing his scenes of pleasure and revelry with anything other than condemnation. But this approach to his art and his audience is not immediately clear to viewers today and can only be appreciated with some understanding of Bosch's worldview. Even compared to other art of his time, Bosch's images were idiosyncratic and unconventional, and his way of thinking particularly pessimistic. Bosch's best-known surviving work, for example, *The Garden of Earthly Delights*, is one of the strangest and most difficult to read paintings in European art history. Now in the Prado Museum in Madrid – where the shop is full of jaunty merchandise bearing brightly coloured details from the piece – the painting was relatively unusual for its time as a triptych that was probably made for a secular setting rather than as an altarpiece for a church. And as such, rather than being limited to Biblical subject matter, it includes images of everyday humans on Earth – although the Earth that Bosch presents on the huge central panel could not be further from the real world. In a cheerfully vivid palette of reds, greens, blues and pinks, the central scene depicts hundreds of naked people frolicking, cavorting, revelling, merry-making and pleasure-seeking in all manner of ways in a fantastical landscape with ponds and rivers, lush vegetation and giant fruit. It is a kind of paradise on Earth in which all humans, uninhibited, have succumbed to all of their desires. Some ride on giant birds or other beasts, some take bites from luscious berries or pluck apples from the trees. There is an orgiastic feel to the whole composition as bodies mix and mingle, tumble and twist, intertwine and embrace.

Indications for how to process this central scene can be found on the side panels, which follow the same visual language but are more overtly religious in their subject matter. On the left, we see God presenting Eve to Adam in the Garden of Eden. She is yet to unleash evil into the world by eating a forbidden apple, but there are signs of what is to come among the creatures around them, which include a cat with a mouse in its mouth and a lion eating a deer. On the right-hand panel, Bosch presents us with a terrible vision of hell where, among the demons and the damned, we are shown, among other oddities, a set of giant human ears with the blade of a knife protruding from between them, a man with a musical instrument up his backside and a pig dressed as a nun. The two outer panels are designed to close, covering the central panel, and on the outside, in grey monochrome, Bosch has painted an image of the newly created world inside a giant bubble, with God looking on. *The Garden of Earthly Delights* was probably commissioned by the aristocratic Engelbert II, Count of Nassau (1451–1504) for his palace of Coudenberg in Brussels between about 1495 and 1504. As early as July 1517, it was seen there by a visitor, who described it as 'bizarre' and clearly didn't quite know what to make of it.[15] The painting, and Bosch's art in general, has been delighting, troubling, amusing and puzzling viewers ever since. But Bosch's own intentions were clear and were much more serious than his art might today suggest.

Hieronymus Bosch grew up as Jeroen van Aken, surrounded by artists. His father Antonius was a painter, as were four of his paternal uncles, and it is likely that young Jeroen (the Dutch version of Jerome) trained in the family workshop. Painting was a paternal family tradition. Both Bosch's grandfather, Jan, and his great-grandfather, Thomas van Aken, had also made their living in this way. In 1404, Thomas had moved from the German city of Aachen to Nijmegen in the Duchy of Guelders in the Low Countries (a geographical region that included modern-day Netherlands, Belgium and Luxembourg). By about 1426, Thomas's son Jan was living in 's-Hertogenbosch, a town in the Duchy of Brabant, now part of the Netherlands and often shortened to 'Den Bosch'. Jeroen van Aken was born there in about 1450. From 1462, the family owned a house off the town's main square, the Markt, which included a workshop. It is not surprising, therefore, that Bosch and two of his brothers joined the family business. As an artist, he styled himself 'Hieronymus Bosch', probably to appeal to an educated elite by using the Latin version of his first name and emphasizing his identification with 's-Hertogenbosch rather than Aachen. Although a relatively lively commercial town, 's-Hertogenbosch was not a leading cultural centre and, unlike nearby Antwerp or Brussels, did not have a thriving artistic community, but Bosch nevertheless remained there for his whole life. This relative isolation almost certainly contributed to the highly idiosyncratic style for which he is known.

Remaining in his hometown, Bosch soon became a big fish in a small pond. In around 1486, he joined the Brotherhood of Our Lady, a local religious association that had thousands of members in the town and beyond, and through which Bosch obtained his earliest commissions, sometimes working alongside his father and other members of the family. Socially, however, his big break came in 1487 or 1488 when he was elevated to a 'sworn' rather than a 'common' member of the Brotherhood, an elite tier comprising members of the clergy, wealthy landowners and businessmen, magistrates, aristocrats and, as seems to have been the case with Bosch, those with exceptional skills. By this time, he was married to Aleid van de Meervenne, a woman from a relatively wealthy local family who owned several properties. The couple were living in a house on the north side of the Markt that Aleid had inherited from her grandfather and which was fancy enough for Bosch to host a dinner for the sworn members of the Brotherhood in 1488. There is no doubt that his position in the organization opened doors for Bosch and as such, it is likely that he waived his payment for much of the work that he undertook for them. This work included wings for an altarpiece featuring St John the Evangelist and St John the Baptist for their chapel in St John's Church, the main church in 's-Hertogenbosch. Painted between 1490 and 1495 and now held in the Gemäldegalerie, Berlin (*St John on Patmos*) and the Lázaro Galdiano Museum, Madrid (*Saint John the Baptist*), these paintings abound with allegorical details and contain elements of Bosch's strange visual world, including a bizarre spectacle-wearing lizard-bird-human-demon. Compared to his later work, however, the scenes are relatively conventional. Bosch also made other paintings for St John's Church, including an altarpiece depicting the *Creation of the World* for the high altar, probably commissioned by the church itself, and panels for other chapels depicting various Biblical scenes. Commissions also came from other patrons in the town, helped by the connections that he made through the fraternity.

Bosch's reputation grew throughout the 1490s, enabling him to make an impact beyond the small pond of 's-Hertogenbosch, despite remaining in the town. His fame was probably enhanced by the handful of engravings based on his paintings made by Alart du Hameel, a printmaker, goldsmith and architect who worked on the Brotherhood's chapel in St John's. Connections among the other sworn members are also likely to have spread the word about his skills and unique style, leading to the sale of his work to some high-profile patrons. In around 1494, for example, he painted a triptych on the theme of the Epiphany for the Antwerp civic leader Peeter Scheyve and his wife, Agnes Gramme (Prado, Madrid). Around this time, he also made work for various international clients, including several Spanish patrons living in Brabant as well as clients in Brussels and possibly Italy, and received his commission from the Count of Nassau. At some point, paintings by him also found their way into the possession of Margaret of

Austria, Duchess of Savoy (1480–1530) and, by the 1520s, the prominent Grimani family in Venice, among other elite collectors. His most prestigious commission, however, came from Philip the Fair, Duke of Burgundy (1478–1506), who visited 's-Hertogenbosch in 1504–1505 and, while there, ordered from Bosch a large altarpiece depicting the *Last Judgement*. He followed this with a commission for the *Temptation of St Anthony* the following year, which he presented to his father Maximilian, the future Holy Roman Emperor.

Like most painters of this period, Bosch took on a wide range of paid work, from painting altarpieces and other works on wooden panels, to adding colour to decorative objects and furniture, and designing stained-glass windows, metalwork and textiles. But the works for which he is best remembered are his panel paintings and specifically his triptychs. Bosch is known to have produced at least sixteen, eight of which survive intact. The earliest are relatively conventional in depicting subjects such as the *Adoration of the Magi* (about 1475, Metropolitan Museum of Art, New York) and *Ecce Homo*, the presentation of Christ to the crowd before his Crucifixion (same period, Städel Museum, Frankfurt). These early examples show the influence of Netherlandish painters of the preceding generations such as Jan van Eyck (died 1441) and Rogier van der Weyden (died 1464), as well as some of Bosch's contemporaries, such as the painter and printmaker Martin Schongauer (1448–91) from whom he borrowed some ideas. By the 1490s, however, Bosch's paintings had become notably unconventional in their subject matter and were populated by the kind of weird and fantastical creatures and imagery that filled the inner panels of *The Garden of Earthly Delights*. The central image of the *Haywain*, for example, a triptych from about 1512–15 (also now in the Prado), depicts a large haystack on a wagon being pulled by demons with the heads of various animals. Merrymakers sit on its top, including a canoodling couple and a trio enjoying some music. Beneath, members of the lower social classes pluck at the hay, jostling and tumbling as they try to get close, while a group of aristocrats follow on horses behind. Violence has broken out at various points amid the chaos, which is surveyed from the sky by a pitying Jesus. On the panel to the left, we again find ourselves in the Garden of Eden, where we follow Adam and Eve from their moment of creation to Eve's acceptance of the apple from the serpent and the couple's banishment from Paradise. In the background, rebel angels are cast down from heaven. On the right wing, we are presented with scenes of torture and destruction in hell. Unusually for the time, the painting on the back of the wings, which forms a full image when the wings are closed, is a secular scene: a travelling Everyman walking along the path of his life with his worldly belongings in a basket on his back. Portentous vignettes mark the route behind him, including an executioner's scaffold, a fellow traveller being robbed and a man playing some pipes. The image carries a moralizing message, warning against the various temptations that might lead to a less-than-virtuous life. Bosch was innovative in painting triptychs in which the exterior image was intended to be read alongside the images inside, and in his integration of religious imagery with scenes of life on Earth.

It is tempting today to look at Bosch and to read his work as light and playful. There is certainly humour in his depictions of naked figures performing handstands, oversized strawberries, fish-headed demons and objects protruding from human orifices. It is also tempting to view Bosch as a kind of proto-Surrealist, or a trippy eccentric on a wild ride. But to do so is to fundamentally misunderstand his intentions. Bosch's paintings were, in fact, deeply moralizing and pessimistic about human nature. He had a particularly dim view of the lower classes, depicting the poor and those on the margins of society, including sex workers and unskilled people, as being those most likely to succumb to sins such as gluttony, drunkenness, idleness and lewdness. These views were not uncommon for the time, however, and his emphasis on the individual to take responsibility for their actions was in keeping with contemporary Christian and humanist thought. In Bosch's view, the pleasure-seeking figures in the central panel of *The Garden of Earthly Delights* are behaving on Earth in a way that will condemn them to hell, showing no self-restraint or moderation and giving in to their base desires and urges. Bosch tells us this by first showing us the creation of the world on the exterior, then the introduction of human beings in the Garden of Eden, where sin will first be introduced, and finally, the terrible punishments of hell. In the *Haywain*, the hay is a symbol for earthly goods, which are all essentially transient (hay will soon wither away) but which humans nevertheless clamour to grab, leading to all manner of bad behaviour. A similar message is delivered on the outer panel, where we see the Everyman besieged by danger as he navigates his path through life, determined to hold on to his material possessions. Bosch created his weird and wonderful visual language to hold a mirror up to society and to warn against folly and sin. In doing so, he employed the tools of satire, a genre practised by ancient writers such as Horace and Juvenal and contemporary writers such as Sebastian Brant and Erasmus, in which aspects of society could be criticized through metaphor in a light-hearted way. In addition to the weirder elements, Bosch's metaphoric language included recognizable imagery that could be more readily understood by his viewers, including references to folk customs, festivals and proverbs. In his world, it seems almost inevitable that humans will disappoint and give in to temptation. The many owls that appear in his works, including *The Garden of Earthly Delights*, are to remind his viewers that they are always being watched and should behave accordingly.

Hieronymus Bosch died aged about 65 during the summer of 1516, from an infectious illness (possibly the plague) that had already claimed the lives of many others in the town. He was given a requiem mass at St John's Church in 's-Hertogenbosch, in the chapel of the Brotherhood of Our Lady. His work was collected enthusiastically in the sixteenth century by King Philip II of Spain, but it seems that within decades of his death, if not earlier, it was already being misunderstood and misinterpreted. For the last five centuries, people have seen what they have wanted to see in Bosch's art, perhaps unwilling to accept the pessimism and judgement in his messages.

4

Leonardo da Vinci: Re-presenting the World

The Louvre in Paris is the most visited museum in the world, attracting around 8.7 million people in 2024. Once inside, around three-quarters of these visitors make their way through the crowds to see an unfinished portrait painting, about 80 cm (31 in) in height, of a woman born in Florence in 1479. Painted by Leonardo da Vinci between 1503 and 1519, the portrait depicts Lisa Gherardini, the wife of Francesco del Giocondo, a silk merchant and important figure in the Florentine government. The painting is known as the *Mona Lisa* ('Mona', a contraction of 'Madonna', was a polite term for a woman in Florence at the time). It is probably the most famous painting in the world. For many years, the identity of the sitter was unknown, contributing to the sense of mystery around it. Viewers were intrigued by the woman's direct gaze and her 'enigmatic' half-smile, and drawn in by the hazy, dreamlike landscape behind her. The dramatic theft of the painting from the Louvre in 1911 increased the public's fascination with the work, which is today reflected in the countless references to the image in art and popular culture. There is no doubt, therefore, that the clamour to view the painting at the Louvre is driven in part by a desire to see this celebrity object and to share the physical space of something so well-known. But it is not just its fame that makes the painting so beguiling. In this 500-year-old portrait of a relatively modest figure, we see a real person with an inner life who appears to be communicating to us through the panel. It is not a stiff representation with a flat background, but a painting of a woman who appears to have relatable thoughts and emotions, set in a landscape that seems to recede into the distance as if we are looking out at it from a window. In viewing this painting, it is easy to feel that we are not only sharing space with the object, but with the woman depicted in the image and the environment in which she sits. We encounter her not just as she might have looked but as she might have *appeared* to us if we had met her in reality, and we encounter her world in a way that we might have experienced it alongside her. Leonardo sought not only to represent the world but to replicate the true experience of interacting with it.

Leonardo da Vinci is widely remembered as a universal genius, a man whose skills and knowledge extended far beyond his expertise as a visual artist. He was the ultimate embodiment of what has come to be known as a 'Renaissance man': a painter, draughtsman, sculptor, architect, designer, engineer, scientist, writer, theorist, cartographer, urban planner and military tactician. It is not surprising, therefore, that his surviving output as a painter is relatively small and he often took many years to complete a project, sometimes failing entirely. He was persistently distracted by other interests including an ambition to build a flying machine based on his analysis of bird flight and studies of the movement of water. But despite absorbing his time, Leonardo's insatiable desire to investigate, analyse and understand the world informed rather than competed with his art. His drawings and paintings were shaped by his comprehension of optics, mathematics, anatomy, topography and the natural world. Leonardo sought to represent the world in a way that made rational, scientific sense. As a result, he produced paintings and drawings that were immediately impactful and set standards for Western art for centuries.

Like Giotto, whom he greatly admired, Leonardo came from Tuscany and trained in Florence, a city with a rich artistic culture and heritage. He was born on 15 April 1452 near the hill town of Vinci. His mother, Caterina, whose last name is not known, was an unmarried farmer's daughter, and his father, Ser Piero da Vinci, was a notary (a lawyer specializing in drawing up documents and contracts). Leonardo grew up in the home of his paternal grandfather, Antonio di Ser da Vinci, while his father's business thrived in Florence. His parents did not marry each other: Caterina married another man in 1453 and Leonardo's father went on to marry four times. At some point in his youth, probably in the mid-1460s, Leonardo entered the studio of the leading Florentine artist Andrea del Verrocchio, who was primarily known as a sculptor but whose workshop took on a variety of commissions, as was typical for the time. Leonardo was a professional painter by at least 1472, when he became a member of the Company and Brotherhood of St Luke, an organization for the city's artists, and remained in Florence for the following decade. In addition to his skills as a painter and draughtsman, he clearly had a natural gift for mathematics, science and engineering, the study of which was encouraged for artists training in Florence. In the decades before Leonardo's birth, pioneering figures associated with the city, including Filippo Brunelleschi (1377–1446), the architect of the city's cathedral, and the humanist writer Leon Battista Alberti (1404–72), developed ideas about art that relied on optical and geometric principles. Both figures advocated the use of linear perspective, whereby the lines in a two-dimensional image are oriented to a single vanishing point to give the impression of three-dimensional forms receding into the distance. In his treatise *On Painting* (1435–6), Alberti also argued that the mathematical and scientific laws that govern the natural world should also be applied to art, an argument that Leonardo absorbed.

In the fifteenth and sixteenth centuries, most European artists made their living from individual sales and commissions, often taken on in collaboration with others. An alternative, however, was court employment, whereby an artist would work for a ruling family and receive a regular salary in return. Leonardo clearly favoured this option. In 1483, he wrote to Ludovico Sforza, the ruler of Milan, which was then an independent duchy. In his letter, he described himself as an expert in military engineering as well as a painter and sculptor, no doubt hoping to appeal to a ruler whose territory was constantly under threat. Leonardo was successful in gaining a role at Ludovico's court and remained in Milan until 1499 when the duchy was invaded by the French. After several years back in Florence – a republic, which could offer him work but not a court position – Leonardo returned to Milan seeking a role under the new French rulers. Between 1507 and 1512, he worked for the French king, Louis XII, and then remained in the city for another year following Sforza's return to power. At this point, he moved to Rome for three years to work for the papacy, another great ruling power, before accepting a role as court artist in France under Louis XII's successor, Francis I, who ascended the throne in 1515 and was a great patron of the arts. Leonardo spent his last years working for Francis and living in relative luxury at a château near Amboise in the Loire Valley in central France, where he died on 2 May 1519. Working as a court artist gave Leonardo prestige, but also some financial security, which was important for an artist who found it difficult to complete commissions. The role also allowed Leonardo to put into practice his engineering skills and the scientific knowledge that he gained through his relentless investigations. Additional tasks that he took on for his patrons included advising on military fortifications and weaponry, undertaking topographical surveys and designing spectacular stage sets for lavish events. In his final years, while working for Francis I, he developed unrealized plans for a new royal palace, which included formal gardens and a network of canals.

The *Mona Lisa* is just one of numerous works that Leonardo is known to have worked on intermittently for years. It was commissioned sometime between 1495, when Lisa Gherardini married Francesco del Giocondo, and October 1503, by which time we know Leonardo had made a start. At some point, however, he set the project aside, returning to it years later but never delivering it to the intended recipients. As a young painter in Florence, Leonardo had received commissions that he had also failed to complete, including a painting of the *Adoration of the Magi* (about 1483) for the altar in San Donato a Scopeto, which remains in an unfinished state in the Uffizi Museum in Florence. Around the same time, he also received the commission for one of his earliest surviving paintings, the *Virgin of the Rocks* (National Gallery, London), which he did complete but was many years in the making. The painting was part of a commission to provide paintings and decorative work for the chapel of the Confraternity of the Immaculate Conception in the church of San Francesco Grande in Milan, for which Leonardo received the contract in 1483 along with two other painters, half-brothers Evangelista and Ambrogio de' Predis. The *Virgin of the Rocks*, which depicts the Virgin Mary with the infant Christ, St John the Baptist and an angel within a rocky landscape, was intended to serve as the central image in the altarpiece. Leonardo probably made a start on it in the 1480s or 1490s, but only completed it and handed it over in 1508, 25 years after the original commission. The details are not all known, but at some point, it seems the three artists decided that they were not being paid enough for what they had produced for the chapel, and a lengthy and complicated legal battle ensued. In other cases, Leonardo abandoned projects altogether. In 1503, for example, he received a prestigious commission for a mural for the great council hall in Florence. Intending to commemorate the *Battle of Anghiari*, a Florentine victory over the Milanese in 1440, the mural progressed slowly and Leonardo left it partially finished in 1508. In addition, during his time at the Milanese court, he had failed to complete a large-scale equestrian monument for Ludovico Sforza to commemorate his father, Francesco Sforza, which had been many years in the planning and had got as far as the production of an enormous, full-size clay model.

As well as being distracted by his other interests, Leonardo's desire to be innovative in his art and experimental in terms of technique also caused him problems. For the *Battle of Anghiari*, for example, he used an unconventional mural-painting technique that led to issues with the paint drying. His experimental approach had also caused problems with his famous wall painting of the *Last Supper*, painted on the end wall of the refectory of Santa Maria delle Grazie, Milan in the 1490s, which was deteriorating only two decades later due to the paint not successfully adhering to the wall. In the case of the equestrian monument for Ludovico Sforza, which he began to work on in 1483, Leonardo's motivation to produce something ambitious and extreme in scale and form slowed down his process. He originally created an impractical design featuring a rearing horse, which proved impossible to realize, and then later spent a huge amount of time trying to work out how to cast his enormous clay maquette in bronze. Unfortunately, the metal set aside to finally produce the monument was sent by the duke to his father-in-law and counterpart in Ferrara, to use as artillery against the advancing French armies, and the clay model was destroyed by the invaders of Milan in 1499. Notwithstanding these failures, Leonardo approached every work of art as if it were a research project, putting many hours of thought and planning into it both before and during the execution. Much of this thinking was done through drawing and Leonardo's many surviving sketches and notebooks provide great insight into his thought processes and ideas. His drawings include quick sketches, more detailed observations from life and diagrammatic plans for engineering projects or mechanical inventions. He also made many notes alongside his drawings, almost always written backwards, from right to left. Leonardo's 'mirror writing' has been viewed by conspiracy theorists as evidence of covert activity, but it seems that as a left-hander, writing in this way was just more comfortable for him when he worked at speed. Around 4,100 sheets of paper containing drawings and notes by Leonardo survive around the world, which tell us that in addition to his art, Leonardo had many unfinished writing projects in progress, including an Alberti-style treatise on painting as well as works 'On Water', 'On the Flight of Birds', 'On the Human Body' and 'On the Elements of Machines'. Leonardo's brain was clearly teeming with knowledge and ideas, almost all of which involved an element of creativity and experimentation. It is no wonder, therefore, that so often he simply ran out of time.

The knowledge that Leonardo gained about the world came from direct observation, reading and empirical research, all of which informed his art. He used the information that he gathered from studying plants and rock formations in paintings such as the *Virgin of the Rocks*, in which the holy figures are situated in a natural environment. In an effort to understand human anatomy, Leonardo studied both live and dead bodies, dissecting at least one full corpse and multiple other body parts. In his surviving notes for his planned treatise *On Painting*, he advises all painters who wish to portray a human convincingly to study the human body in all its myriad forms. In his own efforts to depict humans convincingly, Leonardo also employed mathematical principles, as articulated in his famous drawing *Vitruvian Man*. The diagrammatic image, which depicts a human figure with outstretched limbs inside a square and circle, represents the theory of proportion espoused by the ancient Roman architect Vitruvius. According to the theory, most human bodies, and indeed all natural forms, follow a system of proportional dimensions. A man's full arm span is equal to his height, for example, while his hand is only a tenth of his height and his foot is a seventh. Leonardo also developed ways of painting that took into account the mechanics of the human eye and how we see. In his notes for *On Painting*, he wrote: 'Painting embraces all the ten functions of the eye; that is to say, darkness, light, body and colour, shape and location, distance and closeness, motion and rest.'[16] In his embrace of this, Leonardo developed an artistic technique known as *Sfumato*, meaning smoke, whereby softly lit areas of a composition are blended smoothly into the darker areas, creating slightly blurred transitions. Leonardo employed this technique for the *Mona Lisa*, in which he also sought to replicate the way in which objects and landscapes not only become smaller as they recede but lose clarity and colour. It was important to Leonardo that his paintings depicted not only what we see when we look at the world, but how we see it and experience it.

It was Leonardo da Vinci's ultimate goal to represent the natural world in paint, an art form that he considered to be greater than all others. In painting, he argued, the harmony that we experience in nature can be replicated and received by a viewer in a single moment rather than unfolding sequentially as it does in music. Nobody worked harder than Leonardo to replicate nature's harmony and it is the efforts that he devoted to this that infuse his paintings with the ineffable quality that still makes us want to find hidden secrets and magical meaning within them today.

5

Artemisia Gentileschi: Until her Work is Seen

It may not have escaped your notice that all of the artists I have discussed until now have been male. Artemisia Gentileschi, while not unique in her time as a professional woman artist, was unusual. She was highly accomplished and celebrated in her day, attracting prestigious commissions and achieving recognition as one of the leading Italian artists of her period, so my inclusion of her here is not tokenistic. However, it is primarily because she was a woman that I chose to include her. To understand the way that artists think, we must understand the way in which they experienced their world and there is no doubt that Gentileschi experienced the world in a different way to her male contemporaries. As I hope this chapter demonstrates, Gentileschi's art *was* shaped by her gender. It is true that she was a great artist and not just a great *woman* artist, but to ignore the perspective that her gender brought is to ignore an important aspect of her art.

The story of Susanna and the Elders was a popular subject in art in seventeenth-century Europe. Taken from the Greek additions to the Book of Daniel in the Old Testament (the Apocrypha), it centres around a young married woman, Susanna. One day, while bathing in the privacy of her own garden, two lascivious men spy on the young protagonist and then attempt to coerce her into sex. When she refuses, the men publicly accuse her of adultery and she is condemned to death. Her life is saved, however, when the accounts of the two men are found to be inconsistent. In art, this story is usually depicted at the point when Susanna is bathing, naked, and the men are either watching in secret or approaching. Ostensibly delivering a moralizing message, the subject had the potential to titillate, which no doubt helped to establish it as a staple among the art collections of the elite. Given its popularity, it is not surprising, therefore, that the young Artemisia Gentileschi chose to paint her own version in 1610, as she embarked on her career. In *her* version, the beautiful Susanna is on a bench, naked, a towel draped over her thigh, as the two men leer over her from behind. Her body twists as she turns her face away and raises her arms defensively across her exposed torso. Her brow is furrowed in anguish, her cheeks red and her left breast remains exposed. As the clothed, older men conspire above her, Susanna is left vulnerable and frightened. Gentileschi made this painting when she was only 17. Now in the collection of the Schloss Weißenstein Museum in Pommersfelden, Germany, it is the earliest painting she is known to have signed and dated. It is also her earliest version of this story, which she went on to depict numerous times. Gentileschi operated in an overwhelmingly male profession and made a name for herself as a history painter, a genre that includes biblical, mythological and literary subjects, as well as real moments from history. Her paintings therefore offer a rare female perspective through which to view stories that are usually retold to us by men. Gentileschi's Susanna is not merely an erotic subject; her scene is an exploration of shame, humiliation and abuse, in which we are encouraged to empathize with the preyed-upon young woman.

Artemisia Gentileschi was born in Rome on 8 July 1593. Her father, Orazio, was a painter from Tuscany who had moved to Rome as a child to live with his maternal uncle following the death of his father and at some point took his uncle's name, Gentileschi. When Artemisia was 12, her mother, Prudentia Montone, died in childbirth and she was required to take on the care of her four younger brothers. Despite these domestic responsibilities, her father recognized her potential and she was allowed to train in his workshop, apparently starting to paint around the age of 16. Unlike aspiring male artists who could attend life drawing classes and roam the city to view the myriad works of art that Rome had to offer, Gentileschi was unable to leave her father's house unchaperoned. She did have access to his paintings, however, as well as a collection of prints that he kept in his studio, and attending church provided an opportunity for her to see art beyond her immediate environment. Unsurprisingly, Gentileschi's early paintings are very close in style to those of her father, who was influenced by Caravaggio (1571–1610), an acquaintance and perhaps friend. Indeed, her early work was probably intended to look like her father's as Orazio was well-known in Rome and there was a relatively healthy market for his paintings. It wasn't until she was living in Florence, from around late 1612, that Gentileschi was really able to establish herself as an independent artist and move away stylistically from the art of her father, which her work ultimately surpassed. By the time she died in Naples in January 1654 or later, she had worked in Rome, Florence, Naples and London, and had made paintings for many elite patrons, including Cosimo II de' Medici, the Grand Duke of Tuscany (1590–1621) and Charles I of England (1600–49). She was known across Europe and her fame had been celebrated in poems and prints. Despite this, in the centuries following her death, Gentileschi's achievements were forgotten, buried beneath the male-centred narratives that art historians and dealers constructed and promoted. It has only been in recent years that her career has been reconstructed and surviving paintings that had become separated from her name have been firmly reattributed.

For the most part, Gentileschi painted subjects that were already popular and for which there was a proven demand. Susanna and the Elders was one such subject and the story of Judith and Holofernes was another. In this grisly tale, also from the Apocrypha, a Jewish widow called Judith saves her city from invading Assyrians by enticing their general, Holofernes, into her tent and cutting off his head when he falls into a drunken sleep. Gentileschi painted the brutal moment of decapitation in about 1612–13 and again a couple of years later, presenting Holofernes as naked and vulnerable on a bed as a strong and determined Judith violently cuts into his neck with a sword. Judith is aided in her gruesome task by her female servant, who holds Holofernes down. Blood floods on to the bedsheets and, in the second version, spurts outwards towards Judith. The moment is heightened by dramatic lighting, reminiscent of Caravaggio, that theatrically illuminates the figures and the bed but leaves the background in near darkness. Surviving in collections in Naples (the Capodimonte Museum) and Florence (the Uffizi), Gentileschi's two versions of the scene are very similar although some details have been changed, including the colour of Judith's dress from blue to yellow. Around the same time, Gentileschi also painted *Judith and her Maidservant* (about 1614–15), in which the two women are shown in the aftermath of the horrific act, with the head of Holofernes in a basket.

Gentileschi's dramatic and visceral treatment of the story owes a debt to Caravaggio's own painting of the subject, made in about 1599, as well as versions by her father. However, with knowledge of her biography, it is difficult to view her paintings without concluding that her own experiences informed her creative choices. In May 1611, while working in her father's home, Gentileschi was raped by the painter Agostino Tassi, a colleague of her father's whom Orazio had previously tasked with teaching Artemisia about perspective. Following the attack, Tassi led Artemisia to believe that he would marry her, a depressing but potentially reputation-saving conclusion, but by March 1612, almost a year later, he had failed to follow through on this promise. Indeed, it became clear that Tassi was already married so Orazio instigated legal proceedings against him for 'deflowering' his daughter. A seven-month trial followed, which must have been greatly traumatic and humiliating for Gentileschi. She was forced to describe the rape, which she had violently resisted, and endure accusations that she was promiscuous and had already lost her virginity. Perhaps most shockingly of all, she was forced to undergo a form of torture whereby a vice made of metal and rope called a 'sibille' was tightened around her fingers to test whether she was telling the truth. The surviving transcript of the trial records her cries of 'It's true, it's true, it's true'.[17] Eventually, Tassi was found guilty and exiled from Rome, although his punishment was never enforced. On 29 November, the day after Tassi's sentencing, Gentileschi married the Florentine apothecary and painter, Pierantonio Stiattesi, a union apparently arranged by her father, and moved with him to Florence.

Our detailed knowledge of Gentileschi's rape from the transcript of her trial, which is preserved in the state archives in Rome, both informs and potentially clouds our understanding of her paintings. It is tempting to view all of her dramatic female-centred paintings with this experience in mind, even her first *Susanna and the Elders*, made before the rape occurred. But there can be little doubt that such a violent and humiliating experience influenced both her character and her art, particularly her paintings of *Judith and Holofernes*, made so soon after the event. Judith's physical strength and resolve is surely, at least in part, an expression of Gentileschi's frustration and anger, a revenge fantasy in which she is able to overpower her attacker, a personal *cris de cœur*. Gentileschi was aware of the disadvantages she faced as a woman, and specifically as a woman artist. During Tassi's trial she described being forced to stay home – a measure Orazio took to keep her safe and preserve her reputation – as 'noxious for me' and later in her career she wrote in a letter to a patron that 'a woman's name raises doubts until her work is seen'.[18] But perhaps because of this, she became determined and thick-skinned, and succeeded in establishing an independent workshop in Florence and attracting influential patrons. In addition to the Medicis, she also produced work for Michelangelo Buonarroti the Younger, the great-nephew of the famous Michelangelo, who introduced her to the city's thriving cultural scene. It was also while in Florence that she learned to read and write, having been denied the chance to attend school as a girl, and in July 1616, she became the first woman to enter the prestigious Academy of the Arts of Drawing. But her life in Florence was not without great challenges. Between September 1613 and October 1618, Gentileschi gave birth to five children, three of whom died in infancy. A fourth, her son Cristofano (born 1615) died in 1620 aged four and a half, leaving only her daughter, Prudenzia, to survive into adulthood. In addition, money was a constant worry. Gentileschi was an over-spender and the dowry that her father had promised to pay following her marriage never fully materialized. As a result, she accrued a considerable amount of debt and, in February 1620, was forced to leave the city. Her move back to Rome was probably also due to rumours spreading of her passionate affair with the wealthy Florentine Francesco Maria Maringhi, which threatened to damage her reputation.

Following her time in Florence, Gentileschi spent seven years in Rome before moving to Venice and then Naples, the city in which she would die. Her return to Rome proved difficult to begin with due to the presence of Tassi and strained relations within her family. In 1621, however, Orazio left the city for Genoa, possibly to avoid competing with his successful daughter, and around two years later, Gentileschi's husband, Stiattesi, also disappeared from her life (although it is possible they were living apart at an earlier date). Alongside these changes in her personal life, Gentileschi attracted some new patrons including Fernando Afán de Ribera, 3rd Duke of Alcalá (1583–1637), whose patronage continued into her years in Naples where he was appointed Viceroy in 1629, and Cassiano dal Pozzo

(1588–1657), secretary to Cardinal Francesco Barberini (1597–1679), an important collector. She also became part of an artists' network that included the French painter Simon Vouet, who painted her portrait, and the Dutchman Gerrit van Honthorst, whose candle-lit scenes influenced her work. Following a successful three years in Venice, where she received prestigious commissions including one from King Philip IV of Spain, Gentileschi moved to Naples in 1630, then the largest city in Italy, probably to escape an outbreak of the plague in the north. She disliked living in Naples but continued to flourish as a painter and had a significant influence on the city's artists. Although she was based there until her death between 1654 and 1656, she travelled to England in 1638 at the request of her father who was engaged on the painted ceiling in the Great Hall of the Queen's House in Greenwich, with which she may have assisted. Orazio died in early 1639 but his daughter remained in London for the rest of the year and produced several paintings for the royal collection including *Self-Portrait as the Allegory of Painting (La Pittura)* (about 1638–9), an image of herself in action, with a brush in her raised right hand and her palette in her left. Gentileschi had always used herself as a model and throughout her career made numerous self-portraits, although for the most part she depicted herself in the guise of a figure from history, such as Saint Catherine of Alexandria, or an allegorical personification.

Artemisia Gentileschi did what she needed to do to be a successful artist in seventeenth-century Italy. She promoted herself by writing to patrons and supporters and produced self-portraits to ensure that her face, as well as her work, would hang in elite picture galleries around the world. She moved when she needed to, formed new alliances, friend-ships and networks, and was prepared to paint the subjects that her patrons desired, including female nudes. At the same time, Gentileschi surpassed many of her peers in producing visceral and emotionally profound paintings of great drama and empathy, in which female bodies appear sensual, vulnerable, terrified, subtly erotic and real. As art historians have recently rediscovered, she was one of the great artists of her age – one who painted from a woman's perspective with all the insight and experience that being a woman brought.

6

Rembrandt van Rijn: Things for Which There Are No Words

The lives of Artemisia Gentileschi and Rembrandt van Rijn coincide almost exactly, with only around a decade separating their births and deaths. There are similarities in the way they worked: both used themselves as models, both made use of dramatic lighting and chiaroscuro effects, and both relied primarily on commissions from private patrons to make a living. But there are also considerable differences. Whereas Gentileschi focused on history painting, Rembrandt was most in demand for his portraits and made images of everyday life and real people. In addition, Rembrandt's paintings were increasingly characterized by a loose style with visible brushstrokes, which makes Gentileschi's, and many other artists of the period appear mannered and somewhat old-fashioned. It is partly due to this quality in his art – echoed in his prints by the sketchy manner of his etchings – that Rembrandt's work seems to carry an emotional expressiveness that was new to Western art at the time, one that suggests a level of intimacy between the artist and the viewer. Indeed, to my mind, Rembrandt's art needs very little context for a viewer to feel a connection with the artist, to enter into conversation with him and to understand his thoughts and emotions. Almost all of what we need to know is on the canvas or the sheet of paper, and this is perhaps never more true than in his self-portraits, which become increasingly self-analytical and honest over the course of his career. Rembrandt is an artist's artist, but also an artist for everyone, whose innovations and ideas continue to resonate with both makers and viewers consistently, never falling out of fashion and never seeming irrelevant.

In around 1665, Rembrandt began work on a painting of himself looking out at the viewer, his head and body positioned slightly to his left, leaving half of his face in slight shadow. At the time, Rembrandt was nearing his sixtieth birthday and the years that had passed are evident. His brow bears a deep horizontal line, while his cheeks slide into jowls and then a double chin. His curly hair is white but remains thick and almost touches his shoulders. A white linen cap sits proudly on his head and he wears a working tabard, albeit one lined with fur. In his hands, he holds brushes, a palette and a long stick topped with a padded leather ball known as a mahlstick, a tool that painters used to keep their brush hand steady by holding it against the work. The wall behind him is blank except for two large circles, which are only partially visible. The entire image is painted in muted colours, primarily browns and a dark red, and the paint is applied thickly, loosely and fuzzily with visible brushstrokes. The meaning of the circles is not known, although it has been suggested they represent a world map showing the east and west as separate hemispheres (a convention at the time) or are an allusion to Rembrandt's profession and skill. By this point, Rembrandt had made his name as one of the greatest painters of his age but had also suffered failure and loss and learned much about the human condition. His experiences of life are reflected in the many self-portraits that he made over the years. Known as *Self-Portrait with Two Circles* and now hanging at Kenwood House in London, this late example is one of the most emotionally direct. In earlier pieces, he depicted himself in elaborate clothes and headwear, for example in *Self-Portrait with a Plumed Beret* (1629, Isabella Stewart Gardner Museum, Boston) and *Self-Portrait in Oriental Costume with Poodle* (1631–33, Petit Palais, Paris), or in the guise of an historical figure such as the Apostle Paul (1661, Rijksmuseum, Amsterdam). At times he used self-portraiture to try out expressions and poses, as in *Self-Portrait with Velvet Beret* (1634, Gemäldegalerie, Berlin), in which his head and upper body are slightly twisted, as if he has just turned towards the viewer, and his mouth is partially open as if about to speak. In one etching from 1630 he depicted himself laughing, while in another he looks worried, with knitted brow and wide eyes, his mouth forming the sound of an 'Oooooo'. But in his painting from 1665, he is himself: a successful painter, an old man, an artist in his final years. A work of self-promotion perhaps, but also one of honesty, for which he looked directly at himself in a mirror, while also looking out at us.

Rembrandt made many portraits. After moving to Amsterdam in 1631, he was soon flooded with commissions. But he also made many paintings, drawings and prints of other subjects, including paintings and etchings of biblical or mythological scenes, images of everyday life known as 'genre paintings', depictions of the Dutch landscape and portrait-like images of social types such as beggars, bearded men, children or figures in theatrical costumes. He was instrumental in popularizing the latter, which were known as *tronies*, in which the focus was on facial expression and character rather than individual identities.

Rembrandt was born on 15 July 1606 in Leiden, the second largest city in the Netherlands, centre of the country's cloth trade and a thriving hub of learning and culture. It was the early years of the Dutch Golden Age, a period in which the Netherlands moved towards independence from Spain, became increasingly rich and powerful due to increased international trade and colonization, and thrived in the areas of art and science. Rembrandt's father, Harmen Gerritsz van Rijn, was from a family of millers, and his mother, Neeltgen Willemsdr van Zuytbrouck, was the daughter of a baker. Rembrandt was the second youngest of ten children, three of whom died as infants. It seems he was identified as bright because in around 1616 he was sent to the city's Latin school to receive a classical education and then on to Leiden University in 1620, while one brother went into the family trade as a miller and another became a cobbler.

At some point in his childhood, Rembrandt set his sights on becoming an artist and began his training in around 1622, first with the Leiden painter Jacob Isaacsz van Swanenburg and then in Amsterdam where he took a six-month apprenticeship with the celebrated history painter Pieter Lastman. He decided against travelling to Italy to complete his training, as had become conventional for northern European artists, partly because Italian art was increasingly available to view in the Netherlands, and instead returned to Leiden in 1625. There, he established himself as an independent artist but worked closely with his friend and contemporary

Jan Lievens, with whom he shared resources and ideas. Rembrandt worked in Leiden until 1631, the year in which he received his first major commission from Amsterdam: a portrait of the merchant Nicolaes Ruts (Frick Museum, New York). By this point, he had begun to make his name with *tronies* – for which he sometimes used his parents as models – and history paintings such as *Parable of the Rich Man* (1627) and *Judas Returning the Thirty Pieces of Silver* (1629), in which he employed dramatic light effects. He had also become an accomplished printmaker, producing many etchings between 1629 and 1631. In Amsterdam, however, as the urban population grew richer, the demand was for painted portraits.

By 1631, Amsterdam was the largest port in northern Europe and home to many wealthy merchants and members of the professional classes. The Protestant Reformation of the sixteenth century had decreased demand for art in churches in the Netherlands, so artists now relied on private individuals and governments for work. Rembrandt initially lived with and worked for the art dealer Hendrick van Uylenburgh, who obtained commissions for him and whose cousin, Saskia van Uylenburgh, he married in 1634. It is probable that Van Uylenburgh facilitated Rembrandt's first major commission in the capital city: *The Anatomy Lesson of Professor Tulp* (1632). The painting, which survives in the Mauritshuis Museum in The Hague, is an oil on canvas group portrait made for the city's Surgeons' Guild. It depicts the titular surgeon teaching a group of young doctors by showing them the arm muscles of a corpse. The men gather round, eager to learn. All wear black or dark colours and have large white ruffs, while the professor, who has a lace collar, wears a wide-brimmed black hat. Each face has great character and expression, and their bodies are dynamic: one student leans forward for a closer look while another looks over his shoulder at an open book. The background is dark, but the faces and ruffs of the men are well lit, as is the grey-green skin of the corpse. The red inside the open arm provides a gruesome flash of strong colour. Rembrandt's ability to animate portraits and to give the impression of a real moment in time is one of his great contributions to the genre. In *The Shipbuilder and His Wife* (Royal Collection, London), a double portrait from 1633, the shipbuilder Jan Rijcksen is seen working at his desk, a measuring instrument in hand, while his wife, Griet Jans, rushes in to hand him a letter, steadying herself against the door. He is portrayed as important and professional while she is shown as attentive and dutiful. Despite this contrived gloss, the picture feels like a real moment in their lives.

Rembrandt made many portrait paintings and etchings during his years in Amsterdam. His most challenging commission, however, came in around 1640, by which time he had achieved great fame. In that year, or possibly 1641, he was commissioned to produce a large-scale group portrait for the Kloveniersdoelen, the headquarters of the civic militia in Amsterdam. The painting, which was completed in 1642 and is best-known today as *The Night Watch*, is a depiction of the militia company of Captain Frans Banninck Cocq and Lieutenant Willem van Ruytenburch. Measuring around 3.8 by 4.5 metres (12 ½ x 14 ¾ ft), it is a monumental image in which individual full-length portraits are carefully arranged into a lively, active scene. The captain, situated at the front, gestures with his left hand as if explaining something to his lieutenant. Both wear sumptuous, expensive clothes. Behind them, men stand in a variety of positions, looking in different directions and holding weapons at different angles to create a complex network of lines. The light-coloured dress of a young girl, the company's mascot, glows amid the mass of bodies. The painting was a success and contributed to Rembrandt's fame overseas.

In addition to official portraits made for his clients, Rembrandt continued to make self-portraits and portraits of his family members. He depicted his wife, Saskia, numerous times, from an affectionate drawing of her holding a flower that he made just after they got engaged, to more finished paintings and many drawings in between. He also made double portraits of himself with his wife, including a painting in which he casts them as characters from the biblical story of the Prodigal Son (about 1635, Gemäldegalerie Alte Meister, Dresden) and an etching from 1636 in which Rembrandt is seated at a table drawing and looking out towards the viewer (presumably into a mirror to capture himself) while Saskia sits supportively behind. The couple went through much together, including the loss of their first three children as babies. Their son, Titus, their only child to live to adulthood, was born in 1641. The following year, however, in June, Saskia died of tuberculosis, leaving Rembrandt distraught. His love for Saskia is clear from the many drawings that he made of her, which include images of her with her babies, in bed asleep and sick and dying. Rembrandt depicted bodies – particularly female bodies – in a natural and unidealized way. His images of nudes are fleshy, soft and unacademic. They appear real, not like Greek or Roman sculptures. Rembrandt was a great observer of people throughout his career and he built up an understanding of the human body and its myriad expressions, which informed his *tronies* and genre images as well as his portraits. His sketches of everyday life include children learning to walk, street-food sellers and beggars urinating in public, vignettes that sometimes made their way into his paintings and prints. Rembrandt also looked closely at the art of others, particularly via prints, which he collected and studied. Early in his career, he borrowed ideas from the Dutch artists Lucas van Leyden (c.1494–1533), Maarten van Heemskerck (1498–1574) and Jan van de Velde (1593–1641), and the great German painter-printmaker, Albrecht Dürer (1471–1528). His scenes of everyday life were inspired by his near-contemporary, the French printmaker Jacques Callot (1592–1635), and his biblical scenes of the 1630s owe a debt to the Flemish artist Peter Paul Rubens (1577–1640). In some cases, Rembrandt deliberately followed the style of another artist to appeal to a particular patron or group. He was aware, for example, that the work of Rubens and his Flemish contemporaries was popular with some elite collectors, including Prince Frederick Henry of Nassau, the Stadtholder of the Netherlands, from whom he received some commissions.

Rembrandt had a deep and wide-ranging knowledge of art history, as well as developments in contemporary art. Throughout the 1630s and 1640s, he assembled a large collection of art and 'curiosities', including natural history items and musical instruments. His somewhat compulsive collecting, however, combined with an economic down-turn in Amsterdam, soon created problems. Rembrandt had lived beyond his means and in 1656, he was forced to declare himself insolvent. By this time, he was living with a new partner, Hendrickje Stoffels, and she and Titus took over his business affairs. His collection had to be sold and the family were forced to move out of the house next door to Hendrick van Uylenburgh, which Rembrandt had bought in 1639. Despite this, Rembrandt's reputation as an artist was established and he continued to receive commissions. In 1656, for example, he received a prestigious commission to paint another anatomy lesson, resulting in a compelling but somewhat gruesome image of the physician Dr Deyman revealing a cadaver's brain (Amsterdam Museum).

Although he continued to work, Rembrandt withdrew from the world in his final years, becoming increasingly introspective. Hendrickje Stoffels died in July 1663 and in September 1669, Titus, newly married and with a pregnant wife, succumbed to the plague. Rembrandt died the following month on 4 October 1669. He remains one of the most celebrated European artists of all time, both for his technical innovations – which include his loose, rapid brushwork and use of an etching plate almost like a sketchbook – and the deep humanity in his work. In 1885, Vincent van Gogh wrote to his brother Theo that 'Rembrandt goes so deep into the mysterious that he says things for which there are no words in any language.'[19] Van Gogh particularly loved one of Rembrandt's later works, the painting of a couple known as the *Jewish Bride* (about 1665–9), which he saw in the Rijksmuseum in Amsterdam. The figures probably represent the Old Testament couple Isaac and Rebecca, although they may also depict a real couple whose identities have been lost. Created with paint so thick it is almost sculptural, the image portrays a tender moment between the couple as the man rests his hand on the woman's chest, as she lightly places hers on top. The reds and golds of their clothes and jewellery glisten and shimmer as they catch the light, while the dark browns of the background attempt to envelop them. Their expressions are sombre, although the man seems to carry a slight smile. The painting is enigmatic, the context uncertain, and yet the moment between the couple feels real and, as Van Gogh suggests, there is a magic to it for which there are no words.

7

William Hogarth: The First YBA

Now to England, a country known internationally in the sixteenth and seventeenth centuries for its literary heroes such as Chaucer and Shakespeare, but not generally for its leaders in the visual arts. Indeed, before the eighteenth century, many of the best-known artists working in England had been foreigners, including Hans Holbein the Younger, Anthony van Dyck and Sir Peter Lely. But then came Hogarth. Born in London on 10 November 1697, William Hogarth is best remembered for his modern moralizing tales, which played out in series in both painting and print. A lover of the theatre, Hogarth borrowed from the stage, using dramatic techniques such as choreographed set pieces and visual asides to help tell his stories. His love of drama even spilled over into the traditionally more static genre of portraiture to which he added lively touches and narrative moments. Hogarth was a Londoner through and through, remaining in the city for his whole life and finding endless inspiration in its culture and citizens at all levels of society, of which he could be very critical. Like Hieronymus Bosch, he used humour to deliver scathing attacks on human nature and to warn his viewers of the dangers of straying from a moral path. But Hogarth was less stern than Bosch, and also made images that were playful, cheeky and intended to delight or titillate, cannily being ready to adapt his output to suit his different audiences. Like Chaucer and Shakespeare and the contemporary British writers such as Henry Fielding with whom he was acquainted, Hogarth was a storyteller, albeit one whose stories play out in images rather than words.

Hogarth lived at a time of great change both for London and for the country as a whole. In 1707, the Acts of Union formally united England and Scotland to form the Kingdom of Great Britain. Over the following century, as trade and industry expanded and Britain's overseas territories increased, London became home to a growing middle class that sought entertainment in the form of the theatre, books, newspapers, art and shopping. At the same time, entrenched class divisions continued to cause social inequality, which was heightened by urbanization and the first waves of industrialization across the country. Hogarth was a painter and printmaker who made his name through observing contemporary life and reflecting it back to his audiences. Working at a time when there were decreasing opportunities for European artists to secure patronage from Church or State, he was shrewd in making art that appealed to different tastes and different groups within society, and he found new ways to control the distribution and sale of his work. As such, Hogarth's output was diverse and, while he is best known for his satirical paintings and prints, he also made portraits and group scenes, known as 'conversation pieces', as well as some history paintings. In both his art and his approach to the business of art, Hogarth challenged conventions by skewering elite connoisseurship, lobbying for copyright for artists, selling his prints directly, advertising his services in the printed press and adding moments of levity to traditionally serious genres. At the same time, like all good satirists, he was a social, political and cultural critic whose images not only tell *us*, many years later, about the world in which he lived, but which revealed truths to his contemporaries about their own lives, the lives of the people around them and the potential pitfalls that those lives might hold.

Hogarth's family were lower middle-class. His father, Richard Hogarth, was a schoolmaster who fell into debt after opening an unsuccessful coffee-house where customers were encouraged to speak Latin. His resultant incarceration in Fleet Prison seems to have engendered in his son a determination to achieve financial stability and independence. More immediately, Richard Hogarth's time in prison meant that William was unable to complete a university education and was instead apprenticed to Ellis Gamble, a silver plate engraver based in Leicester Fields (now Leicester Square), London from around 1714, with whom he learned to engrave metalwork and make prints. By 1720, Hogarth had established himself as an independent practitioner in this field, earning a living initially by producing printed items such as trade cards and small illustrations for books. He had bigger ambitions, however, and in 1720 enrolled at the newly founded St Martin's Lane Academy where he received a broader artistic training, which included life drawing classes. From 1724 he continued to develop his drawing skills at an academy run by leading English painter James Thornhill whose daughter Jane he went on to marry in 1729. In print, he began to make satires in 1721, first producing *South Sea Scheme* in response to a financial scandal in which speculation and corruption caused shares in the South Sea Company, a British joint-stock company, to rise rapidly only to crash in 1720, leaving many investors ruined. The print depicts a crowd gathered at the Monument in the City of London while various British archetypes ride a merry-go-round alongside, including a clergyman, a nobleman and a female sex-worker. Elsewhere in the scene, the Devil attacks a statue of Fortune with a scythe and the allegorical figures of Honour and Honesty are publicly whipped by Self Interest and Villainy. The Monument, which was actually built to commemorate the Great Fire of London of 1666, bears an inscription commemorating the destruction of London 'by the South Sea' in 1720. Hogarth followed this print with *The Lottery* in 1724, which satirized state-sponsored lottery schemes, and *The Bad Taste of the Town (Masquerades and Operas)*, which mocked an elite group of powerful figures led by Richard Boyle, 3rd Earl of Burlington, for their penchant for Palladian architecture and Italian masquerades. In each of these prints, the scene is explained by a lengthy inscription in English at the bottom of the page, helping audiences to make sense of Hogarth's somewhat complex imagery.

From the beginning of his career, storytelling was central to Hogarth's art. He was influenced in this by his love of the theatre, an art form that he often referenced directly in his work. In 1728, having recently taken up painting, Hogarth received several commissions to paint a scene from the first performance of John Gay's highly successful satirical play *The Beggar's Opera* at Lincoln's Inn. This resulted in numerous paintings produced between 1728 and 1731 depicting a moment of on-stage action as well as identifiable audience members. Hogarth was a frequent visitor to the theatre and was friendly with leading theatrical figures such as the actor

David Garrick, whose portrait he painted as Richard III in 1745 (Walker Art Gallery, Liverpool). His experience of the theatre no doubt contributed to the composition of his narrative scenes, in which figures are often seen mid-action and in which several plot threads unravel simultaneously. He even liked to add moments of drama to his portraits and conversation pieces, which were traditionally more static, sprinkling a touch of humour or suggesting an unfolding narrative. In his 1732 painting *The Cholmondeley Family* (private collection), for example, he depicts one of the children about to climb on a pile of books, adding life to the posed family scene, while his painting *The Graham Children* (1742, National Gallery, London) includes an excited cat eyeing up a frightened goldfinch in a cage.

Hogarth's knack for visual storytelling really came into its own when he began to tell moralizing stories in a series of paintings and prints. The first was *A Harlot's Progress*, a set of six paintings produced between 1729 and 1731 (now probably destroyed), which was followed by a printed version in 1732. In each of his moralizing series, we follow a flawed protagonist through various highs and lows. In *A Harlot's Progress*, the protagonist is a young woman called Moll Hackabout who arrives in London from York and, through various twists and turns of bad luck and bad judgement, is imprisoned for prostitution and dies from venereal disease. Each image is like a scene from a play, with the main characters in the foreground engaged in an action that moves the story along, and supporting characters behind and alongside. In the final image, set at Moll's funeral, we see a motley ensemble gathered behind and to the sides of the coffin, as if we, the audience, are watching them on a stage. Their interactions and expressions make clear that, for the most part, their grief is insincere, and their attentions are really focused on their own self-interests. Hogarth followed this series with *A Rake's Progress* (eight paintings, about 1733–5), which follows the story of Tom Rakewell, the heir of a rich merchant who leads an immoral life and ends up penniless and insane in London's Bethlem Hospital. By this point, Hogarth had mastered the art of visual storytelling so that the action could be followed with or without written inscriptions.

Hogarth was motivated to make *A Harlot's Progress* partly because he felt creatively frustrated by the group portraits that paid his bills. Throughout his career, he balanced the need to make money with his desire to make art that excited him and allowed him to innovate. He valued invention and had no interest in reproducing work in the manner of artists who came before him, which he considered to be 'little more than pouring water out of one vessel into another'.[20] Happily, *A Harlot's Progress* was very successful. He sold the prints by subscription, requiring half the payment of one guinea per set in advance and half on receipt. Perhaps scarred by the memories of his father's financial failures, from early in his career as an independent artist Hogarth had found ways to maximize the income from his work, which included publishing and selling his own prints rather than going through print sellers and dealers. In addition to adopting a subscription model, which guaranteed his income in advance, he practised innovative marketing techniques such as advertising his art in newspapers such as *The Daily Courant*. But despite his efforts to control his output, pirated sets of *A Harlot's Progress* began to appear shortly after the prints were released, which led Hogarth to campaign for an Act of Parliament that would protect artists from plagiarism. In 1735, he was one of several artists working in Britain to sign a petition leading to the Engravers' Copyright Act, legislation that prevented copies being made of engravings and similar works for a period of 14 years after they were published. Today in the UK, artists (and their estates) retain copyright of their work until 70 years after their death, which not only safeguards their ability to make a living from their work but also preserves their ability to control how their images are used. Plagiarism had been rife before the 1735 Act, which was an important step towards the protections that are in place today. In anticipation of its passing into law, Hogarth had held back his engravings of *A Rake's Progress*, only releasing the series on 25 June 1735, the day after the Act came into force.

Hogarth continued to make darkly humorous moralizing images in the 1740s and '50s, although his output remained diverse. In 1743, he produced *Marriage à la Mode*, another six-painting set (National Gallery, London) followed by engravings in 1745. In this series, Hogarth turned his gaze upon the fading aristocracy, specifically a financially irresponsible nobleman (the Earl of Squander) who is forced to arrange a union between his son and the daughter of a wealthy, socially aspirational Alderman. A disastrous marriage unfolds, full of excess, debt, vanity, adultery, prostitution and syphilis, resulting in the murder of the son (who has become Earl) by his wife's lover. Although Hogarth earned money from the sale of the paintings, the production of the prints was his main aim, for which the paintings served as a model and advertisement. Hogarth was a trained engraver but was unwilling to spend the time perfecting the craft to the levels expected by sophisticated audiences, to whom he marketed these prints, so he employed top-level French engravers to produce his plates. There was also a market, however, for less refined prints, which Hogarth found ways to exploit by producing more cheaply made engravings aimed at an audience who did not traditionally buy fine art. These works include *Industry and Idleness* (1747), a didactic series contrasting the fortunes of the hard-working Francis Goodchild with the lazy Thomas Idle, and *Beer Street* and *Gin Lane* (1751), which, through satire, warned about the evils of unregulated 'foreign' gin (first imported from the Netherlands in the 1690s) while promoting the consumption of wholesome, English beer. Hogarth also produced cheaply made prints that tapped into the widespread interest in true crime in London, with images of famous criminals and notorious figures such as *Simon Fraser, Lord Lovat* (1746), the Scottish nobleman who was executed for treason in 1747 for his role in a Jacobite rebellion.

Alongside his prints, Hogarth continued to paint conversation pieces and portraits and remained open to other genres, continuously adapting his output to suit as wide a range of clients as possible. Among his most celebrated portraits are his much-admired full-length portrait of his friend, Captain Thomas Coram, founder of the Foundling Hospital for orphaned children (1740, Foundling Museum, London), and his famous *Self-portrait with a Pug* (1745, Tate), in which he depicted himself with his pet dog, Trump. In 1747 he received his first commission for a history painting by Lincoln's Inn, one of London's Inns of Court, which resulted in *Paul Before Felix* (1748–51), after which engravings were also made. The following decade, in 1755, he received a rare religious commission, from the church of St Mary Redcliffe in Bristol, to paint a triptych for the altar, which he completed the following year. In stark contrast, throughout his career Hogarth occasionally made titillating paintings for patrons who sought work with a sexual theme, such as the pair *Before* and *After* (1730–31, Fitzwilliam Museum, Cambridge and the J. Paul Getty Museum, Los Angeles), depicting a couple before and after sex, and *Lady's Last Stake* (1759, Buffalo AKG Art Museum) in which a married woman who has gambled away her fortune considers having sex with a young army officer in order to win back her money.

Despite his flexibility in appealing to different consumer demands, Hogarth had strong views and a combative personality. His attacks on particular individuals and segments of society in his art, such as the Earl of Burlington's clique with *The Bad Taste of the Town*, earned him enemies, and he had detractors within the art world in London. When, in 1753, he published *The Analysis of Beauty*, his major work of art theory, he faced criticism from fellow artists including Joshua Reynolds and Paul Sandby, who responded with a satirical etching. Much of this criticism was related to friction that had developed in the art world between those seeking to set up a Royal Academy of Art (including Reynolds and Sandby) and those outside this group, including Hogarth. At other times, however, Hogarth worked with fellow artists towards a common goal, such as the Copyright Act in 1735, and the production of paintings to decorate the Foundling Hospital in 1745, which he coordinated. In 1757, Hogarth's achievements were recognized when he was appointed Sergeant-Painter to King George II, a position that brought him status and a handsome annual salary.

Hogarth died on 26 October 1764 at his home in Leicester Fields after which his wife continued to sell his prints. His art and his stories continue to resonate, as the absurdities, vanities and moral pitfalls of his age continue to feel relevant to a modern audience. Furthermore, the formula that Hogarth invented with his moralizing series established a framework for exploring the contemporary world that many artists continue to use today. In Britain alone, for example, artists such as David Hockney, Grayson Perry, Lubaina Himid and Yinka Shonibare have all appropriated Hogarth's moralizing series as a means of exploring the contemporary world. 'Hogarth was the first YBA', Shonibare has joked, referencing the Young British Artists, the notoriously subversive art movement of the 1990s.[21] Although tongue-in-cheek, his comparison also rings true. Hogarth *was* subversive. He was radical in his way. He was funny and his art was new, fresh and of its day. As such, it helped establish an artistic culture in Britain that paved the way for the likes of Damien Hirst, Sarah Lucas and Yinka Shonibare over two centuries later.

8

Francisco de Goya: Producing Monsters

The Spanish artist Francisco de Goya is also known for his use of satire, but his satirical images are altogether darker and more serious in tone than those of Hogarth. Indeed, towards the end of his life, Goya produced some of the most viscerally disturbing images in Western art history. Between 1810 and 1820, he made 82 etchings that were to form the series *The Disasters of War*, created in response to the period's bloody conflict between Spain and France, the consequences of which he witnessed first-hand as a resident of Madrid. In the series, which remained unpublished until 1863, 35 years after his death, Goya presents the viewer with an uncensored insight into the devastating effects of war. There are scenes of torture and executions, public humiliation, terror, starvation and corpses piled high and left to rot. The series brims with cruelty, death, horror and despair. Immediately after, between 1820 and 1823, Goya painted 14 frescoes on the interior walls of his country retreat in the hills outside Madrid. Collectively known as the *Black Paintings*, the frescoes are dark in both palette and mood. In one scene, inspired by an ancient myth, the Roman god Saturn devours his own son. With wild hair and staring eyes, an unhinged, naked Saturn clutches the headless, bloody body of his child as if it were a chunk of meat. The horror plays out against a dark, brooding background. In another painting from the series, a coven of witches gathers to worship the devil in the form of a goat and a third depicts a drowning dog. In terms of composition, the latter is the simplest and sparest of them all. Towards the bottom of the almost featureless composition in shades of ochre and brown, a dog's head sticks up above a dense mass of something deep and heavy, possibly quicksand. Nose in the air, the dog appears to be in distress. On a recent visit to the Prado in Madrid, where the frescoes hang in a windowless room having been transferred from wall to canvas in the 1870s, I found this painting to be the bleakest of the group. Stripped of its references to Goya's own society, to myth and legend, politics or war, the image is untethered and could have been made at any time in any place, including our own. Read as a metaphor, it seems to express a universal human experience: a dangerous force, oppression, depression, and the instinct to survive. Goya's precise intention is not known, but it seems clear to me as a viewer that he felt something like the weight that is dragging the dog down, and through his art, he was fighting to resist it.

The *Black Paintings* are often viewed as evidence of Goya's distressed psychological state during these later years and it is true that, particularly since the 1790s, he had been troubled both by personal matters and wider factors affecting Spain. He had survived, and indeed thrived, as an artist in Spain during one of the country's most tumultuous periods, adapting to the rules of three Spanish kings and a period of occupation by the French. Portraits of royals and aristocrats, however, did not provide the outlet that he needed to express the despair, anger, disillusionment and sadness that he sometimes felt. Private works such as *The Disasters of War* and the *Black Paintings* did. Darker, weirder subject matter entered Goya's work in around 1794 when he was recovering from a serious illness that had left him permanently deaf. During his period of recovery, he began to make small-scale paintings on tinplate in which his subject matter became more experimental and unconventional. His images of this period include the painting *Yard with Madmen* (1794, Meadows Museum, Dallas) as well as images of cannibals, criminals, a fire and a deluge. In a letter from 1794, Goya wrote of these works 'I have been able to include observations of subjects which in general are offered no place in commissioned work and in which there is no room for fantasy and invention', explaining that he had made them in order 'to occupy my imagination which has been painfully preoccupied with my illness'.[22] Around the same time, he began to make drawings of the world around him, including characters he had seen on the streets and vignettes of daily life, as well as images from his imagination, having previously used drawing primarily to make studies for works in other media. From this time, art became for Goya more than a means of making a living; it became a means of occupying his imagination, confronting his anxieties and expressing his emotions in a way that anticipates the modern period.

Goya lived a long life. He was born Francisco José Goya y Lucientes on 30 March 1746 in Fuendetodos, a village close to Zaragoza in the Spanish province of Aragon, and he died in Bordeaux, France on 16 April 1828 aged 82. He grew up in a lower-middle-class family in Zaragoza, where his father and brother worked as gilders and where he trained in the studio of José Luzán Martínez, initially developing his drawing skills by copying prints. After several years working on various small commissions for churches in Aragon, Goya spent two years in Italy between 1769 and 1771 and then moved to Madrid, Spain's capital, in 1775. He had been invited by the painter Anton Raphael Mengs to work for the Royal Tapestry Factory, a relatively lowly and low-paid role for which he was required to make preliminary drawings and cartoons for tapestries to furnish the various royal residences. Between 1775 and 1792, he produced 63 designs for tapestries, primarily light-hearted scenes of rural merry-making and leisure activities such as hunting (a pastime he loved), which became more inventive and meaningful as he grew in confidence. In his invoice for the *Picnic* (1776, Prado, Madrid), Goya emphasized that the cartoon was entirely his own design, which entitled him to be paid more and which signifies his ambition. In 1780, he was elected a member of the Royal Academy of Fine Arts of San Fernando in Madrid and five years later successfully lobbied for the position of Deputy Director of Painting, achieving the position of Director of Painting a decade later. In the 1780s, he also established himself as a leading portrait painter and received several prestigious commissions to produce religious paintings, including an altarpiece for the Basilica of San Francisco El Grande in Madrid (1781–3). Important early portrait commissions came from the First Secretary of State, José Moñino, Count of Floridablanca and the Infante Don Luis de Borbón, the king's brother. Goya went on to paint other important figures and their families, including King Charles III of Spain who reigned until 1788 and who appointed Goya as Court Painter in 1786. Charles III was a relatively enlightened and forward-thinking monarch, as was his successor Charles IV whose portrait Goya also painted and who promoted him to First Court Painter in 1799.

In 1793–4, Goya suffered the prolonged illness that led to his deafness, attributed by some to lead poisoning, a hazard faced by artists. His illness led to loss of income as he was unable to work on tapestry cartoons and was unavailable for commissions while in recovery, and his deafness brought him other challenges. In 1794, for example, he was forced to resign his teaching position at the Royal Academy due to the difficulties he now faced with communication. In a heart-rending letter to the Academic Secretary written on 5 April 1794, Goya described how his inability to hear a group of beginners 'led to general amusement among the boys and disruption of the class'.[23] His emotional health must also have been tested by the loss of six children and the numerous miscarriages he experienced with his wife, María Josefa Bayeu, whom he had married in 1773. Only their son Javier survived to adulthood. In addition, the world around him was consistently troubling and anxiety-making, and Goya seems to have become increasingly alive, in the 1790s, to the negative aspects of the society in which he lived. By 1797, having spent several years making drawings and small paintings that explored some of his observations and feelings, he conceived of the print project that would become *Los Caprichos* (the fantasies), a set of 80 etchings published in 1799 that satirized Spanish society. Lampooning those who held power, including aristocrats and clerics, and exposing cruelties and hypocrisies, the prints were accompanied by captions that helped to explain the message. In one plate (number 40), Goya takes aim at quack doctors by depicting a physician as a donkey tending to a patient, with the caption 'De que mal morira?' (Of what ill will he die?). In several of the prints, Goya explores his compatriots' attachment to superstitious practices, particularly witchcraft, and in others, he criticizes the institution of marriage and the insidiousness of the sex industry. The most famous plate from the series is number 43, an image of a man sleeping with his head on a desk, a discarded pen to the side, surrounded by creatures of the night: bats, owls and cats. The caption reads 'El sueño de la razon produce monstruos' (The sleep of reason produces monsters). It is an image of a nightmare, of the persistent and ever-present demons that loom larger when we fall asleep and that threaten to overcome us if we lose sight of rationality and sense.

Goya had made prints for sale since the late 1770s, when he produced a group of etchings after paintings by Diego Velázquez in the Royal Collection, but *Los Caprichos* was the first print project in which he really demonstrated his skills as a printmaker. During the course of working on the series, he learned the aquatint technique, which allowed him to produce wash-like areas of tone that could be varied to create shadow, depth and contrasts of light. The series also announced to the public the remarkable development in his imaginative creativity and increasingly unconventional imagery. No doubt concerned about the repercussions if his prints were considered to be critical of anyone in particular, Goya argued that his images were universal in their satire. The advertisement for the first edition of the series, printed in the *Diario de Madrid* on 6 February 1799, read: 'The author ... has selected from among the innumerable foibles and follies to be found in any civilized society, and from the common prejudices and deceitful practices which custom, ignorance or self-interest have allowed, those subjects which he feels to be the most suitable material for satire, and which, at the same time, stimulate the artist's imagination.'[24] The threat of the Inquisition, a judicial system put in place to combat both religious and political dissent, was still very real in Spain at this time, and Goya's criticism of the Church in particular could have attracted their attention. *Los Caprichos* was not commercially successful initially, but the series brought Goya attention overseas and it remains one of the greatest works of satire ever produced in Western art. Goya went on to produce several more celebrated print series including the *Disasters of War* (1810–20), *Tauromaquia* (1816, on the art of bullfighting), *Disparates* (absurdities or follies) (1816–24) and the lithographs, *Bulls of Bordeaux* (1825). In all of his prints, Goya marries imagination with reality. Even in his bullfighting scenes, which feature real-life fighters, moments of drama and daring are heightened to create suspense and wonder.

In 1808, King Ferdinand VII, who had inherited the throne that year, was forced to abdicate by the French and Joseph Bonaparte, brother of Napoleon, was installed on the throne. Four years later, a constitutional government was established in Spain and Joseph Bonaparte abdicated the throne in 1813. This led to the restoration the following year of Ferdinand VII, who revoked the constitution and reinstated both absolute monarchy and the Inquisition. The tumult of these years is reflected in Goya's oil painting *Allegory of the City Madrid* (1810, Museum of the History of Madrid), which initially included a portrait of Joseph Bonaparte in a medallion. In 1812, however, this portrait was painted out and replaced with the word 'Constitution', which was then reversed, reversed again and in 1814, painted over with a portrait of Ferdinand VII. It is little wonder that Goya's head was spinning. (Today, and since 1872, the medallion has borne the words 'DOS DE MAYO' (second of May), commemorating an uprising against the French in 1808.) In addition, during the years of the French occupation, Goya lost his wife in 1812 and Madrid experienced a terrible famine precipitated by the war. Living in the capital and working for the court, whose patronage he generally retained, Goya was painfully alive to the many political twists and turns that his country was subjected to, as well as the social and economic problems that they caused. Following the restoration of Ferdinand VII, with whom he was not politically aligned, Goya was questioned about his conduct during the French occupation, which led him in 1814 to produce the paintings *The Second of May 1808* and *The Third of May 1808* (both Prado), commemorating uprisings against the French, in order to confirm his loyalty. He was also ordered to appear before the Inquisition in 1815 to answer questions about his painting of a naked woman (*The Naked Maja*, 1795–1800, Prado), which belonged to the politician and collector Manuel de Godoy y Álvarez de Faria, but there is no evidence that this came to anything.

Goya purchased the house in which he was to paint the *Black Paintings* in February 1819. Coincidentally, it was already known as the Quinta del Sordo, meaning 'Deaf man's country house'. Once again, he suffered a period of serious illness that year, possibly yellow fever, of which there was an epidemic in Spain. He documented his serious condition in the painting *Self-portrait with Dr. Arrieta* (1820, Minneapolis Institute of Art), which was also a tribute to his friend and physician. In 1824, as Ferdinand consolidated his power, Goya gained permission to travel to France for health reasons, leaving his house and its paintings to his grandson, Mariano Goya y Goicoechea (1806–74). He spent the last four years of his life in Bordeaux and died in 1828 having produced around 700 paintings, 900 drawings and about 300 prints. His art chronicled and commented upon Spanish society during a period of great upheaval, and also revealed much about his own life, his psychological and physical struggles and, more broadly, the human condition.

9

Katsushika Hokusai: Old Man Mad About Art

The Japanese artist Katsushika Hokusai, like Goya, lived a long life and was incredibly prolific. By the time he died on 10 May 1849, he had produced over 300 colour prints, at least 1,000 paintings and hundreds of illustrated books and drawings. But despite this vast output, he always believed that he could be better. As an 89-year-old on his deathbed, he is reported to have said 'If heaven will afford me five more years of life, then I'll manage to become a true artist.'[25] Hokusai's ambitions also extended to his subject matter. He refused to limit himself to what he knew and had experienced and allowed himself to portray fantastical worlds, places he had never visited and creatures he had never seen, basing his images not only on his own observations but on his imagination. Throughout his life, Hokusai worked relentlessly, depicting a vast range of subjects, both real and imagined, with the aim of producing art that would appeal to as wide an audience as possible. He depicted places that he knew well, such as Mount Fuji, which appears in some of his most famous prints, as well as more distant or fantastical places.

Born on 31 October 1760 in the city of Edo (now Tokyo), Hokusai lived at a time when Japan was closed to the rest of the world and Japanese citizens had very little contact with people from other countries, but he allowed his mind to go beyond these physical barriers. In addition to his relentless creativity, he was innovative and inventive, incorporating new ideas into Japanese art, such as the use of a European-style deep perspective, while also drawing on traditions from his own country and from China. His stylistic developments are epitomized in well-known works such as the colour woodblock print *Under the Wave off Kanagawa* (1831, best known as *The Great Wave*), which he made in his seventies as part of the series *Thirty-Six Views of Mount Fuji*. As he grew older, his drive to create seems to have increased, and at the end of his life, he wanted nothing more than to extend his years. He drew every day and was constantly moving, driven by a frenetic energy and perpetual momentum, which also saw him move house over 90 times. Over the course of his life he used at least 30 different names, towards the end calling himself Gakyo Rojin Manji, meaning 'The Old Man Mad About Art'.

Hokusai began to draw aged six, initially depicting animals and plants. Born in the Honjo Warigesui area of Edo, he was adopted aged three by a mirror-maker called Nakajima Ise, who worked for the court of the ruling shogun. Hokusai grew up surrounded by craftsmen and in his mid-teens he was apprenticed to a woodblock carver. Woodblock printmaking involved several figures: the publisher, the artist (who produced the design as a drawing), the block carver and the printer. Later, as an established artist, Hokusai produced designs to pass to a specialist carver in the form of 'block-ready' drawings, but this apprenticeship would have given him a valuable insight into the more artisanal stage of woodblock printmaking. Prior to this, Hokusai also gained a familiarity with printed books, another art form on which he would have a great impact, while working from the age of 12 as a delivery boy for a bookshop. In 1777, Hokusai entered the studio of Katsukawa Shunshō, a master in the *ukiyo-e* style of art. *Ukiyo-e*, which translates as 'Pictures of the floating world', comprised images of everyday Japan including the landscape and popular subjects such as 'female beauties' (or courtesans), Kabuki theatre actors and sumo wrestlers.

In 1778, under the name of Shunrō, Hokusai began to make independent prints, specializing in images of actors. By the mid-1790s, he had left the Katsukawa studio and changed his name to Sōri after the painter Tawaraya Sōri, whose decorative 'Rinpa'-style paintings, characterized by references to the natural world, had a particular influence on him at the time. During this period, Hokusai made a living by producing designs for different types of prints such as picture calendars and single-sheet woodblock prints, including images of beautiful women. In addition, his interest in literature and contact with writers and publishers led to numerous collaborations on illustrated books. He was also a prolific writer himself, producing works of fiction, comic poetry, a treatise on colour and numerous other texts. In his youth he frequented literary clubs and also staged playful public performances to advertise his art. Such events involved the creation of enormous paintings, up to 200 metres (650 ft) in length, which Hokusai would paint in front of an audience using a brush, a bucket of ink and large sheets of paper. On one famous occasion in around 1807, when Hokusai was called to paint in front of the shogun Tokugawa Ienari (reigned 1787–1837), Hokusai drew a band of blue along a long sheet of paper and then produced a chicken, which he let run around the paper after dipping its feet in red ink. He titled the resulting work *Autumn Leaves on the Tatsuta River*.

Hokusai began to use the name by which he is best known today – Katsushika Hokusai – in 1807 when he was in his mid-forties. The name 'Hokusai', meaning 'North [Star] studio', reflected his personal identification with the North Star. Hokusai was committed to Nichiren Buddhism, a branch of the religion based on the teachings of the Japanese monk Nichiren Daishonin (1222–82), and was devoted to Bodhisattva Myōken, a deity associated with the star. Hokusai's faith was important to him throughout his life but increased as he grew older. His later name changes also referenced his beliefs and personal spiritual journey. In 1813, for example, he began to use the name Taito, meaning 'Receiving the Big Dipper' or 'Star-blessed'. Again, this was a nod to the North Star, his guiding light, which he believed had saved his life when he was struck by lightning aged 50 in 1810. In 1820, Hokusai assumed the name Iitsu, meaning to 'become one' or 'one again', in recognition of having reached the age of 60 and the beginning of his life's second cycle, according to East Asian beliefs. As an older man, Hokusai also developed a spiritual identification with Mount Fuji, the highest mountain in Japan, which had long been considered a sacred site. The mountain was to inspire *Thirty-Six Views of Mount Fuji*, his best-known print series, which he produced between about 1829 and 1833. By this point in his seventies, Hokusai put into practice in this series everything that he had learned about composition, perspective, colour and the representation of nature from his study of Japanese, Chinese and some Western art. The prints depict the sacred site from numerous viewpoints, in different weathers and with various details incorporated that provide an insight into nineteenth-century Japan. In some scenes, the mountain is foregrounded, such as *Fine Wind, Clear Morning* (or *Red Fuji*), in which its distinctive shape glows red against a bright blue but cloudy sky. In others, the mountain is in the distance, just visible on the horizon as the focus takes us elsewhere, for example, to a watermill or to a tea house on a snowy day, as a small narrative scene plays out in front. In *The Great Wave*, a distant, snow-capped Fuji is framed by a dramatic cresting wave as the crews of three boats struggle to keep upright in the choppy water. Hokusai took advantage of the recently imported pigment Prussian Blue to achieve the deep, intense colour of the sea. A triumph in woodcut printmaking, the prints were published in a volume in March 1834. Many thousands of impressions of each design were subsequently printed, making each relatively inexpensive. The artist signed the volume 'Brush of Manji, old man crazy to paint, changed from the former Hokusai Iitsu, aged seventy-five' and included a seal that incorporated a stylized image of the great mountain.

The prints in Hokusai's Mount Fuji series, as in the majority of his images, are based on both observation of the real world and his imagination. He combined, distorted and exaggerated details, and added elements that were drawn from his memories and inner thoughts. In his landscape images, he was not aiming for topographical accuracy, but a celebration of the world and its interconnectedness: of nature, of people and of its higher powers. In his print series *Tour of Waterfalls in Various Provinces* (about 1833), he depicted sites to which he had never actually been. In the 1820s, he had embarked on a project to create *A Great Picture Book of Everything*, an ambitious endeavour, which was never finished, to produce an illustrated encyclopaedia covering a vast range of subjects including animals, birds, Buddhism, and the history and cultural practices of India and China. At least 103 of the drawings survive in the collection of the British Museum. Had they been used to make the prints as intended, they would have been destroyed in the process of transferring the designs to the blocks. Hokusai travelled relatively widely in Japan but between 1639 and 1859, the country was effectively sealed. Even within Japan, it was difficult to move around, so Hokusai was largely reliant on books and art to learn about the outside world. From about 1810 he decided to share his knowledge of the world and the skills he had developed as an artist by creating a series of drawing manuals, beginning with *Basic Instructions in Sketching* (1812). Shortly afterwards, encouraged by a group of art enthusiasts he met when he travelled to the city of Nagoya, he produced the first of 15 volumes of *Hokusai's Sketches* (1814–78), each of which contains hundreds of sketches that he called 'manga', intended to help others to learn to draw and also forming a miscellany of Japanese life and culture.

In his final years, Hokusai began to focus on painting after years of making prints of all types, from traditional *ukiyo-e* scenes of actors and beautiful women, *Shunga* prints (erotic subjects), landscapes and many illustrations for books, with which he had achieved considerable success. His painting took several different forms, from hanging scrolls to fans and folding screens. This shift to painting was probably motivated in part by an economic downturn in Japan in the mid-1830s, caused by crop failure that also resulted in a terrible famine and social disquiet. As a result, the market for prints decreased significantly. A final straw may have been the terrible fire in 1839 in which Hokusai lost his home and many of his sketches, materials and books. By this time, Hokusai was living with his daughter Eijo, having lost his second wife in the 1820s as well as another daughter. At some point in the 1820s, he also seems to have suffered a stroke which affected his dexterity. In his final years, therefore, he increasingly relied on the assistance of Eijo, who was a talented artist in her own right, working under the name Ōi. During the 1840s, Hokusai was incredibly productive, producing many paintings – at least 32 in his 89th year alone – and continuing his daily drawing practice, which had become a way through which he continued to explore and understand the world. He also used drawing in an attempt to prevent misfortune and prolong his life by means of 'Daily Exorcisms' – small brush and ink drawings of symbolic creatures such as Chinese lions, which he would make each morning and throw out of the window, although some were rescued from destruction by his daughter and others. During these years, as his spirituality grew in importance, he frequently depicted otherworldly subjects, including devils and the figure of Shōki, a demon-queller, whom it was believed could ward off illness and death.

Over the course of his long career, Hokusai made a great contribution to Japanese art, sharing his observations of the world with his viewers, entertaining them and offering a frequently touching and profound commentary on contemporary life. He had about 200 pupils in total and many others learned from his drawing manuals and texts. Within a few years of his death, Japan opened up to the wider world and Japanese prints, fans and textiles began to flood into Europe, where they were collected by artists including Claude Monet, Vincent van Gogh and Pablo Picasso, significantly influencing their work. Today, Hokusai's images are internationally recognizable, particularly *The Great Wave*, which has even inspired an emoji. In a text accompanying the published volume of *Thirty-Six Views of Mount Fuji*, Hokusai wrote: 'From the age of six I had a penchant for copying the form of things, and from about fifty, my pictures were frequently published; but until the age of seventy, nothing that I drew was worthy of notice … when I reach eighty years, I hope to have made increasing progress, and at ninety to see further into the underlying principles of things, so that at one hundred years I will have achieved a divine state in my art, and at one hundred and ten, every dot and every stroke will be as though alive.'[26] Hokusai may not have made it to 110, or even 100, but through his art, his unique world lives on.

10

J. M. W. Turner: Painting as Poetry

In 2025, as I write this book, it is impossible to ignore J. M. W. Turner, at least in Britain where his 250th anniversary is being celebrated through myriad exhibitions, conferences and books. But even before this anniversary, Turner's legacy loomed large in the country's cultural psyche. In a 2005 BBC poll, his painting *The Fighting Temeraire* was voted 'Britain's Greatest Painting' and both an image of the painting and Turner's self-portrait have featured on the British 20-pound note since 2020. Britain's most prestigious contemporary art prize was named after him when it was founded in 1984, and a contemporary art gallery established in his name opened in the Kent seaside town of Margate in 2011, precipitating something of a cultural renaissance in the area. Today, Turner's art clearly resonates with a wide audience, from art historians and curators who continue to find new and interesting ways to understand and present his art, to a more general viewer, to whom his often hazy, somewhat dreamlike seascapes and landscapes evidently speak.

Turner is best known for his innovative use of light and colour in his paintings. Working in oil and watercolour, he sought to create images that went beyond physical representation, and which captured atmosphere and the specific sensations of being in a particular place at a particular time. Turner's innovative approaches, which included a looser brushwork than was at that time conventional, excited some but displeased others. Despite his enormous success, throughout his career Turner faced criticism from viewers who found his paintings unresolved and lacking in precision and detail. As early as 1799, for example, the year he joined the Royal Academy as an Associate Member at the age of 24, a critic for the newspaper *True Briton* warned that he was in danger of forming 'a habit of *indistinctness* and *confusion*'.[27] The painting that the critic was reviewing was *Harlech Castle, from Tygwyn Ferry, Summer's Evening Twilight* (1799, Yale Center for British Art), a view of a medieval Welsh castle in the distant hills, with a shipyard in the foreground against the yellowing evening sky, and a group of figures seated at the water's edge. The castle is identifiable by its distinct shape, defined by towers at all four corners, but is sketchily painted. Similarly, the hulking carcasses at the shipyard are imprecise and partially silhouetted. Turner did not intend his painting to be a detailed topographical view, but an image of a moment in time, complete with a small human narrative in the foreground, in which light and atmosphere are prioritized. Even after he had established himself as one of the leading artists of his day, his paintings continued to attract negative responses for similar reasons. In 1841, for instance, a critic at *The Times* described his painting *Schloss Rosenau, Seat of HRH Prince Albert of Coburg* (1841, National Museums Liverpool), a depiction of a distant castle with a tree-lined river in the foreground and a yellow sun in the sky, as 'a picture that represents nothing in nature beyond eggs and spinach'.[28] Others, however, found his approach to be intriguing, even exciting. A critic writing for *The Spectator* in 1838 recommended viewing Turner's painting *Regulus* (1828–38, Tate, London) from as far back as possible, to best appreciate the 'glare, turbulence, and uneasiness' of the scene.[29] Today, Turner is often referred to as Britain's greatest ever artist. His hazy, dazzling landscapes, dramatic narratives on land and at sea, and explorations of both past and present are often presented as a bridge between the old masters and the modern, underpinned by ideas akin to those developed by the Impressionists, and providing a path towards a more expressive style of art that led ultimately to abstraction.

Like William Hogarth, Turner grew up at the centre of a bustling London and was witness to everything the city had to offer. He was born in the spring of 1775 and later claimed his birthday as 23 April, an auspicious day for England as both St George's Day and Shakespeare's birthday. His father, William Turner, was a barber and wigmaker based on Maiden Lane in Covent Garden, an area known for its theatres, art societies, print shops, taverns and brothels. His mother, Mary Marshall, was from a relatively prosperous family of small-business owners. Turner's parents recognized and encouraged their son's early artistic talents. He spent part of his childhood, however, living with maternal relatives in Kent and Brentford in Middlesex, possibly due to the death of his younger sister Mary Ann and perhaps also his mother's declining mental health, which led to her admittance to the Bethlem Hospital (popularly known as Bedlam) in 1800. In Turner's time, formal art education in England was dominated by the Royal Academy (RA), which had been founded in 1768, and which also provided an important public arena for artists to exhibit their work. Before entering the Royal Academy Schools in 1789, aged 14, Turner gained some valuable experience as a draughtsman with the architects Thomas Hardwick and Thomas Malton Junior. His drawing skills developed further at the Royal Academy, where his rigorous training involved copying plaster models of classical sculptures and, from 1792, attending life drawing classes. His early exposure to the Old Masters came through the print and book shops in Covent Garden, and John Moreing's auction house on Maiden Lane. This education continued at the RA and through access to private collections as he began to work as a professional artist and receive commissions from wealthy patrons. Turner's early paintings were influenced by the seventeenth-century French landscape and history painters Claude Lorrain (1604–82) and Nicolas Poussin (1594–1665), who were both popular in England at the time. Later, travel both within and beyond Britain increased his opportunities to view art, as did the opening in 1817 of Dulwich Picture Gallery, England's first public art museum, and the National Gallery in 1838. Artists that Turner took inspiration from and paid homage to through his paintings include Raphael, Bellini, Watteau, Canaletto and Rembrandt.

Through his involvement with the Royal Academy, of which he became a full member in 1802, Turner had regular contact with other leading artists of his day and was at times spurred on by friendly and not-so-friendly rivalries. The success of the Scottish painter David Wilkie (1785–1841) in producing genre paintings influenced by the Dutch tradition provoked a direct response from Turner in the form of *A Country Blacksmith Disputing upon the Price of Iron, and the Price Charged to the Butcher for Shoeing his Poney*

(1807, oil on wood, Tate). He also gained creative motivation from his rivalry with fellow landscape painter, and almost exact contemporary, John Constable (1776–1837), whom he first met in 1813. In 1832, when Turner's oil painting *Helvoetsluys; the City of Utrecht, 64, Going to Sea* (Tokyo Fuji Art Museum) was hung next to Constable's *Opening of Waterloo Bridge* at the Royal Academy, Turner worried that his marine painting in greys and blues would be eclipsed by Constable's vibrant, celebratory scene. As a result, Turner used the Varnishing Days (the three days before the annual exhibition opened, during which he would often performatively complete unfinished paintings) to heighten the colour in his painting and add a bright red buoy to the waves in the foreground. On seeing the additions and the dulling effect it had on his own picture alongside, Constable is said to have commented: 'He has been here and fired a gun'.[30] Turner was, by many accounts, a difficult and socially awkward man who was at times bad-tempered and obstinate. Despite his successes, he was never knighted and was considered unsuitable to become President of the Royal Academy, an institution to which he was dedicated and with which he remained actively involved throughout his life. As a businessman, he was shrewd and gained a reputation for his hard bargaining. In addition to the private commissions that he received throughout his life and the commercial work that he undertook, which included supplying illustrations to be engraved for numerous topographical publications, he also sold his paintings on the open market. In 1804, he established his own gallery in Harley Street in the West End of London, where he had lived since 1799, and in his later decades, he employed a dealer, Thomas Griffith, to handle sales and represent him in negotiations with patrons.

As a landscape painter, Turner's living relied in part on his ability to travel, to observe and experience the places that sparked his imagination and that he was commissioned to depict. Turner made his first known drawings as a child in 1786 in the southern coastal town of Margate in Kent, where he was sent to stay with relatives, and made frequent sketching tours for the rest of his life. Travels around the British Isles were often precipitated by commissions. In 1796, for example, aged 21, he was commissioned by the Wiltshire-based antiquarian Sir Richard Colt Hoare to produce watercolour drawings of Salisbury Cathedral and the surrounding area. In his early years as an artist, travel abroad was difficult due to Britain's war with France, but a temporary cessation of hostilities allowed him to visit Switzerland and France in 1802, a tour that included a visit to the Louvre where he saw paintings by Titian, Raphael, Rembrandt and other great Old Masters, and which introduced him to the awesome landscape of the Alps. After the defeat of Napoleon's forces at Waterloo in 1815 finally brought the war to an end, Europe opened up and over the following three decades, Turner travelled across the continent, visiting the Low Countries and Germany in 1817 and taking his first trip to Italy in 1819. He returned from these trips with full sketchbooks and brimming with ideas inspired by both the landscape he had experienced, the culture and history of a place, and the art he had seen. He would make immediate responses, such as the watercolours of the Alps that he exhibited at the Royal Academy shortly after his visit to Switzerland in 1802, but sometimes his ideas and sketches would be set aside for future use. In nineteenth-century Britain, there was still a hierarchy of painting genres that had existed in European art since the

Renaissance, in which landscape painting was considered to be less prestigious than history painting or portraiture. In the eighteenth century, however, artists such as Thomas Gainsborough, Alexander Cozens and Richard Wilson had developed the genre in Britain, taking it beyond the merely descriptive by adding historical associations and narrative elements to their scenes, and in doing so paving the way for Constable and Turner. As part of his mission to confirm the importance of British landscape painting, Turner worked with the printmaker Charles Turner to produce a series of mezzotints after his own designs with the aim of providing a visual guide to the different categories of the genre: historical, mountainous, pastoral, marine and architectural. Available by subscription, the incomplete series was produced between 1807 and 1819 under the collective title *Liber Studiorum* and numbered 71 in total.

As demonstrated by the *Liber Studiorum*, Turner explored the full range of landscape painting. It is perhaps in his marine paintings, however, that his art was at its most dynamic. The first oil painting that he exhibited at the Royal Academy, in 1796, was a marine scene: *Fishermen at Sea* (Tate), based on sketches that Turner had made off the Isle of Wight the previous year. The small fishing boat at the centre of the painting holds its own on the ocean's choppy waters, although a full moon and dark clouds overhead heighten a sense of jeopardy. Between 1796 and 1805, around half the paintings that Turner exhibited at the Royal Academy were sea scenes, including *Dutch Boats in a Gale* (exhibited 1801), in which two boats on stormy water are moments from a collision. The constantly changing nature of the sea and its traffic, and the opportunities to showcase the striking effects of light and other elements on its appearance, provided Turner with a landscape sub-genre that allowed him to flex his dramatic imagination, as well as to incorporate details from history or contemporary life. Wrecks or unfolding disasters often provided the focal point for Turner's marine paintings. The latter, which allowed him to paint glowering skies and swirling seas include *The Shipwreck* (oil on canvas, 1805, Tate) and *A Disaster at Sea* (about 1835), an unfinished canvas that may depict the true-life tragedy of the *Amphitrite*: a British ship carrying female convicts to Australia that broke up in a storm off Boulogne after the captain refused to accept help from the French, killing many of the women on board and some of their children. In Turner's violent and chaotic scene, bodies tumble into the sea, which is almost indistinguishable from the sky as the white churn of the waves is echoed by the clouds. In 1840, Turner painted another disaster at sea, which also allowed him to explore a topical issue of the day in his oil painting *Slave Ship (Slavers Throwing Overboard the Dead and Dying, Typhoon Coming On)* (Museum of Fine Arts, Boston). The painting was inspired by an appalling incident that took place in 1781 involving the British slave ship the *Zong*, whose captain and crew threw more than 130 dead and dying enslaved people overboard after disease spread throughout the ship, in a bid to qualify for compensation available only for those 'lost at sea'. In the painting, Turner once again presents a ship battling a raging sea: its masts list against a fiery sky while in the foreground birds and fish gather to feed on the bodies in the water. A shackled limb, still taut with potential life, remains visible. The slave trade in Britain had been abolished in 1807 and in British colonial territories in 1838, but remained a subject of much public discourse in 1840 as the Empire and its citizens grappled with its legacy. By this point, Turner evidently supported abolition, although he had previously invested in a scheme that relied on slave labour.

During Turner's lifetime, the Industrial Revolution brought radical social and economic changes to Britain. Turner took advantage of newly wealthy industrialists who sought to form art collections, including Charles Birch, who owned a colliery in Birmingham, and Joseph Gillott, who ran a pen nib factory in the same city, both of whom purchased his paintings. Turner also responded in paint to developments in technology, most famously in *Rain, Steam and Speed – The Great Western Railway* (1844, National Gallery, London), in which a steam train emerges through the rain, barrelling across the recently completed, Brunel-designed, Maidenhead Railway Bridge. A few years earlier, in a more melancholy image, Turner had recorded the dying days of a former age in his painting *The Fighting Temeraire* (1839, National Gallery), which shows the final journey of the warship, the *Temeraire*, which was used at the Battle of Trafalgar in 1805, as it is towed along the Thames to be scrapped. A dazzling sun sets as the aging fighter, pale and ghost-like, is led by a steam-powered vessel. Turner's patriotic elegy to the *Temeraire* and what she represented was emphasized by the verses he included in the catalogue for the Royal Academy when the painting was exhibited, which he had adapted from the poem *Ye Mariners of England* by Thomas Campbell: 'The flag which braved the battle and the breeze, / No longer owns her.' Turner had long been in the habit of including verses in the catalogues for the Royal Academy exhibitions, some of which he took from poems by others and some of which he wrote himself. Turner believed that painting and poetry 'flowed from the same source' and complemented each other as art forms.[31]

Turner had a firm belief in his own contribution to British art. Towards the end of his life, he made plans to bequeath the finished oil paintings still in his possession to the nation and attempted to hold on to works that he considered to be particularly important. His frequent references to the Old Masters in his art signalled his identification with these heroes from the past and a conviction that he had earned a place in the pantheon of great artists, in a similar way to Picasso's references to his artistic heroes a century later. Legal wranglings following Turner's death on 19 December 1851 – complicated by the fact that he had been living under an assumed name with his long-term partner, Sophia Caroline Booth, when he died – meant that his bequest was less straightforward than intended. Eventually, however, all the original works that he still held, including thousands of works on paper, were accepted by the British nation in 1856 and are now held by the Tate. Many other works by Turner are in public collections throughout the UK and around the world. Turner transformed landscape painting in Britain and contributed to the emergence of watercolour painting as an important category in its own right. But it is in his radical approaches to light and colour that he made his greatest contribution, through which he was able to evoke wonder and fear, pathos and excitement, and ignite his viewers' imagination.

11

Rosa Bonheur: Art and Animals

It was tempting when making the selection for this book to choose my favourite artists, those whose pictures I would readily hang on my wall or whose company I would happily keep. I resisted this, however, in an attempt to present a broader picture and in recognition of the fact that if I were only to consider the art that I like, I would miss part of the story. Today, Rosa Bonheur's paintings are unfashionable and it is therefore difficult to establish whether it is cultural conditioning or something more personal that would cause me – full disclosure – to walk past them in a gallery. But I include Bonheur here not because I *like* her paintings, but because I admire them, and I find her approach as an artist to be interesting and possibly unique. Bonheur was a painter of animals and the natural world. She found her style as a young woman and stuck with it. She was a highly accomplished artist and she worked hard to achieve a realism and sense of life in her images. Like Artemisia Gentileschi, she was unusual but not unique as a woman artist in her day, and at times she had to navigate social restrictions as a result of her gender. But my interest in her is not limited to her experiences as a woman artist; I find her fascinating for the way in which she physically immersed herself in her art, spending time in unpleasant surroundings such as abattoirs to study the animals that she painted, and in the macho world of horse fairs and markets to observe animal behaviour. I also find it fascinating that she found a genre that she loved and committed herself to it, forging a successful career on her own terms and refusing to be swayed by the market or fashions or what others expected of her. As an artist, Bonheur was relatively conservative in style, but she was both unconventional in her approach to her work and wildly successful in her day. Made during a period of upheaval and war for France – including the Revolution of 1848 and the establishment of the Second Republic, and the Franco-Prussian War of 1870–1 – Bonheur's paintings of rural scenes and animals provided art-viewing audiences with some respite from politics, conflict and human suffering. But her images were not sweet or sentimental; she made naturalistic paintings based on hours of research carried out in slaughterhouses, stables and the natural world, informed by a deep under-standing of animal bodies and behaviour.

Rosa Bonheur decided as a child that she wanted to follow in her father's footsteps and become an artist, rejecting other paths laid before her, including a life as a seamstress. Born Rosalie-Marie Bonheur in Bordeaux, France on 16 March 1822, she was the eldest of four children born to Raymond Bonheur, a painter and art teacher, and Sophie Marquis, the illegitimate daughter of Jean-Baptiste Dublan de Lahet, a well-connected local merchant. Bonheur's childhood was complicated by the fact that when she was around six years old, her father became involved with

Saint-Simonianism, a social reform movement founded by Henri de Saint-Simon (1760–1825), which, among other things, advocated for better conditions for working people and, to some degree, gender equality. On the one hand, Raymond's commitment to the movement seems to have influenced his support of his daughter's wishes to become an artist, but on the other, it took him away from family life and damaged his relationship with his wife. After moving the family to Paris in 1829, where he hoped to find more commissions and better employment prospects, Raymond abandoned the family for a time in 1832 to live with a group of male Saint-Simonians and declared himself to be celibate. For the rest of her life, although she retained affection for and gratitude towards her father, Bonheur blamed him for leaving her mother to care for four children and make ends meet, a burden that she believed contributed to her mother's death in 1833 at the age of 36. Following this loss, Raymond continued to encourage his daughter's interest in art, viewing the success of the portrait painter Élisabeth Vigée-Lebrun (1755–1842) as evidence that a woman could forge a career as a professional artist in France. So, after Rosa was expelled from school for being disruptive and refused to undertake an apprenticeship as a seamstress, Raymond committed to supporting his daughter as an artist and began to teach her.

In 1841, aged 19, Bonheur made her debut at the Paris Salon with two works: *Goats and Sheep* and *Two Rabbits*. The Salon was the official art exhibition organized by the Academy of Fine Arts in Paris and acceptance was determined by a jury. It was an important public forum in which artists could showcase their work, make sales, attract commissions and establish their reputations. Over the following years, Bonheur made her name through the animal paintings and sculptures that she submitted to the Salon, all of which were accepted. In 1847, she attracted the attention of the prominent critic Théophile Thoré, who paid her what he considered to be the ultimate compliment: 'Mlle Rosa paints almost like a man'.[32] The following year, her six paintings and two sculptures accepted by the Salon earned her a gold medal. Bonheur's ability to paint animals so convincingly was the result of close study. As a child, she was allowed to keep small animals at home, including rabbits, ducks and a goat – a practice she continued throughout her life – and she made regular sketching trips to the countryside on the outskirts of Paris to view cows and sheep. In her early twenties, Bonheur made an application to visit the Abattoir du Roule, a slaughterhouse close to where she lived. It was an unconventional request, especially for a woman, and initially Bonheur attracted the mirth and unwanted attention of the workers, but she gained an ally among the senior staff who protected her and facilitated her visits. At the slaughterhouse, she was able to study and sketch animals' bodies, gaining a visceral insight into anatomy that the books she also studied could not provide.

Later in her career, Bonheur also visited livestock fairs and travelled around the countryside on horseback, not only to view animals but to sketch the landscape that would provide the setting to many of her paintings. In 1850, in advance of a planned tour of the Pyrenees with her long-term partner Nathalie Micas (1824–89), Bonheur requested permission from the authorities to wear trousers so that she wouldn't have to ride side-saddle. At the time, it was against the law for women in France to wear 'masculine clothes', supposedly to prevent women from gaining employment in 'male' professions, but the occasional six-month permit was granted on written application to the police, usually for health reasons. Bonheur and Micas were successful in obtaining permits in 1850, and Bonheur received others throughout her life, which allowed her to wear trousers when she visited slaughterhouses and markets. It is generally accepted today that Bonheur was a lesbian and in a committed relationship with Micas, with whom she lived for 40 years. Today, she is often celebrated as an LGBTQ+ and feminist icon, whose appearance – short hair, trousers and smock, cigar – was an indication of her lack of conformity to gender norms. In her lifetime, though, possibly in an effort to protect her reputation and career, Bonheur insisted that she wore 'men's' clothes not to stand out or make some kind of statement, but for practical reasons. In her 'autobiography', which was in fact written and ventriloquized by Anna Klumpke (1856–1942), with whom she lived at the end of her life, Bonheur reminds the reader: 'Don't forget I used to spend days and days in slaughterhouses. Oh! you've got to be devoted to art to live in pools of blood, surrounded by butchers. I was also passionate about horses; and what better place to study them than at horse fairs, mingling with all those traders? Women's clothes were simply always in the way.'[33] On occasions that required a more socially acceptable image, such as meeting potential clients, Bonheur was prepared to wear dresses and hats, but it is clear that she was more comfortable in trousers and a smock, clothes that she also chose to wear at home when she was working.

Bonheur began to sell her paintings in the mid-1840s, initially giving most of her income to her father to help support the family. At the time, some women artists and writers still assumed male or ambiguously gendered pseudonyms to deter prejudice, but Bonheur resolved to use her own name, although she shortened Rosalie to Rosa, the diminutive form her mother had used. Her success at the Salon also brought work, notably a commission from the state to produce a painting on the subject of ploughing (a theme she had successfully depicted in two previous paintings) as part of her gold medal award in 1848. The commission resulted in *Ploughing in the Nivernais* (1849, Musée d'Orsay, Paris), a scene of two lines of oxen being used to drag a plough across a field. The uphill effort of the animals is evident in their hulking frames and the spittle dripping from their mouths. As part of the research for the picture, Bonheur went with Micas to spend some time in the countryside at the home of a family friend. The painting was highly acclaimed. It had originally been intended for the Musée de Lyon, but the government decided to keep it in Paris. A few years later, in 1853, Bonheur painted her most well-known composition, *The Horse Fair*, an oil painting on canvas measuring around 2.5 × 5 metres (8 ¼ × 16 ½ ft), depicting the horse market on the Boulevard de l'Hôpital in Paris. Set against a diagonal line of trees and grey skies, a melee of horses strain, snarl and rear up as their handlers parade them for potential buyers. The scene is full of adrenaline-fuelled chaos and jeopardy. At any moment, a horse might break free and bolt. Bonheur had been studying horses and their anatomy for some years and also took inspiration from the Parthenon Marbles and an 1821 lithograph by Théodore Géricault (1791–1824) titled *Horses Going to a Fair*. The painting was a triumph at the Salon, after which it was exhibited in Britain and the

USA, countries in which Bonheur had gained a considerable following. In 1887, it was purchased by the wealthy American businessman Cornelius Vanderbilt, who donated it to the Metropolitan Museum of Art, New York, in the same year. The success of *The Horse Fair* was due in part to Ernest Gambart, a Belgian art dealer who marketed Bonheur's work in France and overseas, arranging sales, tours and introducing her to wealthy clients.

After the death of her father in 1849, Bonheur moved in with Nathalie and her mother in Paris, and shortly afterwards the three women moved together to a chateau near the Forest of Fontainebleau, called the Château de By. There, Bonheur set up a studio and kept a menagerie of animals, including dogs, a deer, a horse and a monkey called Ratata. In 1873, she was invited by Louis Dejean, director of the Paris Winter Circus, to sketch his tame lioness, Pierrette. Bonheur was wary, having never before interacted with big cats up close, but the opportunity to study a lion without a cage or wall obstructing her view was tempting. So, she and Nathalie travelled to the Château de Saint-Leu near Melun on the outskirts of Paris, where she found the animal to be not only tame and tolerant of human presence, but fascinating and awesome in its anatomy and movement. Gradually, over several visits, the lion grew to trust her to the point that she felt easy in the animal's company as she drew. Bonheur had already begun to paint images of lions, having studied the big cats in the menagerie at the Jardin des Plantes in Paris, but this experience with Pierrette led to a new focus on lions and tigers. Following her encounter with Pierrette, Gambart helped Bonheur to obtain two lions from Marseille Zoo called Néro and Sarah. The lions were shipped to Gambart's home in Nice, where he had built a villa at which Bonheur sometimes stayed and worked. After two months of studying and drawing the lions, Bonheur reluctantly gave them both to the Jardin des Plantes in Paris. In 1885, she was given two lion cubs as a gift, one of which, Fathma, she became particularly attached to and which died in her arms in 1888. The following year, however, she was dealt a much greater blow by the death of Nathalie Micas. Bonheur and Micas had been almost inseparable since they had first met as children and the loss was devastating. In her final years, however, she found happiness with the young American portrait painter Anna Klumpke, with whom she spent the remainder of her life.

When Bonheur died on 25 May 1899, she was famous around the world. She had been commercially success-ful in France and overseas and had received many awards and honours, including the Legion of Honour from the Empress Eugénie of France, wife of Napoleon III, who had also visited her studio. Such was her fame during her life-time that when *The Horse Fair* toured Britain in 1856, it was taken to Buckingham Palace at the request of Queen Victoria, and 'Rosa Bonheur' porcelain dolls were sold in America from the 1860s. Relatively soon after her death, however, tastes changed rapidly, particularly in France, and her art became deeply unfashionable. The emergence of feminist art history in the 1970s brought her name back into public discourse as influential thinkers such as Linda Nochlin acknowledged her importance. Whatever the prevailing tastes, however, Bonheur's commitment to her art and to understanding her subjects cannot be denied. 'Art is a tyrant', she is reported to have said, 'It demands heart, brain, soul, body. The entireness of the votary

… I wed art. It is my husband, my world, my life's dream, the air I breathe.'[34] She was determined to become an artist and to work in a way that suited her. She found her niche and excelled within it, no doubt inspiring many other little girls, including some who owned a Rosa Bonheur doll, to take up art as a result.

12

Claude Monet: Making an Impression

In April 1874, a group of artists calling themselves the Anonymous Society of Painters, Sculptors, and Printmakers, etc., organized an exhibition in Paris that was conceived as an alternative to the Salon, the state-sponsored exhibition organized by the Academy of Fine Arts in Paris in which more conservative artists, such as Rosa Bonheur, excelled. Claude Monet was a founding member of the alternative group, which also included Camille Pissarro, Pierre-Auguste Renoir, Edgar Degas, Paul Cézanne, Alfred Sisley and Berthe Morisot. The exhibition was held at 35 Boulevard des Capucines in rooms recently vacated by the photographer Félix Nadar, and included the work of around 30 artists, many of whom were frustrated with the academy system that still dominated French art. Born in Paris on 14 November 1840, Monet had come of age at a time when exposure and sales as an artist were still heavily reliant on success at the Salon. In 1865, he had been successful on his first submission to the exhibition but over the following years, he faced rejection in 1867, 1869 and 1870. Several of his artist friends, including Sisley, Pissarro and Cézanne, had also been excluded and from around 1867, the idea of mounting an alternative exhibition began to take shape. In general, the artists who formed the Anonymous Society worked in a looser, less precise way than those who exhibited at the Salon, and they also embraced themes relating to modern life, working with lighter, brighter colours.

At the exhibition in 1874, Monet exhibited nine works including a painting of Le Havre, the port city in Normandy to which he had moved with his family in 1845. Painted in November 1872 and depicting a view from a room at the city's Amirauté Hotel, the image depicts the harbour in the early morning fog as a bright orange sun rises, its light leaving a jagged path of short orange brushstrokes in the water. Industrial cranes and smokestacks can be seen in the distance in a hazy purple-blue, while two small boats are silhouetted on the water in the foreground. Above, the sky is ablaze with a messy mass of visible brushstrokes in orange, purple and brown. Titled *Impression: Sunrise* and now in the Marmottan Museum, Paris, the painting attracted the attention of the critic Louis Leroy, who, in his scathing review of the exhibition published in *Le Charivari* on 25 April, used the word 'impression' negatively to emphasize the sketchiness of some of the work on display. His piece was headlined 'Exhibition of Impressionists', which inadvertently named the movement. Throughout his long career, Monet remained committed to this new approach to painting, through which he sought to capture the effects of light and changing weather on the canvas. He was also committed, as far as possible, to painting directly from nature *en plein air* (outdoors). As the leading Impressionist painter, Monet was instrumental in helping to change and diversify French art, opening the door for other avant-garde movements and finding a new way of depicting the world.

Monet's lifelong practice of painting in the open air was inspired by his early training with the artist Eugène Boudin (1824–98) whom he met as a young man at a framing shop in Le Havre. As a schoolboy, Monet, whose father Claude Adolphe Monet was a grocer, had developed a skill for drawing caricatures, which he initially gave away to friends and then went on to sell locally. Boudin was impressed by these drawings but encouraged the young Monet, who then went by his first name Oscar, to try landscape painting and took him on painting expeditions in the surrounding countryside. The paintings that Monet made at this time, including *View from Rouelles* (1858, private collection), show the influence of the Barbizon school: an informal group of French artists of the previous generation, including Charles-François Daubigny and Jean-François Millet, who worked in a realist style and would paint *en plein air* around the village of Barbizon near Fontainebleau. Monet exhibited *View from Rouelles* at the Le Havre municipal exhibition in 1858, thus beginning his public career as a landscape painter. Monet realized, however, that if he was to have a successful career as an artist, he should study painting in Paris. He moved to the capital in 1859 and the following year began to study at the Académie Suisse, an informal art school where he first met Pissarro. Monet's training was interrupted in 1861 when he was conscripted via a lottery to undertake a year's military service in Algeria, but he returned to Paris in autumn 1862 and began to train with the Swiss artist Charles Gleyre (1806–74) alongside Renoir, Sisley and Frédéric Bazille. Like the Barbizon artists before them, Monet's circle occasionally took painting trips together to paint in the open air and Monet began to produce paintings in which he attempted to recreate the light and the sensations of the outdoors on to his canvas. He also began to experiment with working on a large scale, for example, with his unfinished painting *Luncheon on the Grass* (inspired by an 1863 painting of the same name by Édouard Manet), that was to include life-size figures in contemporary dress. It was during this period that he began to find his 'Impressionist' style. The paintings that were accepted into the 1865 Salon, for example, which include *Mouth of the Seine at Honfleur* (1865, Norton Simon Museum, Pasadena, California), demonstrate the beginnings of a looser style of brushwork and a more experimental approach to colour.

Technical innovations in painting materials, including portable easels and the invention of the paint tubes in which ground pigments were already mixed with oil, had made it possible for artists such as those associated with the Barbizon school to paint in the open air. Before the nineteenth century, artists generally sketched outdoors and then painted their canvases in their studios. Monet went to considerable lengths to produce his paintings outside throughout his career. In 1866, in order to work on his large-scale canvas *Women in the Garden* (Musée d'Orsay, Paris), he dug a trench in the garden of the Paris property he was renting, in which to rest the lower part of the canvas while he worked on the upper sections. A pulley system allowed him to raise the canvas to work on the lower areas without altering his viewpoint (although in the end, he was forced to complete the painting in his studio). In the 1870s, inspired by an example set by Daubigny, Monet bought an old boat on which he built a makeshift studio, which he used on the River Seine, a set-up captured by Manet in his 1874 painting *Monet Painting in his Studio*

Boat (Neue Pinakothek, Munich). Working outside in the changeable climate of northern France may have resulted in some dramatic light and weather effects, but it also required Monet, at times, to paint in uncomfortable conditions. While working on his 1868 painting *The Jetty at Le Havre* (private collection), a local columnist described seeing him in the wintery landscape: 'We saw a footwarmer, then an easel, then a man huddled in three overcoats, wearing gloves, and with his face half-frozen; it was Monet studying a snow-effect. There are soldiers of art who lack nothing for courage.'[35] In 1869, while painting *en plein air* with Renoir at La Grenouillère, a resort on the Seine around 12 kilometres (7 ½ miles) west of Paris, Monet produced *Bathers at La Grenouillère* (National Gallery, London), a rapidly produced composition that not only encapsulates the primary features of Impressionism – visible brushstrokes, unblended colours, an emphasis on light – but is also an example of a painting that could only have been produced outdoors. The liveliness and spontaneity of the scene, as a record of a fleeting moment, experienced in real time by the artist, could not have been captured in the studio. Later in his life, after Monet had begun to make work in series in around 1890, he would sometimes set up several easels in a single location, so that he could paint a subject – notably the water lily pond at his home in Giverny – from different vantage points and at different times of the day.

In 1871, Monet settled in the town of Argenteuil, along the Seine to the west of Paris, where he stayed until 1878. In June the previous year, he had married his partner and frequent subject Camille Doncieux, with whom he had a son, Jean (born 1867). In the autumn of 1870, Monet had taken Camille and Jean to London in an effort to avoid conscription following the outbreak of war between France and Prussia. During his time in England, Monet had seen works by Constable and Turner, and been introduced to Paul Durand-Ruel, who became his first dealer. He had also produced his first paintings of London, which included *The Thames below Westminster*, showing the Houses of Parliament in the fog (National Gallery, London) and *Hyde Park, London* (Rhode Island School of Design). During his time living in Argenteuil, Monet produced numerous paintings that reflected modern life in a rapidly industrializing France. In 1872, for example, while on a visit to Rouen, he painted *The Goods Train* (Pola Museum of Art, Hakone, Japan), an image of a steam train hurtling through a landscape populated by factories and billowing chimneys. The railway became a recurring subject in his work, culminating in a series of paintings of St-Lazare Station in Paris made in 1877. To produce these works, Monet obtained permission to paint in the station and also worked from an apartment close by that was paid for by Gustave Caillebotte, his patron and fellow painter. Caillebotte was one of a number of artists who travelled to Argenteuil to visit Monet, who had become the linchpin of the group that would become known as the Impressionists. With the support of Durand-Ruel, Monet and the others experienced some commercial success in the first years of the 1870s but by 1873 Durand-Ruel was no longer able to purchase as many works and the idea of holding an independent exhibition was revived, partly through economic necessity. The First Impressionist Exhibition, as the 1874 show was to become known, sparked a tradition that lasted until 1886 and resulted in eight exhibitions. Monet participated in all but the fifth in 1880 and the sixth in 1881. By this time, Monet had lost his wife, Camille, who had died in 1879 shortly after the birth of their second son Michel, in 1878. He was also struggling financially as paintings by the Impressionists were not selling well and had made the decision to submit, again, to the Salon in 1880, which he did successfully but for the last time. The devastation that Monet felt at the loss of Camille, who probably died from cancer, is expressed in his painting *Camille Monet on her Deathbed* (1879, Musée d'Orsay), a near-abstract portrait of his dying wife that has all of the rawness and pain of a work by the Norwegian artist Edvard Munch (1863–1944).

Shortly before Camille's death, Monet's family had moved to Vétheuil, around 65 kilometres (40 miles) from Paris, to set up a joint household with his patron, Ernest Hoschedé, who had fallen on hard times. After Camille's death, Monet began a relationship with Hoschedé's wife Alice and in 1883, after Alice and Hoschedé had become estranged, the couple moved to a rented house in Giverny, a village in Normandy on the right bank of the Seine, along with his two sons and her six children. They married in 1892 following Hoschedé's death the previous year. Monet was to find great inspiration from his surroundings in Giverny, where he was to spend the rest of his life. By 1890, partly due to the success of his work in the USA where it was marketed by Durand-Ruel, he had gained enough financial security to purchase the house. It was around this time that he also began to produce paintings in series, through which he was able to explore a subject in different light and weather conditions, and at different times of the day. In 1890, he began a series on the subject of haystacks and poplars, and two years later, he started to depict the façade of Rouen Cathedral, resulting in over 30 canvases. During this period, he would often work on multiple canvases in a single day, restricting himself to an hour or less for each. Between 1899 and 1901, he visited London several times to visit his son Michel who was studying in the city and made many paintings of the Palace of Westminster on the Thames, which he worked on either from his room at the Savoy Hotel on the Strand or a terrace at St Thomas's Hospital on the south side of the river. Meanwhile, at Giverny, he was developing a large garden that included a pond and stream. The design included a Japanese-style bridge, reflecting his long-term interest in Japan and its visual culture. Like many French artists of this period, Monet had been influenced by the influx of Japanese prints, fans and textiles into the country from the 1850s, an enthusiasm that is expressed in his 1876 painting *La Japonaise (Camille Monet in Japanese Costume)* (Museum of Fine Arts, Boston). In the garden at Giverny, Monet also filled his pond with water lilies originating from South America and Egypt, and in his final years his house and garden, particularly the bridge and water lilies, became the dominant subjects in his art, which included an immersive cycle.

Claude Monet died on 5 December 1926, aged 86. From around 1912, cataracts had affected his vision, resulting in a shift in his painting from dominant blues and greens to a palette with more reds and yellows. Following surgery to remove the cataracts in 1923, he destroyed or reworked many of the paintings he had made during this period. During these last years, artists from around the world travelled to Giverny to meet Monet and learn from the Father of Impressionism, as he was known. His work and approach to art – painting *en plein air*, depicting the contemporary world and using expressive, unblended brushstrokes as well as strong, sometimes unnatural colours, and untouched areas of ground – have had a profound influence on the art of the twentieth century. In America, for example, the Abstract Expressionist painters took inspiration from his loose brushstrokes and use of colour to suggest emotion or mood, while the Pop artists picked up his thread of repetition and seriality. Following Monet's death, several of the monumental paintings from his water lily cycle were installed at the Orangerie Museum in Paris, creating, in the words of the French artist André Masson, a 'Sistine Chapel of Impressionism'.[36] Monet had first offered the paintings to the French State on 12 November 1918, the day after the Armistice, as a symbol of peace. In 1918–19, he also produced a series of ten paintings of Weeping Willows, which he dedicated to the conflict's fallen soldiers.

13

Vincent van Gogh: Feeling Deeply

As with Artemisia Gentileschi, it can be tempting to proj-ect aspects of Van Gogh's biography on to his whole career and view his output as an artist through the lens of what we know of his later life. For Gentileschi, it is knowledge of her experience of sexual violence that can skew our read-ing of her work, but with Vincent van Gogh it is knowledge of his mental ill-health and death by suicide at the age of 37. But in some respects, the life of Van Gogh *was* tinged by melancholy from the start. Exactly one year before he was born on 30 March 1853 in the southern Netherlandish province of Brabant, his parents had suffered the loss of their first child, a son who was born stillborn. He, too, had been called Vincent. The Vincent that survived is today one of the best-remembered and most recognized artists in the world, but during his lifetime he achieved little recogni-tion, and he died from a self-inflicted gunshot wound in 1890 just as he seems to have been on the verge of success. Van Gogh's posthumous fame is no doubt due in part to his compelling biography, but also reflects his great contribu-tion to Western art and the fact that he made paintings and drawings that continue to resonate with people on a deep emotional level, something that he always hoped his work would achieve. 'I want to reach the point', he wrote to his brother Theo just two years after taking up a brush, 'where people say of my work: that man feels deeply.'[37]

Van Gogh was not a prodigy. He spent much of his early adult life trying different jobs and searching for the purpose that art would eventually give him. After he failed to complete school, his supportive family arranged work for him aged 16 with the international art dealer Goupil & Cie, initially in The Hague and then in London and Paris. Although he was interested in and well-informed about art, he first directed the obsessive and fanatical energy that he later poured into his drawings and paintings towards religion, which he threw himself into after he was dismissed from Goupil in 1876. The letters that he wrote during these years to his brother and other family members (hundreds of which survive) reflect the intensity with which he pursued his newfound calling, to such a degree that his family were concerned – even his father Theodorus, who was himself a Protestant minister. Despite his zeal, however, Van Gogh's inability to focus academically eventually led him to abandon his intention to study theology, and after several years working variously as a teacher, in a bookshop and as a lay preacher, he took the advice of his brother Theo and, in 1880 aged 27, decided to become an artist.

Van Gogh's relationship with his younger brother, one of his five surviving siblings, not only generated this initial impetus, but provided the love, patience and support that was to sustain Van Gogh throughout his life. Theo, who lived in Brussels, where he also worked for Goupil & Cie, recognized Van Gogh's drawing skills in the illustrations that occasionally peppered the text of his letters. Somewhat exasperated by his brother's lack of direction, Theo probably envisaged for him a career as a professional illustrator or draughtsman, but with typical fervour Van Gogh began to practise drawing intensively and set his sights on a more creative path. Financially supported by Theo, he took painting lessons with renowned Dutch artist Anton Mauve in The Hague, a cousin by marriage, and devoted himself to becoming an artist, later studying for a short time at the academy of art in Antwerp, Belgium. From the beginning, Van Gogh took inspiration from the natural world and his physical environment, often painting *en plein air*. The countryside provided the subject for many of his early paintings, which were influenced by Mauve and his fellow realist artists in the Netherlands and France, such as Jean-François Millet and Jules Breton, who made romanticized images of the countryside and sympathetic scenes of rural life in earthy tones. In 1885, he completed his best-known work from this period, *The Potato Eaters* (Van Gogh Museum, Amsterdam), an ambitious painting in dark colours of a family of peasants seated around their kitchen table eating potatoes and drinking coffee. With their coarse-featured faces and gnarled hands, the figures appear weary, while their eyes are downcast or transmitting worried glances. Their light comes from a single source, a lamp hanging above them, their surroundings are simple and their meal well-earned. The painting was an important work for Van Gogh, who hoped that it might launch his career. But disappointingly, it met with disapproval from friends and remained unsold at his death. Although far from the vibrant, dynamic images that he would later produce, *The Potato Eaters* demonstrates the development of Van Gogh's singular, recognizable style and his ability to infuse a composition, whatever the subject, with meaning and emotional expression.

In early 1886, Van Gogh moved to Paris, then the centre of the art world in the West. During the two years that he lived there, his art came to life. He became familiar with recent developments in contemporary art, including Impressionism and Neo-Impressionism, the movement led by Georges Seurat and Paul Signac, who created images from juxtaposed dabs of complementary colours in an effort to capture the transient effects of light. In Paris, Van Gogh also found an avant-garde artistic community through the studio of the painter Fernand Cormon where he took lessons and became friends with Émile Bernard and Paul Gauguin, among others. This exposure to such new and exciting art and artists encouraged Van Gogh to experiment, which he did by loosening his own brush-work and adding brighter colours to his palette. Although he was influenced by Seurat and Signac, he was less rigid and more instinctive in his approach to applying colour. He often used himself as a model during this period, painting 27 self-portraits during his time in Paris, which chart his stylistic development. In addition, he pursued his newly found interest in Japanese *ukiyo-e* woodcut prints, which he had started to collect in Antwerp and continued to buy in Paris. The prominent outlines, vivid colours and unusual crops and perspectives found in these images had a profound influence on his work. It was partly the influence of Japanese prints, and his desire to find an environment that provided the lush, vibrating landscapes and potent light that he felt would help him to create similarly dramatic scenes, that led him to the south of France. There, he found olive groves, sunflowers and lilacs, and the dazzling sun of the Mediterranean.

When Van Gogh moved to the Provençal city of Arles in February 1888, he intended to establish an artistic retreat where artists he had known in Paris could come and work, producing drawings and paintings for Theo to sell in the capital. To this end, he rented four rooms in a house known as the Yellow House and he persuaded Paul Gauguin to join him. Gauguin and Van Gogh were close and initially worked side-by-side, inspiring each other and sharing ideas. But the two artists had different approaches to their work – Gauguin, for example, worked primarily from memory and the imagination, while Van Gogh worked from life – and their personalities clashed. The experiment turned sour at a time that Van Gogh's mental health was worsening, and, on 23 December, following a violent argument precipitated by Gauguin's threat to leave, Van Gogh cut off part of his ear, wrapped it in newspaper and presented it to a sex worker in the city's red-light district. Unable to remember much of the incident afterwards and clearly experiencing an acute crisis, Van Gogh was admitted to hospital the following day where he was visited by Theo, who had rushed down to see his brother. This incident, which Van Gogh memorialized shortly afterwards in two self-portraits with a bandaged ear and his subsequent year-long stay as a voluntary inpatient at a psychiatric hospital at nearby Saint-Rémy-de-Provence, makes it difficult to look at his art from this time without viewing it with his anguish in mind. But Van Gogh's years in the south of France were the most productive and creatively brilliant of his career and there is joy and wonder to be found in later work – in the vivid colours and swirling brushstrokes through which he expressed the beauty of nature – as well as the deep sadness that is also visible in his art.

Van Gogh recognized his own propensity for what might now be called depression and tendency to feel deeply throughout his life. He also recognized the role that his creativity could play in, if not overcoming it, finding a way to live with it. He expressed this to Theo in July 1882: 'Even though I'm often in a mess, inside me there's still a calm, pure harmony and music. In the poorest little house, in the filthiest corner, I see paintings or drawings. And my mind turns in that direction as if with an irresistible urge.'[38] In the depths of his misery in Saint-Rémy, he found comfort and a ceaselessly inspiring subject in the walled garden of the hospital. He also painted other areas of the hospital, such as his room and the corridors, the surrounding landscape including olive groves, and he reimagined works by artists of the past whom he admired, such as Rembrandt and Eugène Delacroix. Altogether, he produced around 150 paintings during his time there, as well as many works on paper, all the time pushing himself to develop his art and find new ways to combine on the canvas or paper what he saw with his eyes and what he understood in his mind with what he felt in his heart. Van Gogh's approach to art epitomizes this combination of observation from life, knowledge gained from studying the theories and the work of others, and emotional expression. Although Van Gogh tended not to paint purely from his imagination, he sometimes added fantastical elements. For example, one of his most famous paintings, *Starry*

Night over the Rhône (1888, Musée d'Orsay, Paris), in which lovers take an evening walk along the River Rhône, was painted outdoors at the actual location, but it has been noted by art historians that if he were facing south-west, as he appears to be, the Ursa Major constellation that gives the painting its name would not have been visible.[39] In addition, it is probable that the strolling figures were also an embellishment. The idea for the painting had percolated in Van Gogh's mind for a while before he finally produced it. In June 1888, he wrote to Émile Bernard: '…when will I do the starry sky… that painting that's always on my mind?'[40] Van Gogh clearly composed elements of his pictures in his head. The paintings that he made in the walled gardens at Saint-Rémy, for example, undoubtedly include imaginative elements. 'I sometimes make changes to the subject', he wrote to Bernard the following October, 'but still I don't invent the whole of the painting; on the contrary, I find it ready-made – but to be untangled – in the real world.'[41]

During Van Gogh's time in the hospital in Saint-Rémy, his art was beginning to attract attention. In January 1890, the critic Albert Aurier had written favourably of his work in the influential magazine, *Mercure de France* and the following month his painting *The Red Vineyard* (Pushkin Museum, Moscow), which was on display in Brussels alongside two paintings of sunflowers that he made in Arles, sold for 400 francs to the Belgian painter Anna Boch, a sale that, if perhaps not the only one he made in his lifetime as has often been said, was surely the most significant. Momentum was building, Theo was continuing to submit his paintings to exhibitions, and in March 1890, ten of his works were selected for inclusion at the prestigious Salon des Indépendants in Paris. When Van Gogh finally left the psychiatric hospital in May 1890, he moved to Auvers-Sur-Oise near Paris, where he was closer to Theo and in contact with other artists. A doctor based there, Paul Gachet, who was himself an amateur painter, advised him to keep painting, which he did, working daily in the gardens and wheatfields. In July, however, his health deteriorated significantly, partly due to the intense anxiety he felt on learning that Theo, on whom he was still financially reliant, intended to leave his job and start his own business. Theo had married Johanna Bonger in 1889 and their son Vincent was born in January 1890. It is probable that Van Gogh felt that he was a burden on his brother, who now had a family to support. On 27 July, Van Gogh walked into a wheatfield and shot himself in the chest with a pistol. He died two days later.

Van Gogh's contribution to art history has been immense. His work was emboldened by the colour of the Impressionists and Neo-Impressionists, liberated by the loose brushworks of his fellow Dutch artists Frans Hals (1580–1666) and Rembrandt, and given a new sense of perspective by Japanese printmakers such as Katsushika Hokusai and Utagawa Hiroshige (1797–1858). He channelled his fanatical drive into extreme hard work and found a way to present the way he *experienced* the world, as well as the way he saw it. Today, the Van Gogh Museum in Amsterdam, which houses many of the works that were in his possession when he died, is one of the most visited museums in the world, and visitors flock to see his paintings at other institutions, eager to take selfies that prove they once shared the same space with his art. Elsewhere, his images are reproduced on phone cases, umbrellas and as Lego sets. 'I can do nothing about it if my paintings don't sell', he wrote to Theo in 1888. 'The day will come, though, when people will see that they're worth more than the cost of the paint and my subsistence, very meagre in fact, that we put into them.'[42]

14

Käthe Kollwitz: Artist as Advocate

As I hope this book demonstrates, all artists are shaped by the circumstances in which they live, both in their ways of thinking and the art that they choose to produce. Born in 1867, Käthe Kollwitz lived in Berlin during the first half of the twentieth century during both World Wars in which she lost her son and her grandson. The wife of a doctor, she was exposed to the hardships and sufferings of his patients and became acutely aware of the particular challenges facing working-class people, especially women. Her art, which took the form of drawings, prints and sculpture, is not cheerful. It reflects the times in which she lived and the personal tragedies that she experienced. I often wonder what she might have produced if she had lived in a different time and a different place, and whether she was innately drawn to the dark side of life, or if she simply responded to the world as she found it.

In 1903, Kollwitz completed an etching titled *Woman with Dead Child*. The seated mother clutches the child's body in her arms, burying her face in his torso as his lifeless head falls backward. Her solid, naked limbs wrap around him, clenched in agony, while her fingers clamp around his fragile body, refusing to let go. What little we can see of her face is distorted by pain. The two figures are fused together in a dark mass against a featureless background, as if the mother is trying to absorb the child back into her body; in this most intense moment of maternal grief, the rest of the world no longer exists. When making this print, Kollwitz used herself and her seven-year-old son, Peter, as models, using a mirror to capture their pose. The composition resembles a pietà, a traditional subject in Western art depicting the Virgin Mary cradling the lifeless body of Jesus Christ after his violent crucifixion. Indeed, it evolved from another print, a lithograph titled *Pietà* that Kollwitz made in the same year, in which a mother stands over and embraces the laid-out body of a dead child. Both are powerful, but the etching has an emotional intensity that makes it difficult to view without feeling as if one is intruding on an acutely private moment.

The themes of motherhood and death feature prominently in Kollwitz's art, as do the experiences of women more generally, particularly the hardships faced by women from the lower social classes. In 1914, Peter, Kollwitz's second and youngest son, was killed in action on the Western Front, a few months into the First World War. He was 18 years old and Kollwitz was overcome by a grief of the kind that she had expressed in this etching 11 years earlier. She could not have known then what her son's fate would be or that the print would foreshadow a personal experience so accurately, but in 1903 she had observed this kind of grief in others. Growing up in Königsberg, East Prussia (now Kaliningrad, Russia) where infant mortality rates were relatively high among the largely agrarian population, and then living from 1891 with her husband Karl Kollwitz in the working-class neighbourhood of Prenzlauer Berg in Berlin, Kollwitz had witnessed the hardships that working women faced, from tough physical work to domestic violence, unplanned pregnancy and the loss of their children. From the beginning of her career, the experiences of the poor featured heavily in her art, as did the wider, but not unrelated, themes of war, oppression, revolution and death. After the First World War and the death of her son Peter, she became focused on exposing the futility of war and the horrors it brought, not on the battleground, but at home, among those left behind. Making prints, drawings and sculptures provided comfort to her during difficult times, helping her to work through her grief and to feel as if she was contributing to change. But making politically and socially engaged art was also something she felt duty-bound to do. 'I have no right to withdraw from the responsibility of being an advocate', she wrote in her diary in 1920, 'It is my duty to voice the suffering of men, the never-ending sufferings heaped mountain-high. This is my task, but it is not an easy one to fulfil.'[43]

Kollwitz lived between 1867 and 1945, a period which saw Germany unified into a single nation-state following the Franco-Prussian war, the Russian Revolution, both World Wars and all the social, economic and cultural repercussions that these conflicts brought with them. She was born into a family with socialist leanings, the fifth child of Carl Schmidt and Katharina Rupp Schmidt. Her father recognized her artistic talents and did everything he could to make it possible for his daughter to become a professional artist. As a girl, Kollwitz was unable to enter the local academy, but her father enrolled her in private art lessons in Königsberg from the age of 14 and then from

1886 she spent four years studying at schools for women artists in Berlin and Munich. A previous trip to both cities with her mother and sister when she was 17 had introduced her to the work of the Old Masters, including the Flemish artist Peter Paul Rubens (1577–1640), whose paintings of muscular, fleshy bodies made a great impression. At art school, Kollwitz found that she had no real affinity with painting, finding colour to be a particular stumbling block, and gradually realized that she could better express herself through drawing and printmaking – a decision she reached in part after studying the writing and prints of the German artist Max Klinger (1857–1920). In 1890, Kollwitz established her first studio in Königsberg and dedicated herself to drawing and printmaking, building on the little technical knowledge she had of the latter through hard work and experimentation. In June the following year, she married and moved with her husband to Berlin into a house that also functioned as her studio and Karl's surgery. Berlin was rapidly industrializing, and many members of the local community were engaged in the cheap labour that enabled the city's development. Kollwitz's first-hand experiences of Karl's patients, and the stories that he told her, no doubt stiffened her resolve to make work about disadvantaged people. But her art had already taken this direction, initially in the form of genre paintings and then in a planned series work based on *Germinal*, the 1885 novel by Émile Zola that explored the harsh conditions faced by coalmining communities in France in the 1860s. Influenced by the egalitarian views of her family, as well as the cultural milieu in which she came of age, Kollwitz was personally left-leaning but her interest in the lower classes also transcended politics. In working people, she saw a beauty and a sense of humanity and freedom that moved her, in contrast to the middle classes, whose 'pedantic' lives held no appeal.[44]

Kollwitz's first major achievement as an artist was her print portfolio *A Weavers' Revolt*, made between 1893 and 1898. Prior to this, Kollwitz had been working on the series related to *Germinal* but in February 1893, she attended the private première of Gerhart Hauptmann's play *The Weavers*, which explored an uprising in 1844 by a group of Silesian weavers in protest against their poor conditions and the incoming mechanization that would leave them redundant. 'The performance was a milestone in my work', Kollwitz later wrote, 'I dropped the series on *Germinal* and set to work on *The Weavers*.'[45] Although relatively small, the series took several years to complete, largely because Kollwitz was inexperienced as a printmaker and thus made many studies, trial proofs and discarded images before finishing the final six plates. She was also now a mother, having given birth to her first son Hans in 1892, who was followed by Peter in 1896. Although ostensibly about the 1844 Silesian revolt, the series, like Hauptmann's play, was intended to draw parallels with contemporary Germany. The themes of motherhood and death were present from the start. The first plate, *Need*, a crayon and pen lithograph, depicts a desperate mother at the bedside of her sick child, head in her hands, while her weaving loom calls for her attention in the background. The second, *Death*, shows the figure of death, a skeleton, reaching out to a starving woman as her husband and child helplessly stand by. The series goes on to explore the planning of the revolt, the uprising itself and the fatal consequences for some of the protesters. The series was a critical success when it was shown at the Great Berlin Art Exhibition in 1898 and, importantly for Kollwitz, it also delighted her father who had maintained such faith in her artistic abilities, although to her great regret he died before he could see the works exhibited. The series was not without its detractors, though, and official disapproval prevented Kollwitz from receiving a medal for the series. Emperor Kaiser Wilhelm II (1859–1941), who had acceded to the throne in 1888, disapproved both of avant-garde art and art that was critical of Germany or too negative in tone. In a speech given in 1901 he argued that art should assist in educating the lower classes and offering them the opportunity to 'refresh and strengthen themselves' and that rather than portraying misery, art should elevate and 'not lower itself into the gutter'.[46] Despite this, the series made her name and attracted the attention of Max Lehrs, Director of the Dresden Prints and Drawings collection, who became an important champion of her work.

In 1901, Kollwitz visited Paris for the first time, which broadened her awareness of Modernist art movements, a trip she followed with a longer visit in 1904. Her early work was influenced by artists such as Klinger and Wilhelm Leibl (1844–1900), who worked in a realist style, but in the first decade of the twentieth century, Kollwitz began to move away from the naturalistic scenes of *A Weavers' Revolt* to produce images that focused more on the forms, gestures and expressions of her figures, who were often isolated from their surroundings as in *Woman with Dead Child*. In 1902, she began work on her second major print series, *Peasants' War*, a group of seven etchings on the subject of a revolt by German peasants in 1524–5 against their religious and feudal overlords. Again, Kollwitz was interested in the contemporary parallels and once more she focused on the experiences of women. The second plate, *Raped*, for example, shows a violated and broken woman lying in her garden while her terrified child looks over the fence. In the sixth plate, *Battlefield*, a mother stands over the body of her dead son. The women in the series are not only portrayed as victims, however, but as active protagonists. The figure standing over the dead child is 'Black Anna', the nickname of Margarete Renner (c.1475–1535), a woman from the Black Forest, who was one of the leaders of the revolt. The third plate is a closely cropped image of a determined peasant woman sharpening her scythe. Again, the series had a powerful impact and brought Kollwitz considerable attention, as well as the Villa Romana Prize that allowed her to spend several months in Italy.

Around this time, Kollwitz's attention began to turn towards sculpture, which she had studied briefly at the Académie Julian on her second visit to Paris in 1904. During that trip she had visited Auguste Rodin, whose work made a significant impression. She made her first sculptural work in 1908, a bronze portrait relief of her maternal grandfather Julius Rupp, a Protestant theologian. It was the death of Peter in October 1914, however, that led to her almost abandoning printmaking and focusing on sculpture for almost four years. In the weeks following the terrible news, she wrote in her diary that she had conceived of an idea for a memorial, which eventually became *Grieving Parents*: a stone sculpture of a man and woman kneeling, both with their arms wrapped around themselves, the mother with her head bowed. The granite sculpture, which took 15 years to complete, was installed in 1932 at Peter's grave in Belgium. Her protracted work on the memorial and on the theme of her loss was at times comforting and at times painful. In 1916, she wrote in her diary 'Made a drawing: the mother letting her dead son slide into her arms. I might make a hundred such drawings and yet do not get any closer to him. I am seeking him… I feel… that Peter is somewhere in the work and I might find him.'[47] She also described her attempts to distance herself from her personal experiences when working, for fear that 'I again feel myself the mother who will not give up the sorrow.'[48] But writing in 1920, she reflected, 'Tranquility and relief have come to me only when I was engaged on one thing: the big memorial for Peter. Then I had peace and was with him.'[49] It is clear that the monumental nature of a stone sculpture was important to Kollwitz when making the memorial to her son. Its three-dimensionality brings the suffering of the parents to life, while the resilient nature of the stone offers some hope that life might go on.

Kollwitz's interest in printmaking was reignited when she saw a group of woodcuts by sculptor Ernst Barlach at an exhibition in June 1920. She admired the expressive nature of the prints, which she felt were powerful and profound. Between 1922 and 1923, she made the seven woodcuts that make up her series *War*, which explored the experience of women whose sons and husbands went off to fight in the First World War, as well as the hardship that German people were continuing to endure. After Peter's death, Kollwitz was increasingly outspoken about her commitment to pacifism. In October 1918, *Vorwärts*, a newspaper published by the Social Democratic Party, published a letter by her written in response to a call for men to volunteer, in which she pleaded, 'There has been enough of dying! Let not another man fall!'[50] In 1924, she produced a poster titled *War – Never Again!*, one of several posters she designed during this period that included *Help Russia* (1921) – an image of an emaciated man collapsing as disembodied hands reach out to catch him – which was produced for the International Workers' Aid organization to raise money for Russians affected by famine. Kollwitz's increasing despair at the world in which she lived was reflected in *Death*, her series of eight lithographs made between 1934 and 1937, as the National Socialists under Adolf Hitler tightened their grip on Germany and the world moved towards another great war. In 1932, Kollwitz had signed a petition calling for unity organized by the left, which led, in 1933, to her dismissal from the Prussian Academy of Arts, where she had been made a professor in 1919, the year she also became its first female member. Despite being denied the opportunity to exhibit over the following years, she continued to make work, driven by the sense of duty that she increasingly felt. In the late 1930s and early 1940s, she concentrated once again on sculpture, producing several works on the theme of motherhood. *Tower of Mothers* (1938), for example, was a bronze sculpture of a group of women forming a protective ring around their children. She made her final print in 1942, *Seeds for the Planting Shall Not be Ground Up*, a lithograph depicting a woman holding three boys close to her body with her arms forming a protective barrier between them and the world. In the same year, her grandson, also called Peter, was killed fighting in Russia. Both Kollwitz's personal experiences and her dedication to her politically and socially engaged art clearly took their toll. She experienced periods of deep depression throughout her life, a life that she examined and recorded in over 100 drawn and printed self-portraits and written diaries. Despite this, her son Hans remembered his mother as someone who loved laughter and longed for opportunities to laugh, and there are moments of lightness and pleasure in her work, including an etching made in 1910 that shows a happy mother smiling at her little child. But the troubled times in which Kollwitz lived, and the empathy that she felt for those less fortunate than her, required her to sacrifice some of that happiness and repeatedly confront the darkest elements of the human experience.

15

Henri Matisse: Seeking Colour and Light

Had it not been for a serious bout of appendicitis, Henri Matisse might never have become an artist. Born at the home of his grandparents in Le Cateau-Cambrésis in Picardy, northern France on New Year's Eve 1869, Matisse grew up in nearby Bohain-en-Vermandois and initially studied law in Paris but found his chosen career uninspiring. Back in Picardy, he soon became bored of his job as a legal clerk and it was at this time, in 1890, that Matisse became ill. During his extended recovery, he brought a box of paints with which he began to experiment. Matisse was not from a family of lawyers but a family of artisans and crafts-people who were creatively inclined. Le Cateau-Cambrésis was a textile town, and Matisse was descended from several generations of weavers. During his childhood, his parents ran a shop that sold hardware goods and house paints where his mother, Anna Héloïse Gérard, who was a good amateur painter of porcelain, advised customers on their domestic colour schemes. It is possible, therefore, that Matisse may have chosen a creative path regardless of his illness, but the forced break from the law was certainly a catalyst. Shortly after he returned to work, he began to take drawing classes and in 1891 he abandoned the legal profession completely. 'Once bitten by the demon of painting', he later said, 'I never wanted to give up.'[51] He rented his first studio in Paris, on the quai Saint-Michel, in 1894, after studying at the city's École des Beaux-Arts. In Paris, he immersed himself in art and became familiar with the work of the Impressionists as well as Vincent van Gogh, who had died just a few years before, and Paul Cézanne who was a major influence. By 1905, Matisse was at the forefront of contemporary art as a leader of the Fauves, a group known for their daring use of colour. He went on to produce a considerable body of paintings, drawings, prints, sculptures and *papiers découpés* – paper cut-outs – an art form he innovated in his later years. At times radical and revolutionary and at times working in a way that was out of step with the avant-garde, Matisse always remained faithful to his chosen mode of expression, specifically his pursuit of representing space and light through colour, refusing to be pulled in directions with which his creativity didn't align. Describing his aims in 1908, at a time when Pablo Picasso was battling with Cubism, Matisse wrote: 'What I dream of is an art of balance, of purity and serenity, devoid of troubling or depressing subject matter, an art that could be for every mental worker, for the businessman as well as the man of letters … a soothing, calming influence on the mind.'[52]

In many ways, Matisse was successful in his aims. His work has brought calm, and indeed joy, to many, not least through his use of bold and uplifting colour. Like Van Gogh, he originally worked in a much duller palette, which he referred to as his 'old-master palette' in reference to the painters whose work he studied at the Louvre. It was in Brittany, where he spent several summers working *en plein air* from 1895, that he realized that brighter colours would better help him to achieve on canvas the effects of natural light that he sought to capture. 'The search for colour did not come to me from studying paintings', he later explained, 'but from the outside – that is from the revelation of light in nature.'[53] But, also like Van Gogh, Matisse's depictions of what he observed in nature were combined with the expression of his feelings. He sought not only to express the physical phenomenon of light, but the sensations it elicited in him. In 1898, he experienced a different kind of light, this time in the south of France when he visited Corsica with his new wife, Amélie Parayre. Having felt inspired by the southern light, colours and landscape, he spent the summer of 1904 in Saint-Tropez where he experimented with colour division whereby dabs of pure colour were juxtaposed on a canvas with the intention that they would merge in the eye. Divisionism, or Pointillism, as it is sometimes known, was practised by the Neo-Impressionists, including Paul Signac with whom Matisse exchanged ideas. The following year, Matisse returned to the south with his family, this time to Collioure, a fishing village near the Spanish border. There, he was joined by André Derain, a fellow artist whom he had met five years earlier. For several weeks, the two artists worked side-by-side. Their shared aim was to move away from using colour merely to describe the subject that they were representing, but to use it to express feeling, which resulted in bold and unnatural colour choices. Their efforts resulted in Matisse's breakthrough painting *The Open Window* (National Gallery of Art, Washington DC), an image of fishing boats seen through an open window in bright reds, browns, pinks, blues and greens, applied with thick, urgent brushstrokes that captured the sunlight dancing on the water and flooding into the room.

Matisse showed *The Open Window*, and other paintings that he had made that summer, at the Salon d'Automne in Paris later in the year. They were displayed in the infamous Salle VII alongside Derain's Collioure works and paintings by other artists with a shared approach, including Maurice de Vlaminck and Albert Marquet. After seeing their vivid paintings together, the critic Louis Vauxcelles wittily named the movement the Fauves, meaning 'wild beasts'. Matisse's radical use of colour was cemented the following year, in 1906, when he exhibited the large-scale painting *The Joy of Life* (Barnes Foundation, Philadelphia), at the 1906 Salon des Indépendants. An Arcadian scene of merry-making, dancing and pleasure-seeking, the painting caused outrage among some, who objected to its unnatural oranges, yellows, greens and blues, the semi-abstracted bodies of the figures, and the lack of coherence in scale and perspective. To others, it was dazzling. It was purchased by Leo and Gertrude Stein, the influential American brother-and-sister collectors living in Paris, and it is thought to have spurred a rivalry in Picasso that contributed to the completion the following year of his landmark painting *Les Demoiselles d'Avignon* (Museum of Modern Art, New York).[54] By 1908, however, Matisse had moved on from Fauvism, recognizing the limitations of the approach: 'Fauvism … was a brief time when we thought it was necessary to exalt all colours together, sacrificing none of them. Later we went back to nuances, which gave us more supple elements than the flat, even tones.'[55]

Just as travelling to Brittany and the south of France helped Matisse to realize the ideas that he expressed in his Fauvist works, seeking and experiencing new locations helped him to move on. First, he found an inspiring subject in the garden of a villa he purchased in the Paris suburb of Issy-les-Moulineaux, to which he relocated with his family in 1909. Unable to serve in the First World War as the result of his fragile health, he spent the war years in Paris and Issy, experimenting with new ideas including Cubism. But finding himself at odds with this new mode of representation, he eventually abandoned his attempts and accepted that this was not the kind of art he wanted to make: 'A will to rhythmic abstraction was battling with my natural, innate desire for rich, warm, generous colours and forms....'[56] His move to Nice in 1918, where he had spent time the previous year to recover from bronchitis and was to spend most of the rest of his life, brought this battle to a definitive end. During his first decade in the Mediterranean city, Matisse's output was dominated by paintings of interiors and posed models with theatrical backdrops informed by an interest in Islamic art and culture, to which he had been exposed on visits to Algeria in 1906, and Morocco in 1912 and 1913, trips he had taken in part in pursuit of more intense light. In addition, a visit to an exhibition of Islamic art in Munich in 1910 and a trip to southern Spain in the same year also stimulated this interest. At the time, both Algeria and Morocco were under French colonial control, and colonial channels also enabled Matisse to collect non-Western art objects. It is within this context that he painted images of eroticized 'odalisques' (female members of a harem), posed by models in his studio with costumes and props, and other images infused with references to the 'Orient', a vague and fictionalized Eastern world in which people and objects from Asia and North America were presented as 'exotic' and somewhat homogenized. It was not this aspect of the work that received criticism among his contemporaries, however, but rather the relatively conventional nature of the paintings following the audacity of his Fauvist period. But this period in his work allowed Matisse to explore not only the light of the Mediterranean and his experiences of the landscape, colours and atmosphere of Morocco, but also new ways of depicting objects and textures, putting into practice what he had learned about colour and perspective during his years based in Paris. Yet by the end of the 1920s, he had reached a dead end. Another direction was to come, but not before he went on a journey.

On 27 February 1930, looking for new creative ideas, Matisse set out at the age of 60 to Tahiti in French Polynesia. Once again, he was motivated by the light: 'What can it be like on the other side of the hemisphere?', he wondered.[57] He travelled to the South Pacific via the United States, visiting several cities including New York, Chicago and San Francisco. He stayed in Tahiti for three months, making drawings, which although they were often devoid of colour, helped him to think through ideas about light and space. It took a long time for the experiences he had in Tahiti to find direct expression in Matisse's work. Before they did, a commission that he received to design a mural for the Barnes Foundation in Philadelphia gave him a focus on his return to Nice and marked a new period in his art. Set within the architectural space above the windows in one of the galleries, *The Dance* is a site-specific three-panelled painting depicting dancing figures in grey, which tumble and cavort in concert against a background of blue, pink and black. The project engendered a new freedom in Matisse's art and a move to a more abstract, decorative and immersive style. Matisse worked on *The Dance* for three years, eventually finishing it in April 1933. Everything that Matisse achieved was the result of hard work and deep thinking. Just as Van Gogh spoke of thinking about *Starry Night* for many months before he eventually painted it, Matisse also created in his mind before picking up his brush. Much of his thinking was also done on paper through drawing. 'To draw is to make an idea precise', he said in 1949, 'Drawing is the precision of thought.'[58] He also worked relentlessly throughout his career, beginning work punctually in the morning, breaking for meals and then continuing into the evening. It is unsurprising, therefore, that a major operation and brush with death in 1941 failed to quell his creativity.

In 1941, Matisse underwent emergency surgery to remove an intestinal tumour. Complications during his recovery nearly cost him his life and he was left in pain and with severely reduced mobility. Forced to spend much of his final decade in bed or a wheelchair, Matisse was unable to work in the way that he was used to. These circumstances led to the development of his cut-out technique from 1943, whereby studio assistants painted sheets of paper in gouache colours of his choosing, which were then left to dry before Matisse cut shapes from them, which he described as 'drawing with scissors'.[59] At first, he worked with a board on his lap on which he arranged the shapes himself, but he soon established a system whereby his assistants pinned the shapes to the walls at his direction. During these years, while war was raging across Europe, Matisse worked in a studio-apartment in the Hôtel Régina in Cimiez, an area in Nice, and at the villa Le Rêve in nearby Vence, where he went to escape the air raids. Visitors to each location would have found walls covered in his cut-out shapes, from which he created over 200 works of art. One of the first was his art book *Jazz*, published in 1947 but begun in 1943,

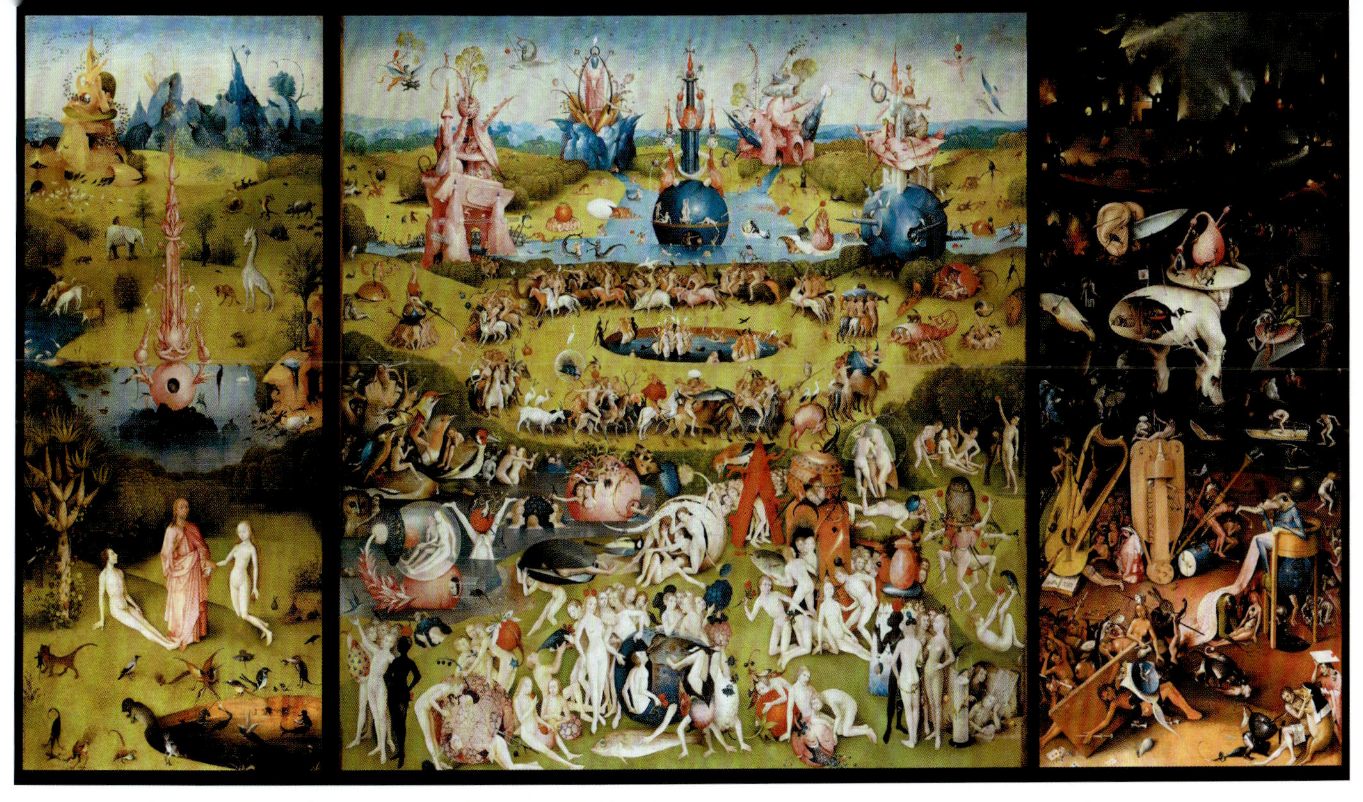

Hieronymus Bosch (*c.*1450–1516), *The Garden of Earthly Delights*, 1490–1500, oil on oak panel (Museo del Prado, Madrid)

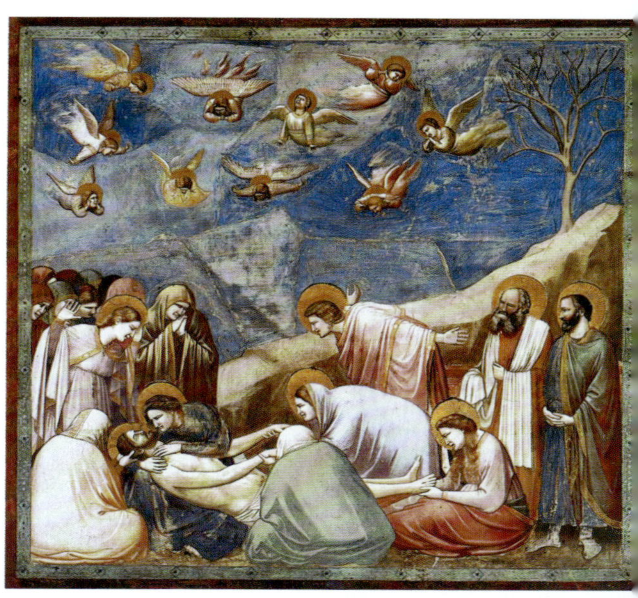

Giotto
(1266/7–1337),
*Lamentation
(The Mourning
of Christ)*, about
1305, fresco
(Scrovegni
Chapel, Padua)

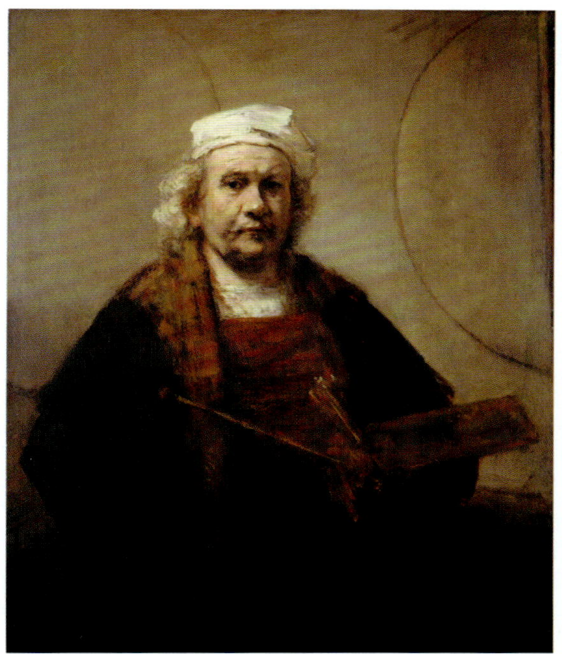

Rembrandt van
Rijn (1606–69),
*Self-Portrait with
Two Circles*,
about 1666,
oil on canvas
(Kenwood
House, London,
English
Heritage)

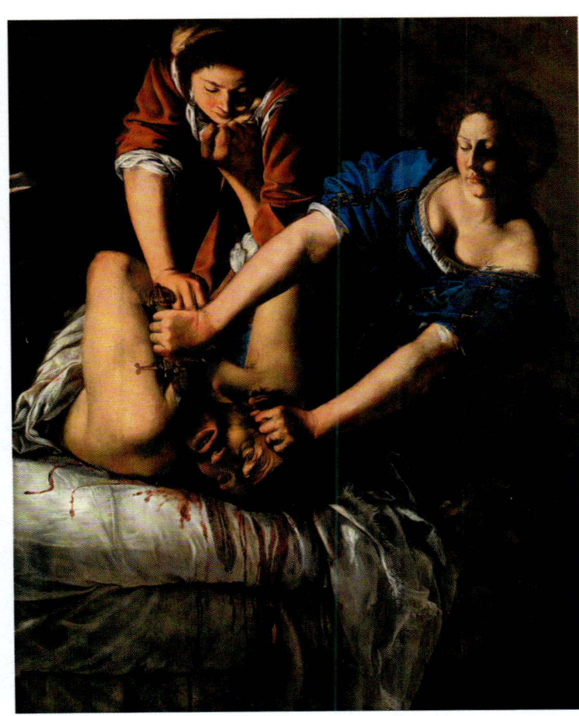

Artemisia Gentileschi (1593–1654 or later), *Judith beheading Holofernes*, 1613-14, oil on canvas (Museo e Real Bosco di Capodimonte, Naples)

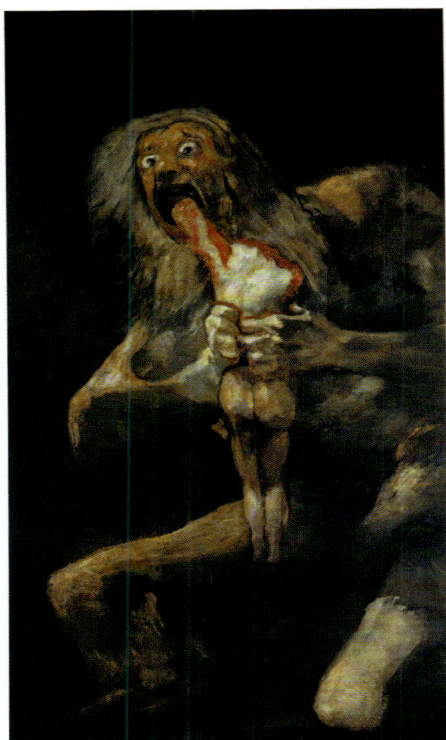

Francisco de Goya (1746–1828), *Saturn* from the *Black Paintings*, 1820-3, mural transferred to canvas (Museo del Prado, Madrid)

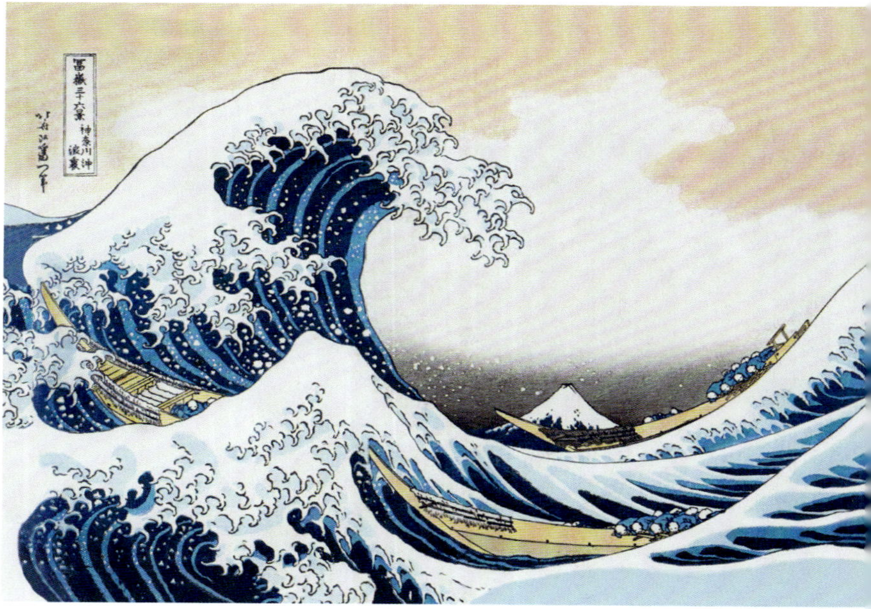

Katsushika Hokusai (1760–1849), *Under the Wave off Kanagawa* or *The Great Wave* from *Thirty-six Views of Mount Fuji*, about 1830-2, woodblock print (Metropolitan Museum of Art, New York)

Vincent van Gogh (1853–90), *Starry Night over the Rhône*, 1888, oil on canvas (Mus d'Orsay, Paris)

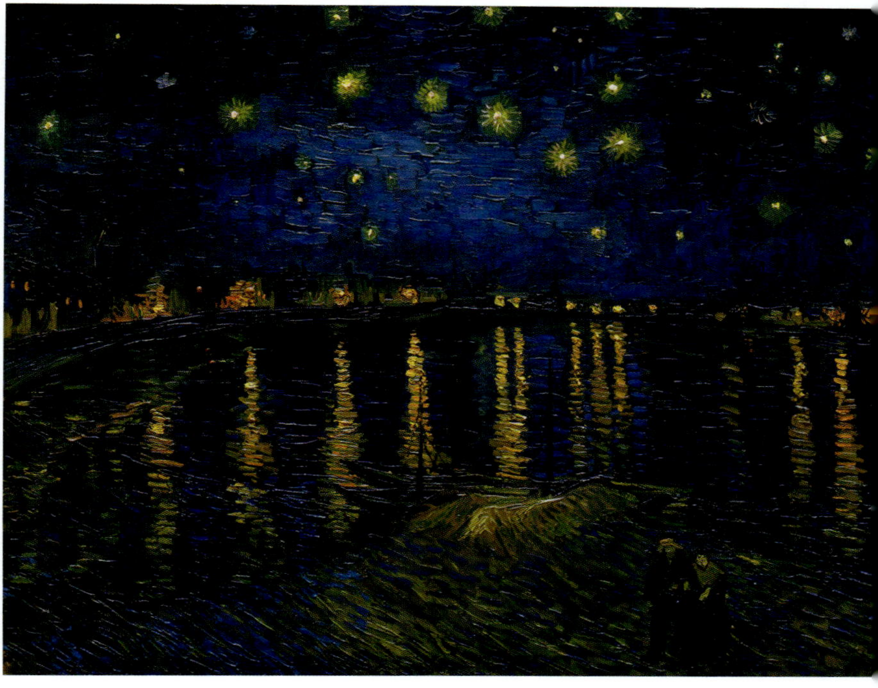

the Kollwitz (1867–1945), *Woman with Dead Child*, 1903, etching and soft ground
hing with black chalk, graphite and metallic paints (National Gallery of Art,
shington DC)

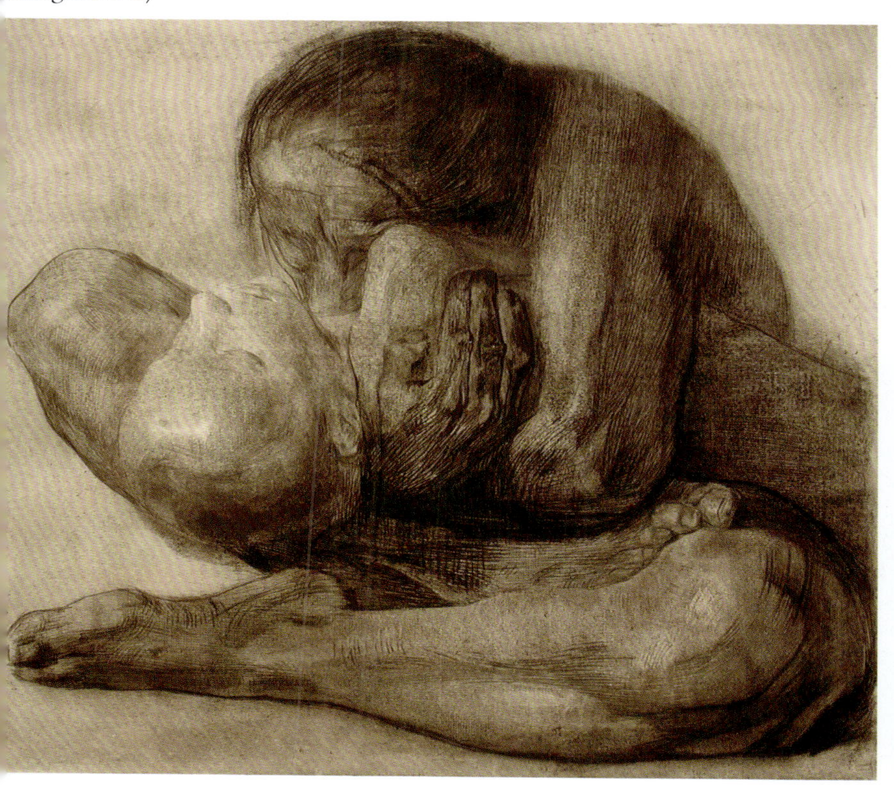

Henri Matisse (1869–1954), *The Joy of Life*, 1905-6, oil on canvas
(The Barnes Foundation, Philadelphia)

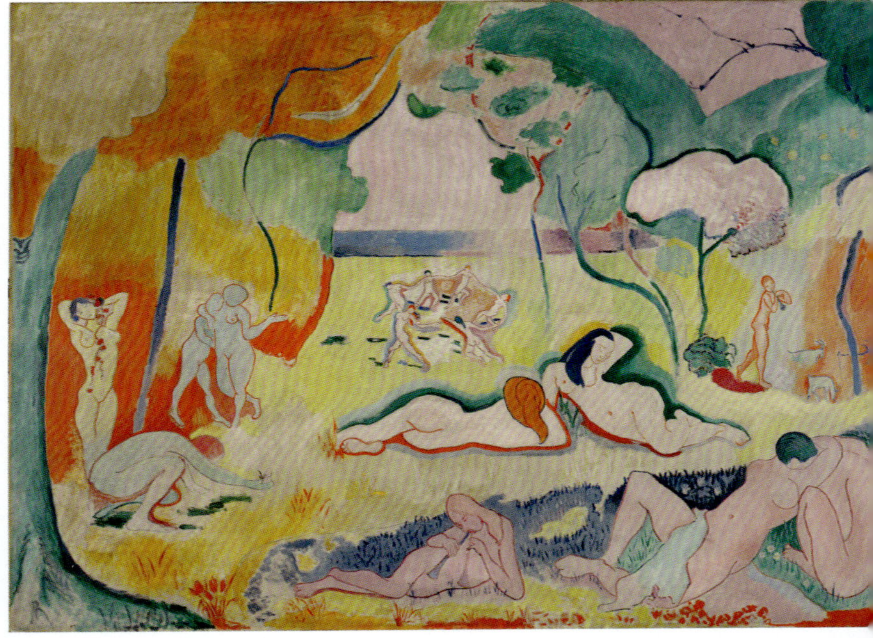

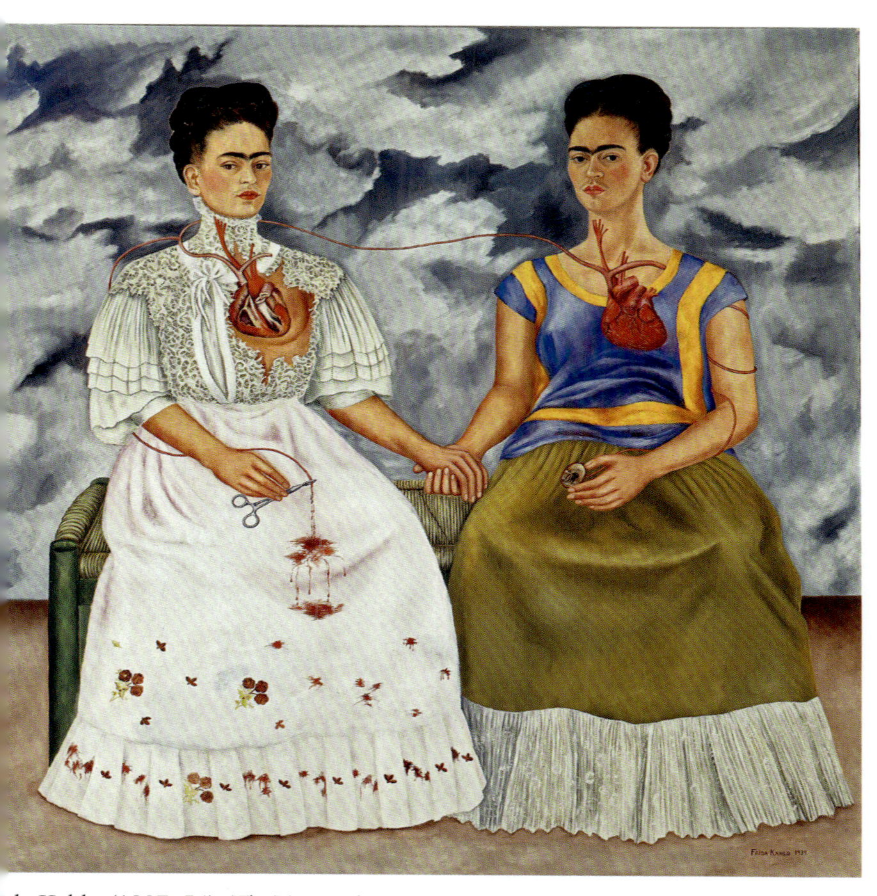

da Kahlo (1907–54), *The Two Fridas*, 1939, oil on canvas
useo de Arte Moderno, Mexico City)

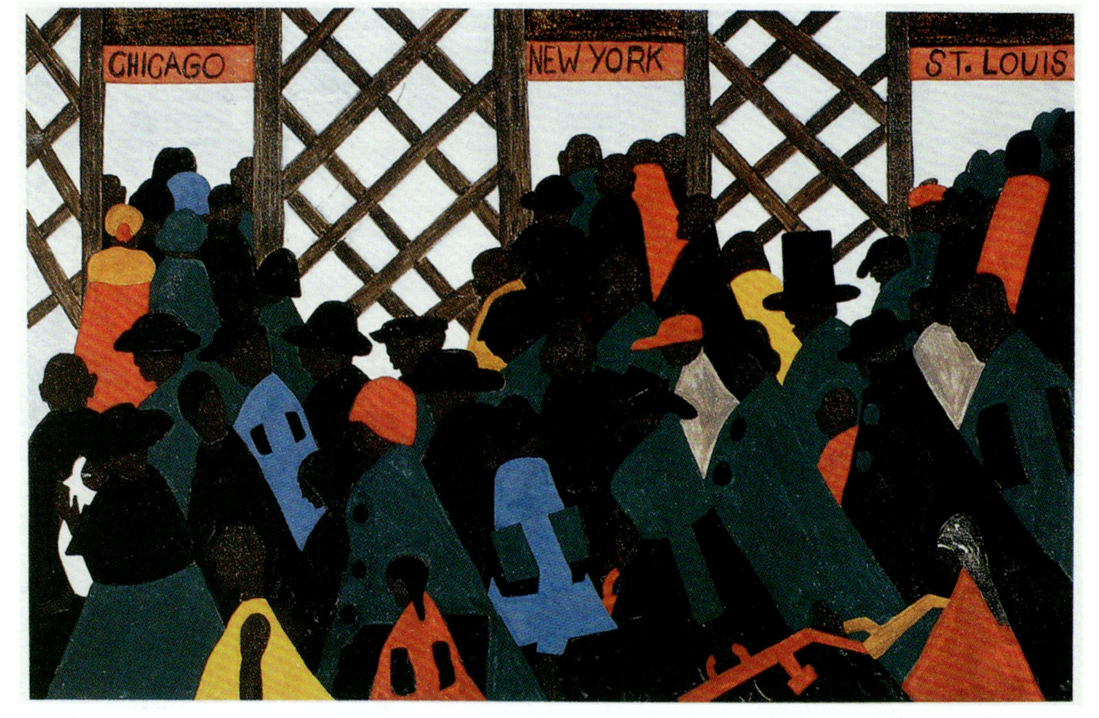

Jacob Lawrence (1917–2000), *The Migration Series*, panel no. 1, Casein tempera on hardboard, 1940–41. (Phillips Collection, Washington DC)

which included 20 colour prints of his cut-paper compositions and his own text on various subjects including his art, travel, religion and happiness. His experiences in Tahiti also found their expression in his cut-paper works, in his designs for two screenprint on fabric editions for the textile company Ascher. Made in 1946 and titled *Oceania, the sky* and *Oceania, the sea*, they comprise white cut-out shapes representing birds, sea creatures and vegetal forms against beige backgrounds that give the sense of a light so dazzling that all colour is obscured. These works were followed by the tapestries *Polynesia, the sea* and *Polynesia, the sky*. Matisse described how the effect of the light in Tahiti gave him 'the same feeling I had when I looked into a large golden chalice.'[60] In his cut-outs, Matisse distilled everything that he had learned and discovered about light and colour throughout his career. The apotheosis of this came between 1948 and 1951, with his work for the Rosary Chapel in Vence, which included designs for the stained-glass, walls, furniture and vestments. Matisse used the cut-out technique for the blue, yellow and green stained-glass, through which light pours on to black and white murals on the walls, as well as for the liturgical vestments. Matisse considered the work to be his masterpiece and reflecting on it in 1952, two years before his death on 3 November 1954 at the age of 84, he acknowledged that his illness had given him a sense of freedom in his art that he had never felt before.

16

Pablo Picasso: That Guy Missed Nothing!

When I was tiny, just one year old, I was taken by my mother to the 1981 exhibition *Picasso's Picassos* at the Hayward Gallery in London. According to her pencil annotations in the catalogue, I was transfixed by the swollen belly of Picasso's bronze sculpture of a goat and compared the Spanish artist's Cubist compositions to my elder sister's efforts at playgroup. But despite this critical slam, I seem to have been engaged by his work. Picasso loved children and recognized the directness with which they were able to communicate through drawing, before they became burdened by expectations around style and skill. On visiting an exhibition of children's drawings, he is said to have remarked, 'When I was their age I could draw like Raphael, but it took me a lifetime to learn to draw like them.'[61] This appreciation seems to have been reciprocated. Despite his often esoteric references to artists and literature and Greek myths, Picasso found a way of communicating through his art to as wide an audience as possible. As I can anecdotally testify, Picasso's art appeals to children through his bright colours and images of animals, to fellow artists through his innovations in technique and composition, and to those who simply wish to be told a story or to be shown an alternative way of seeing the world.

Artists who have come after Pablo Picasso have often struggled with the weight of his enormous legacy. One day, at home in East Hampton, New York, the twentieth-century American artist Lee Krasner was startled by a crash coming from elsewhere in the house. When she went to investigate, she found her husband Jackson Pollock on the floor, staring at a book he had thrown across the room. It was a book about Picasso, probably an exhibition catalogue from the Museum of Modern Art, covering the first 40 years of his art.[62] 'God damn it', Pollock exclaimed, 'that guy missed nothing!'[63] Like many artists who have come after him, Pollock was both inspired by the Spaniard's work and intimidated by the great legacy that Picasso left. During his lifetime, Picasso produced around 20,000 works of art. He was incredibly prolific, working across media in painting, drawing, printmaking, sculpture, ceramics and theatre design. He was endlessly curious, always seeking to move his art forward and discover new ways of making images, of exploring a subject and expressing his ideas. He often oscillated between different media and styles, moving at times between semi-abstraction and a much more naturalistic imagery, refusing to progress along a linear path in his art without exploring alternative routes and occasionally turning back. He took inspiration from everywhere, including books and magazines, literature, film and TV, the work of other artists, the world around him and his own life and relationships. Often the sources that he referenced would sit in his brain for years, percolating, only to appear somewhat spontaneously, particularly when he was making drawings or prints. Picasso was eager throughout his life to take opportunities to explore new ways of working, taking up ceramics, for example, when he moved to a town where there was a pottery in the mid-1940s. Half a century after his death, Picasso's work is still widely exhibited, reproduced, written about and explored from all angles. Artists continue to grapple with him; some love his work, consciously learn from him and pay homage to him, others react against him and critique him, but few are able to ignore him. In recent years, aspects of his character and personal life have increasingly been scrutinized, particularly his treatment of women, which could be cruel and abusive, and which cannot be untangled from his art, but his influence endures and he remains one of the most famous artists of all time.

Although Picasso spent most of his career in France, he was born and brought up in Spain and his Spanish heritage shaped his art throughout his life. He was born in the nineteenth century, on 25 October 1881 in Málaga, Andalusia on the Mediterranean coast. His father, José Ruiz Blasco, was a painter and art teacher. Picasso took his name from his mother, Maria Picasso López. In 1891, the family moved across the country to La Coruña in north-west Spain, where Picasso attended art school. He went on to study in Barcelona, where his father took a teaching job in 1895, and Madrid, at the Royal Academy of Fine Arts. Picasso had drawn from a young age and had been taught to paint by his father. He had a natural talent and by his late teens was a highly skilled draughtsman but felt restricted by the traditional training he received in the academy. By 1899, he was living in Barcelona among a group of bohemian artists and writers, centred around Els Quatre Gats (The Four Cats), a café and art centre where he would have his first solo exhibition in 1900, aged 19. In the same year, he visited

Paris for the first time, which was then the centre of the art world in the West. Paris offered more opportunities for a young artist than Barcelona, as it had a well-established infrastructure of studios, galleries and dealers, and a ready market, and was then abuzz with avant-garde writers and artists from across Europe. Picasso's first solo exhibition there came quickly, in 1901, at the gallery of the influential dealer Ambroise Vollard, who had previously championed the work of Van Gogh, Gauguin and Cézanne – all artists whose work Picasso admired. After several years of living between the two cities, Picasso moved permanently to Paris in 1904 and took a home-studio in a run-down building in Montmartre nicknamed the Bateau-Lavoir because it swayed in the wind like the laundry boats on the River Seine. In Montmartre, he was surrounded by artists, some of whom he'd known in Spain, and became friends with writers including Guillaume Apollinaire, Max Jacob and André Salmon. The area was also home to performers, including erotic dancers from the nearby clubs and acrobats from the Cirque Medrano, which Picasso frequently attended. Many of the figures from the circus and the streets of Montmartre, including sex workers, addicts and those living in poverty, found their way into his early work.

In February 1901, Picasso's great friend and fellow Spanish artist Carles Casagemas publicly shot himself in Paris following a period of depression and alcohol misuse partly triggered by unrequited love. He had accompanied Picasso on his first visit to Paris the previous year and the two had shared accommodation and explored the city together, taking advantage of all it had to offer, including its bars and its women. The death of Casagemas had a significant impact on Picasso's work. He responded to the loss in a number of paintings, including a portrait of his dead friend in repose, closely cropped around his head with a candle burning alongside (Picasso Museum, Paris), the unnatural colours and loose brushwork of which show the influence of Van Gogh. Picasso's grief brought a sense of melancholy to his work, which found expression in a primarily blue palette and images of poor, emaciated figures. Although greatly influenced at this time by the generation of artists who came before him, including Édouard Manet (1832–83) and Henri de Toulouse-Lautrec (1864–1901), Picasso had also become very familiar while studying in Madrid with the greats of Spanish art, including El Greco (1541–1614), Diego Velázquez (1599–1660) and Goya, whose work he had studied in the Prado Museum. The art of his Blue Period, as it has become known, shows the influence of El Greco in particular in the elongated limbs and long, bony figures and necks of his wretched protagonists. *The Frugal Meal*, his first etching as a professional artist, made shortly after he arrived in Paris in 1904, exemplifies this. A hungry-looking couple sit in a drinking tavern, an empty bowl and a looming bottle on the table before them. The man, who is blind, drapes his arm over the left side of his partner, his fingers falling down her shoulder, while the fingers of his other arm rest on her right arm, partially fanned out and extending up like a climbing ivy. The woman looks out at the viewer with an intense gaze, while the man turns away. Picasso was untrained as a printmaker but soon realized that making prints, which could be produced in multiple copies, was a way of reaching a larger audience and attracting buyers who were unable to afford paintings or sculpture. Paris was a printmaking hub, with a network of established professional print studios and publishers, including Vollard, who could facilitate and distribute artists' editions. From 1904 onward, Picasso produced around 2,400 prints using a variety of techniques including etching, aquatint, drypoint, lithography and linocut. He found that printmaking offered a respite from his painting, but also provided him with an alternative creative output, one that continued to inspire him throughout his life.

Picasso's most radical moment came in 1907 when he painted *Les Demoiselles D'Avignon* (The Ladies of Avignon, Museum of Modern Art, New York), an audacious, large-scale image of five female sex workers in a brothel, standing naked, some with their arms raised, confronting the viewer provocatively. Picasso's early work in Paris had been relatively naturalistic, despite the exaggeratedly bony limbs and figures of his subjects, but in this painting the bodies of the women are partially abstracted and composed of jagged geometric shapes, while their faces are blank and mask-like, with over-large eyes. In addition, Picasso had abandoned linear perspective, breaking up the picture plane so that it is unclear where each body stands in relation to the others and the objects around them, which include a curtain and a table holding a bowl of fruit. Like many others in his circle, Picasso had recently become interested in non-Western art objects from Africa and Oceania, as well as ancient art from the Iberian Peninsula (which includes Spain and Portugal). In 1905 he saw an exhibition of Iberian art in the Louvre and it soon began to influence his art. Three of the women in this painting have simplified, blank faces with large eyes reminiscent of the recently excavated objects he had seen. The heads of the other two women are closer in style to the African objects that some of his friends had begun to collect, including Matisse and Apollinaire, and which he started to buy after finishing the painting. Picasso's attitude to non-Western art is often criticized today. Collectors in Paris were able to acquire these objects through colonial channels, and the objects were often referred to as 'primitive art'. Picasso was attracted to objects for their aesthetic values, primarily their shapes, and was uninterested in their makers, use or cultural significance, an attitude that was widespread at the time. *Les Demoiselles d'Avignon* shocked many of those who saw it, including Picasso's closest friends and supporters. In addition to the allusions to non-Western art, Picasso was radical in breaking up the picture plane, a move towards Cubism, the style he developed over the following years in close collaboration with the French artist Georges Braque. Cubism was an attempt to find a new way of representation, which Picasso and Braque felt was closer to the true way of seeing. Between around 1908 and 1914, when Braque left Paris to fight in the First World War, the two artists made work that was strikingly similar and increasingly abstract – although never completely so – that depicted objects, often still lifes, from multiple viewpoints simultaneously. Picasso, who as a Spaniard was not conscripted, continued to make Cubist works into the 1920s and eventually found that he had taken his explorations as far as they could go, but that he had altered the course of modern art in the process.

In the 1920s and '30s, Picasso returned to a more naturalistic style, which was very influenced by the ancient Greek and Roman art he saw on a visit to Italy in 1917 when he was working with Russian ballet company the Ballet Russes. Picasso's interest in classical art had previously been stimulated by the work of French Neo-Classical artist Jean-Auguste-Dominique Ingres (1780–1867), whose elegant lines were inspired by Greek sculpture and ancient objects such as painted vases and engraved bronze mirrors. At the time, Picasso spoke about his change in style, which found its expression in paintings, drawings, prints and sculpture, explaining: 'The several manners I have used in my art must not be considered as an evolution, or as steps toward an unknown ideal of painting … If the subjects I have wanted to express have suggested different ways of expression I have never hesitated to adopt them.'[64] Much of Picasso's so-called 'classical period', particularly the first half of the 1930s, reflects his complicated personal life at the time. In 1918, he had married Olga Khokhlova, a Ukrainian-born ballet dancer whom he had met while working with the Ballet Russes, and in 1921 they had had a son, Paulo. In 1927, however, Picasso, who was by this point in his mid-forties, met Marie-Thérèse Walter, who was 17, with whom he soon began an affair. Picasso's art from this time contains multiple images of Walter and references to their secret meetings, which often took place at the beach when he was on holiday with his wife and child, or time spent together in his sculpture studio just outside of Paris. Much of this work is erotically charged, reflecting Picasso's desire for his young lover, sometimes violently so – for example, in his etchings of the Minotaur, the dangerous and hungry half-man, half-bull of ancient Greece. Picasso's marriage came to an end around 1935 and his relationship with Walter ended soon afterwards.

In 1936, civil war broke out in Spain and Francisco Franco, leader of the Nationalist forces, took over the ruling of the country as a dictator. The war was a political awakening for Picasso who had been largely unpolitical until this point. He made numerous works of art in response, most famously the mural-sized oil painting *Guernica* (1937), depicting the horrific aftermath of the bombing of the Basque town by German and Italian fascist forces. Picasso painted the scene in black, white and grey as a response to newspaper images. An anguished woman carries her dead child, a horse twists in agony and broken bodies flee in terror. At the time, Picasso was in a relationship with the Surrealist photographer Dora Maar, who documented the making of the painting and increased Picasso's political awareness. Famously, Maar was the model for the *Weeping Woman*, a series of paintings and prints also made in response to the war, portraying a grieving woman, her face contorted with pain, with the reflection of flying bombers in her eyes and tears falling from her eyes. The motif was in part inspired by a letter from Picasso's mother in which she described how all the fires in Barcelona made her eyes water, and partly by the tradition in Spanish art of representations of the Virgin Mary in sculpture with glass tears. In 1937, *Guernica* was displayed in the Spanish Pavilion of the International Exposition in Paris with two impressions of his *Weeping Woman* print alongside. The painting was sent to the United States in 1939 and was toured around the country, and internationally, where it was viewed by many. It then hung at the Museum of Modern Art, New York, until it was given to Spain in 1981. It now hangs at the Reina Sofía Museum in Madrid and continues to carry a powerful anti-war message. Sadly, Picasso himself never returned to Spain, vowing not to visit while Franco was in power. Franco died in 1975, two years after Picasso. In the mid-1940s Picasso moved to the south of France with his new partner, Françoise Gilot, first settling in the town of Vallauris near Antibes, later living in Cannes and then finally in nearby Mougins with his final partner Jacqueline Roque. Life in the south of France brought him closer to his native Spain, allowing him to attend bullfights again, a sport he had enjoyed since boyhood that he frequently referenced in his work.

In 1966, a huge retrospective exhibition was held in Paris, across the Grand Palais, the Petit Palais and the Bibliothèque Nationale, to celebrate Picasso's 85th birthday. Although he had become somewhat out of step with developments in art (he disliked contemporary movements including Abstract Expressionism and Pop Art) and had received negative reviews for some of his recent work, Picasso had secured his place in art history, alongside his great heroes Michelangelo, Velázquez and Rembrandt. Throughout his career, Picasso frequently referenced the artists he admired, showing both irreverence and respect. In 1934, for example, at a time he was particularly influenced by the prints of Rembrandt, he found a caricature of the great artist appearing spontaneously as he drew on an etching plate. Later, in the 1950s and '60s, he made several series of paintings that explored specific works of art, including the *Women of Algiers* by Eugène Delacroix (1798–1863), Velázquez's *Las Meninas* and *Dejeuner sur l'Herbe* by Manet. In 1968, when he was 86 and his health was failing, he made a group of 347 etchings over a seven-month period, working on the etching plates at home before handing them over to the printers Aldo and Piero Crommelynck who had set up a studio nearby. The prints emerged as a kind of visual diary, containing references to friends, lovers, works of literature and subjects that had interested him throughout his career including the circus, brothel scenes and allusions to artists such as Rembrandt, El Greco and Degas. Picasso's interest in erotic Japanese prints is also evident, particularly in a group depicting the Renaissance artist Raphael having sex repeatedly with his model 'La Fornarina' (the baker's daughter). In addition, elements of popular culture found their way into the scenes including references to the televised wrestling that Picasso had become obsessed with and films that he had recently watched, such as *The Lives of a Bengal Lancer*. Picasso clearly enjoyed making these prints, reflecting on his past, fantasizing about the sex he was no longer having, and inventing characters and escapades. At the same time, he continued to experiment, using grease and solvent on the plates to create unusual textures. Picasso continued to work into his final year. He died on 8 April 1973 in his 92nd year, having created an enormous body of work and leaving an indelible mark on the twentieth century.

17

Kazimir Malevich: Nothing in Common with Nature

As Western art moved into the twentieth century, artists began to challenge the notion that good art was art that convincingly represented aspects of the physical world. Picasso sought to unburden himself from the refined style that had developed over centuries as an ideal in Western art to reach a simpler, more candid form of visual communication, but for others this move away from replicating the world in a realistic way led to an abandonment of representation altogether and the embrace of pure abstraction. Few artists followed this path as vehemently as Kazimir Malevich, who was uncompromising in his belief that art should be liberated from the burden of representation, be it representation of the physical world, of stories or experiences, or of an artist's inner thoughts, feelings and fantasies. Art, he believed, should be subject-less, object-less and should not depict or signify anything. This approach – which required an artist to free themselves from the rules of European art history, including ideas about space, perspective and light that had developed over hundreds of years – was, he argued, the only way to achieve total creative freedom. Malevich called his radical approach 'Suprematism', the principles of which he laid out in 1915 in his treatise *From Cubism and Futurism to Suprematism: The New Pictorial Realism*. In that work, he argued 'The artist can be a creator only when the forms in his picture have nothing in common with nature' and, along with his fellow Suprematists who included Ivan Puni, Ivan Kliun and Kseniya Boguslavskaya, called upon the Academy to 'renounce the inquisition of nature.'[65] In art, Suprematism was a form of pure abstraction, best exemplified by Malevich's *Black Square* (1915, State Tretyakov Gallery, Moscow), an oil painting of a black square against a white background on an unframed canvas measuring around 80 × 80 cm (31 ½ × 31 ½ in). Reduced to the most simple form, the painting existed purely on its own terms, with no references to a subject or meaning. Suprematism derived its name from the Latin word *supremus*, meaning superior or perfected and Malevich certainly believed in the superiority of his ideas. Radical movements that had come before, such as Cubism and Futurism, the Italian avant-garde movement led by Filippo Tommaso Marinetti, were, in Malevich's view, important developments on the path to Suprematism, but he felt that none had gone far enough. The creation of *Black Square* felt so momentous to him that he couldn't eat, drink or sleep for a week after it was completed, but once recovered, his energy poured into disseminating his ideas, which he embarked upon with the conviction and zeal of an evangelical preacher.

Malevich's life and career coincided with a period of great change in Western art. He was born to Polish parents in Kiev (Kyiv), Ukraine, which was then part of Tsarist Russia, on 23 February 1879, the eldest of 14 children. During his childhood, his father, Seweryn Malewicz, worked in the sugar beet industry in various locations, including Belopolye (Bilopillya), in northeastern Ukraine. Malevich began to draw aged about 12, initially sketching horses, people and his surrounding landscape. As a teenager, he briefly attended the Kiev School of Art before his family moved to Kursk in 1896, then from 1903 trained at the Moscow School of Painting, Sculpture and Architecture, where he learned to paint in an Impressionist style. In Moscow, he met some of the key figures of Russian Modernism including Wassily Kandinsky, Mikhail Larionov and Natalia Goncharova, and in 1910 joined the avant-garde arts association Jack of Diamonds, with whom he exhibited in 1914. Malevich and his fellow Russian artists were aware of contemporary developments in French art, such as Fauvism, Cubism and Futurism, as well as the work of the German Expressionist group known as Der Blaue Reiter (The Blue Rider), based in Munich. Malevich's early work, which included paintings of peasant life, carried these influences, as well as references to traditional Russian folk art and religious icon painting. In the early 1910s, his paintings became increasingly abstract as he combined geometric shapes with recognizable objects in paintings such as *Lady at a Column* and *Englishman in Moscow* (both 1914, Stedelijk Museum, Amsterdam). It was in December 1915, however, at *The Last Futurist Exhibition of Paintings: 0.10* in Petrograd (now St. Petersburg), that his Suprematist style was made public with the display of *Black Square*, the most radically abstract painting known to have been created in Western art at that time. Critics and visitors to the exhibition were bewildered and, in some cases, angered and dismayed by Malevich's audacious presentation. Malevich described the reaction in his book *The Non-Objective World* (published in 1927): 'When … in my desperate attempt to free art from the ballast of objectivity, I took refuge in the square form and exhibited a picture which consisted of nothing more than a black square on a white field, the critics and, along with them, the public sighed, "Everything which we love is lost. We are in a desert … Before is nothing but a black square on a white background!"…The square seemed incomprehensible and dangerous to the critics and the public … and this, of course, was to be expected.'[66]

Despite the criticism, Malevich persisted with his Suprematist paintings, following *Black Square* with *Black Cross* and *Black Circle* (both 1915) and he made three more versions of *Black Square*, which became a repeating motif in his art and symbol of his artistic mission. During 1916, he collaborated on a journal called *Supremus* with the painter and composer Mikhail Matyushin and poet Aleksei Kruchenykh, with the aim of spreading the message about non-objective art. Malevich's own paintings became more dynamic at this time. His compositions were still formed from simple geometric shapes, but they increasingly involved multiple elements and colours that interacted in complex ways (see, for example, *Dynamic Suprematism*, 1915/16, Tate, London). By the time the first edition of *Supremus* was ready to launch in early 1917, the February Revolution was underway, beginning with a series of mass protests that led to the abdication of Tsar Nicholas II. This first wave was followed by the October Revolution and the start of the Soviet regime. Initially, avant-garde art movements were encouraged by the new government and Malevich was able to continue freely along his Suprematist path. He found favour under the new rulers, joining the Fine Arts department of the People's Commissariat for

Enlightenment (known as Narkompros), in which he had a role contributing to the preservation and development of museums. He also became a teacher at the Free State Art Studios (Svomas) in Moscow and was commissioned to design theatre sets, posters and book covers. In 1918, Malevich produced a series of white paintings including *White on White* (Museum of Modern Art, New York), in which an off-centre, tilted white square appears to float above a slightly lighter shade of white. These paintings were exhibited in the *Tenth State Exhibition: Non-objective Creation and Suprematism* in Moscow in 1919, and in the same year, Malevich had a solo exhibition in the city at the Sixteenth State Exhibition. But life in Moscow was difficult due to shortages of food and fuel caused by the civil war that began in 1918, and Malevich found working for Narkompros challenging, in part due to internal wranglings with other artists including Kandinsky. In 1919, therefore, he accepted an offer to work at the People's Art School in the Belarusian city of Vitebsk, which had been set up by the Modernist painter Marc Chagall. At Vitebsk, Malevich found a receptive audience among the staff and students, some of whom formed a Suprematist group called Unovis, meaning Champions of the New Art. Under Malevich's direction, the group sought to apply Suprematism to all aspects of life, from clothing, wallpaper and kitchenware to furniture and architecture. Having reached something of an endpoint with his white-on-white paintings, Malevich stopped painting and dedicated himself to teaching, writing and translating his theories into non-functional architectural ideas, which found their forms in plaster models that he called 'architektons'. In 1922, under pressure from Narkompros, Malevich left Vitebsk and moved to

Petrograd, along with some members of Unovis, where he began to work for the Museum of Artistic Culture, which became the State Institute of Artistic Culture (Ginkhuk) in 1924.

During the years of the First World War and the Russian Revolution, Russian artists had become increasingly isolated from their counterparts in the West, so in the early 1920s, Narkompros made efforts to introduce developments in Russian art to the rest of Europe. In 1922, for example, an exhibition of contemporary Russian art was sent to the Galerie Van Diemen in Berlin and the Stedelijk Museum in Amsterdam, which featured six works by Malevich, including *White on White*, and numerous works by other Unovis artists. In 1927, Malevich's profile outside of Russia expanded considerably due to his three-month tour of Poland and Germany and exhibitions in Warsaw and Berlin. While in Germany, he made contact and exchanged ideas with leading European Modernists including Jean (Hans) Arp, Naum Gabo and Kurt Schwitters, and visited the Bauhaus design school, which had a similarly integrated approach to art, design and architecture to that of Unovis. In Russia, however, the attitude to avant-garde art was beginning to shift and it is possible that Malevich was considering moving to Germany, as he left many of the works and manuscripts he had taken in the care of his German hosts when he returned to what was now Leningrad. Over the following few years, the government's approach to art became increasingly conservative, favouring a realist style of painting, and Malevich became sidelined. Possibly due to the pressure that he faced when he returned to Russia from Germany, he took up painting again and returned to a figurative style, albeit one that incorporated elements of Suprematism. His painting *Suprematist Female Figure* (1928–32, State Russian Museum, St Petersburg), for example, depicts an obvious human figure, but one constructed from simple shapes in various shades of green. Without any distinguishing features, the figure is essentially a universal human representing no one in particular. In 1930, however, Malevich was banned by the government from making art on the basis that his work did not serve society, and he was imprisoned for two months, partly due to his contact with artists in Germany. After his release, he was able to practise as an artist once more, but never again made a work as radical as *Black Square*, although he continued to sign his figurative paintings with the symbol. When Malevich died in 1935, a black square was painted on his coffin, along with a black circle.

For several decades after his death, Malevich's legacy was suppressed and his work remained little known. In the mid-1950s, however, the Stedelijk Museum in Amsterdam acquired many of the works that Malevich had left in Germany in 1927 and interest in his art increased. A retrospective exhibition in 1973–4 at the Solomon R. Guggenheim Museum in New York and Pasadena Museum of Art in California came at an important moment when a generation of American artists, including Donald Judd, Ellsworth Kelly and Sol LeWitt, were producing hard-edged Minimalist compositions. Reacting against the emotionally expressive canvases of the Abstract Expressionists, the movement that included Jackson Pollock, Lee Krasner and Willem de Kooning, as well as the exploration of the everyday by the Pop artists, the Minimalists of the 1970s were interested in form, colour and materials over subject and meaning, and so Malevich's vision resonated with them.

Despite the zeal with which he preached his Suprematist message, however, Malevich believed that stasis equalled death and that everything, including art, should keep moving. He might have freed the world from the object, dragging it out of 'the rubbish-filled pool of Academic art' as he put it,[67] but he also expected art to change and develop, as it always has and it likely always will.

18

Mark Rothko: Basic Human Emotions

Unlike Malevich, who preached his message loud and proud, Mark Rothko insisted that he was not an 'abstractionist'. For those familiar with his art, this might seem puzzling, as the works for which he is best known – large-scale canvases on which fuzzy-edged rectangles appear to float in front of a different coloured background – are devoid of people and recognizable objects. But for Rothko, these paintings, which he began to make in around 1949, were an extension of the figurative works with which he started his career, a continuing exploration and expression of the human condition, and as such are intended to represent *something*. In this, he differed significantly from Malevich. 'I'm not interested in relationships of colour or form or anything else,' he told the American writer Selden Rodman in 1956, 'I'm interested only in expressing basic human emotions – tragedy, ecstasy, doom, and so on … if you … are moved only by their colour relationships, then you miss the point!'[68] Rothko also insisted that his paintings were intended to be universal in scope and not a representation of his personal emotions or those felt by specific individuals. Individualized or particular references in his work, he felt, would act as a barrier between the art and the viewer, with whom he wanted to communicate directly and powerfully. 'The fact that lots of people break down and cry when confronted with my pictures shows that I *communicate* those basic human emotions,' he told Rodman, 'The people who weep before my pictures are having the same religious experience I had when I painted them.'[69] Rothko took pains to achieve clarity in his art by removing all obstacles between the artist and the idea, and then the idea and the viewer. He sought to achieve this not only through his pared-back compositions, but also by presenting his art in an environment in which there would be as few distractions as possible. He was particularly concerned that his paintings could appear decorative if shown in the 'wrong' way. To this end, from the 1950s, Rothko became increasingly specific about the space in which his paintings were displayed. He considered the optimal environment to be a relatively intimate, dedicated space, away from work by other artists and without strong lighting or spotlights (which he believed could 'romanticize' the works). He also specified that his large canvases should be hung unframed, as close to the floor as possible.[70] Rothko wanted viewers to *feel* his art, not to intellectualize it or to focus too much on its formal or aesthetic qualities. 'One does not paint for design students or historians but for human beings,' he said in 1952, 'and the reaction in human terms is the only thing that is really satisfactory to the artist.'[71]

As a young man, Rothko had not intended to become an artist. In 1921, he took up a scholarship at Yale University where he studied a wide range of subjects, including maths, philosophy and history, with the intention of becoming a lawyer or engineer, but left in 1923 without graduating.

He was born Marcus Rothkowitz on 25 September 1903 in Dvinsk, Russia (now Daugavpils, Latvia), the youngest of four children. In 1910 his father, Jacob Rothkowitz, emigrated to the USA, where he worked in the clothing business in Portland, Oregon. Rothko's two older brothers followed in 1912 and the family was reunited the following year when Rothko, his sister and mother, Anna Goldin Rothkowitz, joined them. Sadly, however, Jacob died the following spring from cancer and the Rothkowitz children were all forced to take on part-time jobs in addition to their studies. Despite this, Rothko excelled at school. He was interested in literature, music and the theatre, and briefly considered a career in acting. It was not until he moved to New York City after leaving Yale that his interest in art really took hold. There, he began to attend courses at the Art Students League, a leading art school in Manhattan, and educated himself about art history and contemporary developments in art by visiting museums and artists' studios. One of his tutors at the Art Students League was the American painter Max Weber, who had spent time in Paris and introduced his students to European Modernism, including the work of Cézanne, Picasso and Matisse. These ideas were reinforced by the Armenian American painter Arshile Gorky, with whom Rothko also took classes, at the New School of Design. Around this time, in 1925, Rothko met the American painter Milton Avery, whose figurative paintings made an impression, particularly the use of simplified forms and flat areas of unnatural colours, which showed a movement towards abstraction. Rothko's own paintings from this time were also figurative, depicting landscapes, still lifes and scenes of figures engaged in everyday activities. During the Great Depression of the 1930s, like many American artists, Rothko was paid to produce paintings under the Works Progress Administration as part of the Federal Government's New Deal programme. These works included a series of scenes in subway stations that showed the daily grind of urban life. It was during this decade that he began to make a name for himself as an artist. He had participated in group exhibitions since the late 1920s, but in 1933, he had his first solo shows: at the Museum of Modern Art in Portland, his hometown, and at the Contemporary Art Gallery in New York.

Marcus Rothkowitz became an American citizen in 1938 and began to use the name Mark Rothko in 1940 at the start of a politically turbulent decade that was to see important developments in American art. It was during these years that the centre of the Western art world shifted from Paris to America and the New York School emerged, an internationally significant movement of artists whose work was characterized by expressive, gestural brushstrokes and large expanses of colour, known as colour fields. Rothko became a leading figure of the New York School, along with Jackson Pollock and Willem de Kooning. It took almost a decade of being 'Mark Rothko', however, for the distinctive paintings for which he is best known to first emerge. During the 1930s, his figurative paintings had become increasingly loose and abstracted. In the early 1940s, his images of people and everyday life gave way to compositions influenced by European Surrealism and the theories of Sigmund Freud and Carl Jung, who both placed considerable importance on the unconscious mind. Influenced by the Surrealists, Rothko experimented with automatic drawing, whereby he aimed to make spontaneous marks on paper that would directly express his inner thoughts and feelings and would be unmediated by his conscious mind. During this period, he also became very interested in the stories and symbols of ancient mythologies and the human drama that they carried. His paintings from the early 1940s contained references to Greek myths, for example, including the stories of Oedipus and Leda and the Swan, and featured symbolic creatures that have been meaningful to different civilizations, particularly birds. This imagery soon developed into biomorphic forms, resembling but not quite representing organic objects such as plants, shells or animals, as well as expressive marks, some of which were created through automatic gestures.

Around the mid-1940s, as recognizable figures disappeared from his work, Rothko began to experiment with layering and overlapping colours in both watercolour and oil. In watercolour, he diluted the pigments and also added ink into still-wet watercolour to achieve blurring and bleeding between his colours and marks. He took a similar approach when working on canvas, staining areas with thin layers of paint. Rothko titled few of his works, leaving the ideas behind them open to interpretation. Others had vague or enigmatic titles such as *Memory* or *Vision at End of Day* (both 1946, National Gallery of Art, Washington DC). In the second half of the decade, shapes defined by linear marks began to disappear from Rothko's paintings and he began to make compositions comprising amorphous patches of colour that fizzed and fuzzed around the edges. In 1949, these areas of colour became horizontal and were soon reduced to simple rectangular shapes, initially in bright colours of reds, oranges, greens and yellows. The boundaries between them were deliberately blurred, which gave them a sense of movement. By this time, Rothko had cemented his position as a leading New York painter, gaining representation by the city's leading avant-garde dealers including Peggy Guggenheim and Betty Parsons, and attracting the attention of museums, such as the San Francisco Museum of Modern Art, which held a solo exhibition of his work in 1946. With the emergence of what is generally called his 'mature style', he had arrived at a language in his painting through which he was at last able to explore and communicate the deep human experiences that had interested him throughout his career.

In 1958, Rothko received an important commission to produce a group of paintings for the Four Seasons Restaurant in a new skyscraper called the Seagram Building in Midtown Manhattan. The paintings that he produced are darker in palette than some of his earlier work, dominated by maroon, dark reds and black. His horizontal shapes are replaced by vertical lines and window-like rectangles, through which light appears to emanate. The aim was to install the paintings in a continuous frieze, creating an intense, immersive experience. In making the works, however, Rothko concluded that the restaurant, which he described as 'a place where the richest bastards in New York will come to feed and show off', was not the best environment for the works.[72] As a result, he turned down the $35,000 that he was to be paid for the commission and in 1969 donated nine of the canvases to the Tate Gallery in London on the proviso that they be exhibited in their own room, which opened in May 1970. A decade earlier, the Phillips Collection in Washington DC became the first museum to establish a permanent Rothko room where visitors could experience his paintings as he intended. Throughout the 1960s, Rothko was given other opportunities to create groups of paintings, including a commission in 1961 from Harvard University to produce a series of murals for a newly designed building, and an invitation in 1964 to provide paintings for a chapel in Houston, Texas, for the private art collectors John and Dominique de Menil. The latter project occupied Rothko for several years as he not only produced a series of large-scale, meditative canvases in black and maroon but also became involved in the design of the octagonal chapel. When Rothko met Selden Rodman in 1957, he spoke about the 'religious experience' that his work could elicit, and the De Menils had chosen Rothko largely because of this spiritual element to his art. Rothko wanted his paintings to be dramatic and to mine the depths of human feeling. He wanted his viewers to participate in his work, not simply to observe. 'A painting is not a picture of an experience; it is an experience', he told *LIFE* magazine in 1959.

The De Menil Chapel was an important commission for Rothko but a year before it was inaugurated, he died by suicide in his New York studio, on 25 February 1970. In his later years, Rothko had suffered from depression and his mental health had declined further in 1968 after an aneurysm left him unable to paint large-scale works. He began to drink heavily and shortly afterwards separated from his second wife, Mary Alice ('Mell') Beistle, with whom he had a five-year-old son. In the years since his death, Rothko's paintings, particularly those with a darker palette from his later years, have often been read with his depression and suicide in mind, and it seems impossible that his own emotional state did not affect his work. But throughout his life, during which he wrote extensively about art, Rothko expressed his view that an artist's ego or biography could become an obstacle between the art and the viewer, and that his work was about the universal. In 1961, on the occasion of his exhibition at the Whitechapel Art Gallery in London, a journalist from the *Yorkshire Post* who attended the opening reported, 'Mr. Mark Rothko … did not like to talk of himself or his work. "You see the pictures. You look at them and think about them. This is what interests me."'[73] Rothko refused to centre himself in his art and as a result, I aim to resist that urge when looking at his paintings.

19

Barbara Hepworth: Every Hill and Valley Becomes a Sculpture

Barbara Hepworth decided aged seven that she wanted to be an artist. A pupil at Wakefield Girls' High School in the West Riding of Yorkshire, northern England, she had attended a lecture on Egyptian sculpture and been fascinated by the slide show of the Pyramids and ancient sculptures that accompanied it. Three-dimensional forms continued to fascinate her throughout her childhood, particularly those she would see in the natural landscape when she would accompany her father, a civil engineer, on car journeys around the county. The town of Wakefield, where Hepworth was born on 10 January 1903, was industrial, a mining and mill town full, as she remembered it, of 'cobbled streets, stunted and most ungracious houses … slag heaps, warehouses, noise, dirt, and smell.'[74] When she travelled into the countryside of the Yorkshire Dales with her father, however, 'every hill and valley became a sculpture.'[75] This way of viewing the world, seeing sculptural forms in her surroundings, remained with Hepworth throughout her life. In an interview in 1946, she revealed 'all the time I am not working I am thinking about sculpture. Looking out of a window or walking down the road it is impossible not to be aware of form and colour.'[76] By this point, Hepworth was living in St Ives in Cornwall, a fishing town where the strong natural light and coastal beauty had long proved attractive for artists, and she had become a leading member of the abstract art movement in Britain. The natural world offered inspiration for Hepworth throughout her life, as did the human figure and the relationship between the two. Hepworth found that this relationship was most evident to her in the countryside or on the coast and was ever present in Cornwall, where 'the human figure … becomes a free and moving part of the greater whole'.[77] But in Hepworth's view, art did not have to be representational in order to respond to the human experience. Nor, as a politically engaged artist, did she believe that artists had to create realist or overtly political art to contribute to change. In her view, abstract art could carry universal truths that transcended political and cultural barriers. Just as the images of ancient Egyptian art spoke to her in a school lecture hall when she was seven years old, her sculptures, she hoped, might speak to others around the world, who would understand their silent language of peace, nature and human connectivity.

When Hepworth trained at Leeds School of Art (1920–1) and the Royal College of Art in London (1921–4), sculpture in England was generally made by modelling and casting, rather than 'direct carving'. Most sculptors made models in clay that were given to craftsmen to produce in bronze or stone, often via a plaster cast. In contrast, direct carving required the artist to cut into stone or wood themselves.

Hepworth may have tried direct carving at the Royal College of Art but it was in Italy in 1925 that she really learned to carve under the guidance of the Italian master carver Giovanni Ardini. Hepworth had travelled to Italy on a West Riding Scholarship to spend a year in Florence, during which she studied Romanesque architecture and Renaissance art. While on a visit to Rome, she met the English sculptor John Skeaping (1901–80), who had been awarded a scholarship at the British School of Rome, which she had also applied for, and whom she married at the Palazzo Vecchio in Florence six months later. Living and working together in Rome, the couple encouraged each other's interest in direct carving, a practice that had been revived in England by artists of the previous generation including Eric Gill, Jacob Epstein and Henri Gaudier-Brzeska, and which was championed on the continent by Constantin Brâncuși and Amedeo Modigliani. Ardini's teaching not only inspired Hepworth's commitment to direct carving but also led to a deeper interest in the materials that she used. 'Marble changes colour under different people's hands',[78] Ardini told her, and with that, Hepworth realized the importance of getting to know each type of stone or wood that she worked with and responding to the particular qualities of each accordingly.

Hepworth's first sculptures were figurative, but working with wood and stone, as well as the influence of European Modernism, led her towards abstraction. Her earliest surviving carving is *Doves (Group)* (1927, Manchester Art Gallery), a small marble sculpture of two birds with their heads nestled into their feathers, resting side by side.

The rounded forms of their heads and bellies are emphasized by the smooth marble, in contrast to the roughly cut base on which they rest. While living in Rome, Hepworth was inspired by the forms of the doves that she and Skeaping kept. Hepworth's time in Italy also opened her eyes to the importance of strong, natural light, which revealed and sharpened forms, contours and colours in ways that the light in Yorkshire rarely did. Later, she would find a light that suited her in Cornwall but when Hepworth and Skeaping returned to England, they first settled in London, moving to a house in Hampstead in 1928. There, they became part of an artistic circle that included Henry Moore, a fellow Yorkshire artist whom she had studied alongside in both Leeds and London. Hepworth and Skeaping began to exhibit together and her work soon attracted a number of influential supporters including the major collector George Eumorfopoulos and the British Museum curator Laurence Binyon. The collections of the British Museum were important for Hepworth, Skeaping and Moore, as they provided ready access to non-Western art of the type that had influenced many of the Modernist artists in Paris, including Picasso, Matisse and Brâncuși, specifically sculptures and masks from Africa and Oceania. Hepworth's exploration of form and materials over the following years, which involved closely looking at the work of others, as well as her continual studies of nature, gradually led to her thinking about space and shape in a less representational way. By the end of 1934, her work was almost completely abstract. By this time, her marriage to Skeaping had ended and she was living with the artist Ben Nicholson (1894–1982) in whose abstract 'white relief' paintings, which he began to produce from 1933, she found an approach to form and composition that chimed with her own work. Both Nicholson and Hepworth were interested in simple shapes: circles and spheres, ovals and ovoids, as well as holes, curves, contours and planes. Both were influenced by developments in Paris, to which they travelled together in the 1930s, meeting leading members of the avant-garde, many of whom were experimenting with abstraction, including Brâncuși, Picasso, Georges Braque, Hans Arp, Joan Miró, Naum Gabo and Piet Mondrian. In 1933 they were invited to join the Paris-based group Abstraction-Création, an association of abstract artists with which Hepworth exhibited in 1934. The couple's close contact with these artists continued through the 1930s, particularly with Mondrian and Gabo who both moved to London as the world moved towards war.

The ideas to which Hepworth was exposed through her contact with European artists in the 1930s not only strengthened her commitment to abstract art but also helped shape her views of the purpose of art and the ways in which she, as an artist, could contribute to society. She was particularly influenced by Constructivism, a movement that originated in Russia that was brought to the West by Gabo, who was also a sculptor. The Constructivist artists sought to make art that reflected the modern world, that was integrated into everyday life, that was for everybody and that could contribute to social change. Aesthetically, their work was often based around elementary shapes that could be found in nature. Hepworth became a leading proponent of Constructivist art in Britain, producing works such as the small-scale teak sculpture *Ball, Plane and Hole* (1936, Tate), an abstract arrangement of a ball resting on a curved wedge alongside an irregularly shaped block of wood bearing a perfectly round hole of similar dimensions to the ball. In 1937 this sculpture was included in an exhibition in London titled *Unity of Artists for Peace, Democracy and Cultural Development* organized by the anti-fascist group Artists' International Association. Hepworth believed that the ideas communicated through abstract art could transcend social and political barriers, as she expressed in the 1937 publication *Circle: International Survey of Constructive Art*: 'The language of colour and form is universal and not one for a special class … it is a thought which gives the same life, the same expansion, the same universal freedom to everyone.'[79] Hepworth remained committed to opposing fascism and other oppressive regimes throughout her career. Her work was underpinned by these views, often silently, but sometimes in a more overt way such as in 1938–9 when she made a wooden sculpture titled *Project (Monument to the Spanish War)* (destroyed in the Second World War). In 1964, in a speech at the unveiling of her large-scale bronze sculpture *Single Form* at the United Nations Headquarters in New York, Hepworth expressed her belief that 'The United Nations is our conscience. If it succeeds it is our success. If it fails it is our failure.'[80] Art, she believed, had an important role to play in these collective efforts, a view that she shared with Käthe Kollwitz who also felt a duty to use her art for the greater good.

By 1939 Hepworth had established herself as a leading sculptor and a leading member of the abstract art movement in Britain, but her life in London was soon to end. In August of that year, just before the outbreak of the Second World War, Hepworth and Nicholson moved to Cornwall to escape the inevitable bombing, along with their triplets, who had been born in 1934. They settled near the coastal town of St Ives, which had been popular with artists since the nineteenth century due to its mild climate, the clarity of light, and the beauty of the ocean and surrounding cliffs and moorland. Initially, Hepworth found it difficult to make sculpture due to a lack of space and her domestic responsibilities as a mother (in addition to her triplets, she had an older child, Paul Skeaping, who had been born in 1929). In what little time she had, she made drawings, producing studies for sculptures and thinking through her ideas on paper. She was able to resume her sculptural practice after the family moved to a larger house in 1942, by which time her art had absorbed the influence of the Cornish landscape. Her sculptures of this time became less rigidly abstract and include references to some of the forms that she found in the world around her, including the rock formations, the contours of the landscape and the movement of the ocean. Her sculpture *Wave* (1943–4, Scottish National Gallery of Modern Art), for example, comprises a curved wooden form that resembles a cresting wave. The painted white interior heightens the curling brown of the exterior wood, suggesting motion, while a series of taut strings stretching across the central space create a sense of tension, a finely balanced moment suspended in time. Hepworth used string in many of her sculptures from this period and added colour to some, which she applied sparingly and usually to the concave interiors of her curved works. In a statement about her work that was published in 1952, she explained: 'The colour in the concavities plunged me into the depth of water, caves, or shadows deeper than the carved concavities themselves. The strings were the tension I felt between myself and the sea, the wind or the hills.'[81]

Like most successful artists, Hepworth worked on her art as often as she could and thought about it when not working. She liked to have an idea fully worked out before she began to carve, so thinking through ideas both in her head and on paper was important. When her children were small, she would do much of this thinking during the day while cooking or carrying out other domestic chores, after which she would often work into the night. Hepworth enjoyed the physicality of her life as a sculptor, just as she enjoyed dancing and, as a young woman, skating. There was a rhythm involved in carving that required her to be in step with the materials with which she was working. By the time she moved to Cornwall, she had learned how to work with many different types of wood and stone and was able to anticipate their challenges and lean into their particular qualities. During the war, she was unable to obtain many of the imported woods that she favoured, so learned to work with wood from the trees that grew around her in Cornwall. In the mid-1950s, Hepworth began to make sculptures in metal, which required her to use a modelling rather than direct carving technique. This allowed her to make sculptures on a larger scale and to cast small editions, during a time her work was increasingly popular in Britain and overseas. Throughout the 1950s and '60s she made numerous sculptures that were intended to be shown outdoors, including two for the Festival of Britain in 1951 as well as *Winged Figure* (1961–2) for the exterior of the John Lewis department store on Oxford Street in London and *Single Form* for the United Nations Headquarters in New York.

In 1949, Hepworth had purchased Trewyn Studio in St Ives, a two-storey building with a garden, where she lived alone after her divorce from Nicholson in 1951. In 1975, she tragically died in a fire there. By this time she was regarded as one of the world's greatest modern sculptors and had been exhibited widely in Britain and elsewhere. She had suffered many personal challenges and tragedies in her life, including her daughter Sarah's serious illness in the 1940s and the death of her son Paul in an RAF plane crash over Thailand in 1953, but she had continued to believe in her duty as an artist to make work that contributed to society in a positive way. She believed passionately that the arts should be funded by the state, so that those with the drive and talent to make a difference in this way could be free to do so. Hepworth had found that freedom herself, as well as the personal integration with her surroundings that she also felt was imperative for a sculptor. She continued to work into her final years, making a series of marble sculptures in the 1970s, including her last major work *Fallen Images* (1974–5), a return to the material that she had learned to carve as a young woman in Italy.

20

Frida Kahlo: Identity and Self

Art has always been informed by the personal experiences of the artist, but over the course of the twentieth century and beyond, artists have increasingly explored the self. Today, identity is perhaps *the* dominant theme in contemporary art, as artists explore what makes them who they are, how they experience the world and the wider social and political themes that these investigations bring to the surface. Frida Kahlo was one of the first artists to make work that was explicitly about herself, her identity and body, including her intimate experiences of sex, fertility and illness. He art goes beyond the personal reflections that we find in the self-portraits of Rembrandt or Van Gogh, for example, which are guarded and enigmatic by comparison, and it was truly autobiographical, albeit contextualized by and offering comment upon the wider world in which she lived. In her paintings and drawings, Kahlo laid bare the physical challenges that she faced as a result of a devastating bus accident, the emotional pain that she endured in her struggle to have a child and her relationship with the artist Diego Rivera (1886–1957), as well as her personal history and identity as a Mexican woman who had a part-European and part-Indigenous heritage. Over the course of her life, Kahlo made nearly 200 paintings and drawings, including about 55 self-portraits. Much of her art includes fantasy elements and dreamlike imagery, which led the French Surrealist leader André Breton to claim her for his movement. But speaking in 1953, Kahlo rebuffed this affiliation, stating: 'I never painted dreams. I painted my own reality.'[82]

The bus crash that had such a profound effect on Kahlo's life occurred in Mexico City on 17 September 1925. Kahlo was 18, a young woman just entering the adult world. She was travelling in a flimsy wooden bus with her first serious boyfriend, Alejandro Gómez Arias, when a tram ploughed into them. Several people were killed and Kahlo sustained horrific injuries from which it is miraculous that she did not die. Kahlo's body had already been damaged by polio, which she contracted aged six and which left her with a withered leg. Following the crash, in which she fractured her damaged leg 11 times as well as her spinal column, collarbone, ribs and pelvis, Kahlo was forced to remain in hospital for three months – an echo of the nine months she spent at home recovering from polio in 1914. During this second period of enforced convalescence, Kahlo read books about art and took up painting with the aid of an easel that she could use from bed and a mirror fixed to a canopy above, which allowed her to see her own image. She was encouraged in this by her parents, Guillermo Kahlo, a German-born commercial photographer of Hungarian-Jewish descent, and Matilde Carlderón y González, who had both Spanish and Indigenous ancestry. Kahlo was the third of their four daughters, born on 6 July 1907 in the Coyoacán district of Mexico City. Guillermo Kahlo had moved to Mexico in 1891, changing his name from Wilhelm, and had obtained a relatively lucrative commission from the state to photograph the country's pre-Columbian monuments. This work had come to an end, however, with the start of the Mexican Revolution in 1910 and the fall of the dictator Porfirio Diáz. This led to a significant loss of income for the family, which required Kahlo to take part-time jobs in the holidays and after school. Despite this, she found time to learn about photography from her father, who also taught her to hand-colour photographs with a brush. Prior to the crash, Kahlo had also taken art classes at the National Preparatory School and completed a paid apprenticeship with the commercial printer Fernando Fernández, but she had not previously envisioned a career as an artist. She was drawn to science and considered becoming a doctor or a scientific illustrator. Later, she was to claim that it was boredom while stuck in hospital that drove her to take up painting, along with the availability of a box of paints that belonged to her father and the easel that her mother had asked a carpenter to specially make.

In her first self-portrait, *Self-portrait in a Velvet Dress* (1926, private collection), Kahlo presents herself to the waist, looking out towards the viewer, her head turned slightly to her right. She wears a burgundy-red dress with a patterned collar and holds her right arm up across her body so that her elegantly splayed hand is prominent. Her hair is neatly parted and slicked back, while stylized ocean waves curl and crest in the background. Kahlo's pose in this portrait, which she painted for Arias in the hope of reviving their stalled relationship, is reminiscent of a Renaissance portrait, while her elongated neck and hand suggest the influence of the Italian Modernist Amedeo Modigliani

(1884–1920). In the early years of the twentieth century, Mexican painting was significantly influenced by European art but during and following the Revolution (1910–20), painters such as Diego Rivera, David Alfaro Siqueiros (1896–1974) and José Clemente Orozco (1883–1949) sought to establish an independent Mexican style, which incorporated Indigenous and folk-art traditions. They were facilitated in this by a government-funded programme whereby artists were commissioned to paint murals on the walls of schools, hospitals and other public buildings. The large-scale paintings on the theme of Mexican history and culture carried social and political messages. Kahlo first met Rivera in 1922 when he was painting a mural at her school, but it was in 1928 that she really got to know him and his circle of artists and intellectuals. Kahlo and Rivera soon became a couple and married in 1929 despite their 21-year age difference. Kahlo was influenced by Rivera's painting, particularly his strong outlines and subject matter, and he and his friends also strengthened her awareness of Mexican culture and her personal identity, which had a significant impact on the way she presented herself. In her second self-portrait, titled *Self-portrait – Time Flies* (1929, private collection), she portrays herself wearing a simple, lace-trimmed white cotton blouse of a type worn by ordinary Mexican women. Her prominent jade necklace references pre-Columbian jewellery, while her dangling earrings are of a style popular during Mexico's colonial period, reflecting Kahlo's identification with both Mexico's Indigenous and European heritage.

Kahlo recognized the symbolic power of clothes, jewellery and hairstyles. During her relationship with Rivera, she generally wore Tehuana costume, clothes worn by the

Indigenous Zapotec women on the Isthmus of Tehuantepec, whose society was perceived as matriarchal: an embroidered blouse, a long skirt (usually red or purple) and long gold necklaces. She often wore her hair in braids and sometimes an Indigenous-style headdress. As an adolescent, Kahlo had learned that long Mexican skirts or trousers could be useful in hiding her withered leg, which fellow children had made fun of, and as a young woman she had sometimes dressed in men's suits, asserting both her individualism and independence. Clothes were important to her as a means of self-expression as well as a tool through which to communicate social and political messages and personal affiliations. The deep personal significance of the clothes that she chose to wear is exemplified in her painting *The Two Fridas* (Modern Art Museum, Mexico City). Kahlo made this painting shortly after she and Rivera divorced in 1939, following several years of infidelity on both sides and after Rivera's deeply hurtful affair with Kahlo's sister, Cristina. In 1934, when she first learned of the affair, Kahlo stopped wearing the Tehuana clothes that Rivera favoured her in and cut her hair short, fully aware that he loved it long. In *The Two Fridas*, Kahlo presents two versions of herself seated side-by-side and holding hands, both looking out at the viewer. On the right side, she wears colourful Tehuana dress and holds a miniature portrait of Rivera as a child. Her heart, which is visible, appears healthy. On the left side, she wears a European style white dress with a high collar and her exposed heart is damaged. A blood vessel connecting the two hearts ends in the lap of the European-style Frida, clamped with a medical tool yet bleeding into her lap. The painting seems to express Kahlo's belief that Rivera loved the version of her that wore

Tehuana attire and rejected other aspects of her identity. This was a rich period for Kahlo's self-portraiture and the following year she painted *Self-portrait with Cropped Hair* (1940, Museum of Modern Art, New York) in which she sits on a simple yellow chair wearing a man's suit and shirt and with short hair. The chair and the floor around her are covered with locks of shorn hair and she holds scissors in her hand. An excerpt of text and musical notation above references a popular Mexican song that translates as 'Look, if I loved you, it was for your hair. Now that you are without hair, I don't love you anymore.'[83] After remarrying Rivera in December 1940, Kahlo painted *Self-portrait with Braid*, in which she is shown wearing her hair in a looped braid of a type worn by some Indigenous women in Mexico, and wearing a pre-Columbian style necklace. Kahlo agreed to remarry Rivera on the agreement that she would remain financially independent, as she had determined to become when they divorced, and that they would not resume their sexual relationship. They remained together for the rest of her life.

The damage done to Kahlo's body by both polio and the bus crash continued to cause her severe pain throughout her life, and as her body deteriorated further, she had to undergo many surgeries and other medical interventions. As well as exploring her physical pain in her art, Kahlo addressed the psychological distress that this suffering caused and the other ways her disabilities impacted her life, including her inability to have a child. In 1930, Kahlo was forced to undergo an abortion as her body was not able to carry a child to full term. Two years later, in July 1932, while on a visit to Detroit, USA, where Rivera had been commissioned to paint a mural for the Ford Motor

Company, she suffered a miscarriage. During the resultant 13 days that she spent in hospital, Kahlo made a number of drawings exploring the experience, which led to the oil painting *Henry Ford Hospital* (1932, Dolores Olmedo Museum, Mexico City). In the painting Kahlo lies naked and bleeding on a bed, the frame of which is marked with the name of the hospital and the month and year. Her swollen belly still appears pregnant but her child, a boy, floats above. His body is tethered to her by an umbilical red thread. Other objects float around the bed, also bound to her by red threads, including a set of pelvic bones, a snail, a purple orchid and a model of a uterus. The painting is relatively small in size – around 31 × 38 cm (12 × 15 in) – and painted on a metal plate, echoing the format of traditional Mexican *retablo* paintings, which were intended to thank a saint or religious figure for the avoidance of a misfortune. Kahlo's mother had been a devout Roman Catholic and Kahlo would have seen many of these types of paintings in churches. She began to collect them as an adult after the Revolution made many objects from churches available on the open market. *Henry Ford Hospital* was her first major painting to deliberately reference the genre. In *retablos*, stories were often told in sequential ways through non-naturalistic imagery that might include imagined elements. Usually, the saintly figure to whom thanks were being offered was also pictured, although in this case, nobody had intervened to prevent Kahlo's misfortune. In the 1940s, Kahlo's health worsened considerably, and she was forced to wear a series of painful corsets, which she references in her painting *The Broken Column* (1944, Dolores Olmedo Museum), produced shortly after she had spinal surgery. In this image, Kahlo depicts herself with her torso split in two and a crumbling stone column in the place of her spine. Her naked body is strapped into a surgical corset and multiple nails protrude from her face and body. The nails echo traditional representations in art of St Sebastian, who is generally shown semi-naked and pierced with arrows, the method by which he was martyred. Kahlo referenced the story of St Sebastian more explicitly in her 1946 painting *The Wounded Deer* (private collection), a self-portrait in which she has the body of a deer, which has been shot through with arrows. In 1953, when she was forced to have her right leg amputated at the knee as the result of gangrene, Kahlo processed the experience in a drawing of two disembodied feet with text beneath that read 'Feet what do I need them for / If I have wings to fly.'[84] In her darkest moments, she used art to explore her pain.

In an interview published in 1945, Kahlo claimed that she painted herself 'because I am so often alone and because I am the subject I know best.'[85] In addition to painting herself repeatedly, she also explored her life and experiences through drawings and, from 1944, a journal, which combined drawings and text. But Kahlo's art was not all autobiographical – she also made many portraits of others and paintings on wider themes, including Mexican society. Kahlo's art and lifestyle, and that of the muralists including Rivera, contributed significantly to a greater awareness of Mexican history and culture, and the establishment of a distinctive Mexican school of painting. Beyond her self-image, Kahlo referenced Mexican culture in her art through references to the civilizations of the Aztecs, Olmecs and Toltecs and their beliefs, including images of pyramids and temples. She also incorporated representations of Mexico's native flora and fauna into her paintings. In 1941, Kahlo was selected by the government as one of the founding members of the Seminar of Mexican Culture, a group of 25 artists who were tasked with spreading knowledge of the country's heritage. From 1929 onward, Kahlo spent a significant amount of time in the United States, both with and without Rivera, and these experiences helped her to view Mexico from an outside perspective. Her painting *Self-portrait on the Borderline between Mexico and the United States* (1932, private collection) shows her standing full-length in a pink dress between an ancient Mexican landscape and an industrialized, technology-heavy USA. Kahlo had been sympathetic to communism since her youth (even having an affair with Leon Trotsky in 1937) and, in addition to her distaste for certain aspects of American society, she found the gap between the rich and the poor in the United States to be particularly troubling.

When Kahlo first visited the USA, she did so as Rivera's wife, but she soon obtained recognition in her own right and her work was shown in several group exhibitions at institutions including the Museum of Modern Art, New York, and the Institute of Modern Art, Boston. In 1939 a group of her works was exhibited in Paris and her self-portrait *The Frame* (1938) became the first work by a twentieth-century Mexican artist to be acquired by the Louvre. It was not until 1953, however, that Kahlo received her first solo exhibition, which was held at the Gallery of Contemporary Art in Mexico City run by the Mexican photographer Lola Álvarez Bravo. By this time, she had very little mobility, so her four-poster bed was brought into the gallery for the opening and decorated so that she could lie in it and greet the attendees. Over 200 people came and she was celebrated with Mexican ballads into the small hours. Kahlo died aged 47 on 13 July 1954 after years of suffering. The last drawing in her diary was an image of an angel in thick boots or heavy wrappings around its lower legs. Her last words, written as she was about to be discharged from yet another visit to hospital, were both enigmatic and poignant: 'I hope the leaving is joyful – and I hope never to return.'[86]

21

Emily Kam Kngwarray: Life and Landscape

In 1977, Emily Kam Kngwarray joined a batik-making workshop for Aboriginal women from the Sandover region of Australia's Northern Territory.[87] Then in her mid-sixties, she was the oldest woman in the group. Making art of a type that could be hung on a wall or sold to collectors was new to Kngwarray but, like most women from her community, she had practised ceremonial painting for much of her life, specifically ritualistic body painting and sandpainting. Over the following 11 years, Kngwarray made many batiks on cotton and silk before she was introduced in 1988 to acrylic painting on canvas, a less labour-intensive medium that she found suited her better in her eighth decade. Kngwarray made thousands of works of art during these years, continuing to paint until shortly before her death in 1996. By the late 1980s, she was recognized as a leading Australian painter and her work was collected by public museums and private collectors around the world. To Western audiences, schooled in the histories of European and North American art, Kngwarray's batiks, paintings and works on paper appear abstract and related in style

186

to the gestural works of the Abstract Expressionists, but Kngwarray's art emerged from an entirely different tradition. For Kngwarray and other Aboriginal artists from the desert region of Central Australia in which she lived, visual art and other forms of creative expression were part of everyday life and, like the songs and dances that they performed collectively, were deeply connected to the histories, physical landscapes, flora and fauna, and traditions of their ancestral homelands, or Countries. As a senior Anmatyerr woman from Alhalker Country, Kngwarray's art reflects her deep knowledge of her homeland, of which she was a custodian, with references to topographical features, plants, bush food, animals and rituals. Her work also draws on Indigenous beliefs connected with the land, specifically the concept of Dreaming (*Altyerr*), a philosophical framework through which all aspects of the world and beyond are understood, and the relationships between time, land, ancestors, living things, natural phenomena and social and cultural practices are ordered and remembered. Place names, songs and ceremonies carry, preserve and communicate this inherited knowledge and belief system, and from her early work with batik, Kngwarray's art was also deeply rooted in, and a part of, this worldview.

Emily Kam Kngwarray was born in about 1914 in Alhalker, the traditional Country of the Anmatyerr people in the Central Desert area of the Northern Territory, Australia. Kngwarray was her skin name, a family name, and Kam her personal given name. Kam is the Anmatyerr word for the seeds and seedpods of the pencil yam (*anwelarr*), a creeping plant with edible roots that had a particular cultural significance in Alhalker and was an important source of food. It was not until Kngwarray was in her teens, by which time white pastoralists had begun to encroach on Aboriginal land in the region, that she was given the 'Whitefella' name of Emily. Growing up, Kngwarray learned about her land from her elders. Living in a grass shelter, she was taught to dig for witchetty grubs, pencil yams and bush potatoes, and to hunt for lizards and other animals that she could eat. She became a skilled hunter and gatherer, often walking miles to find food, as well as a butcher and cook. From the mid-1920s, white settlers were granted land leases and grazing licences in the region, bringing with them unfamiliar animals such as sheep, goats, horses and cattle. Ways of life began to change and, in some cases, Indigenous people were forced to leave their traditional lands. In the late 1930s, a cattle station was established in the area adjoining Alhalker, called Utopia by the colonizers. Many people from Alhalker and the surrounding Countries, including Kngwarray, worked for the white pastoralists at Utopia and other stations, although relationships were tense and complex. It was not until the 1960s and '70s that the land rights of Aboriginal people began to be recognized and land began to be returned to the Indigenous communities. The land occupied by the Utopia Station was returned to its traditional owners in the 1970s and Alhalker Country followed in 1986.

The workshop at which Kngwarray learned to make batiks grew out of a literacy and numeracy programme that was established by the Institute for Aboriginal Development at the Utopia Station homestead in 1976. There, Kngwarray and other Aboriginal women learned to write their names so that they could sign documents, including pension cheques. They were also taught other skills, including sewing and driving, with the aim of increasing employment opportunities and improving living standards. In 1977, the batik workshop was trialled by Jennifer Green, a linguist working on the programme. Batik is an art form that has been practised for centuries in Asia and South America but is particularly associated with Indonesia. It involves creating a design by applying hot wax to fabric, usually cotton or silk, which is then dyed. The wax resists the dye, preventing the areas it covers from changing colour, and when the dyeing process is complete, it is removed with hot water. Although there was little support from the funding agencies for the initiative, the workshop proved to be of interest to the female participants and the Utopia Women's Batik Group was formally established the following year, with Julia Murray as its coordinator. Murray argued that the women in the group could achieve financial independence by producing batiks that could be sold. From the beginning, Kngwarray and the other members of the group were encouraged to be original and experimental in their designs; only the technique was taught. They painted directly with the wax on to strips of cotton or items of clothing, without making any preparatory designs. Soon, the women began to create batiks that drew inspiration from their land and everyday lives. Kngwarray's batiks are, for the most part, untitled, but some include recognizable figurative imagery, such as the lizards (goannas) that appear in a batik on cotton from 1981 (National Gallery of Australia, Canberra), skeletal-like forms that have been identified as relating to emus, and references to plants such as the pencil yam, with its sprawling network of vines. Kngwarray's colours were generally restricted to ochres – red, yellow and brown – with some greens and black. She continued to produce batiks until the summer of 1988, at which point she was introduced to acrylic, which allowed her palette to expand to include pinks, purples and brighter hues.

In 1988, Kngwarray was around 74 years old and the process of making batiks had become overly arduous. The women worked outside, but even so, working with fires, hot wax and boiling water was uncomfortable. Batik often involved multiple rounds of dyeing and boiling the fabric and although Kngwarray was strong, age was taking its toll and her eyesight was beginning to fail. Working with acrylic was introduced to artists in the region by CAAMA (the Central Australian Aboriginal Media Association), an Aboriginal-led organization based in Alice Springs (around 250 km – 155 miles – southwest of Alhalker), which had taken over the Women's Batik Group the previous year. In her transition to canvas, Kngwarray carried both the themes and motifs of her batiks and the free, gestural style of her mark-making from one medium to the other. Over the following eight years, she produced more than 3,000 paintings in acrylic. As with her batiks, she made her works on canvas by laying the fabric on the ground and sitting alongside it, or sometimes on it, in much the same way she would if she were sitting to prepare meals or dig for food in the ground. As her work found an audience and a market among collectors, her canvases were stretched and displayed upright on gallery walls, but she did not generally experience them this way. She worked speedily and confidently, using a long brush that allowed her to paint on a large scale, and often applying multiple layers of dots and linear marks to the canvas.

A number of Kngwarray's earliest works on canvas include iconography related to the emu, an important animal in Anmatyerr culture. *Emu Woman* (1988–9, Janet Holmes à Court Collection, Perth), for example, was one of her first acrylic paintings. Measuring 92 × 61 cm (36 × 24 in), the canvas is covered in forms that seem to depict either a plant with various branches, or spines with ribs which are painted in white and yellow against a black ground and covered in dots in brown, black and yellow. It is possible the forms represent the fan-flower (*intekw*), which is eaten by emus, or the skeletons of the emus themselves. The 1990 painting *Untitled (Country and Emu Tracking)* (Albertina Museum, Vienna) depicts emu footprints, with lines indicating the paths that they take. Other early canvases relate to the flora of the region, such as *Ntang Dreaming* (1989, National Gallery of Australia), which probably represents the seeds of the woollybutt grass (*alyatywereng*) and *Pencil Yam* (1990, National Gallery of Australia). A number of Kngwarray's canvases also relate to the ceremonies that are performed by women from her community, known as Awely. Held on special occasions and to promote community and wellbeing, the ceremonies involve communal body painting and dancing. Together, women participants 'paint up' their chests, breasts and arms using natural pigments mixed with emu fat. These linear designs were directly referenced by Kngwarray in a series of oval paintings in acrylic on board that she made in 1990, and other paintings of the period were inspired in less direct ways by these rituals.

Although Kngwarray's style developed and changed at various points during the eight years that she made works on canvas, her repertoire of subjects remained consistent: the pencil yam with its tangle of vines, carrot-like root, bright green leaves, yellow flowers and seeds (*Kam*); other vegetation including the fan-flower, woollybutt grass, the desert raisin (*katyerr*) and wild fig (*tywerrk*); emus; goanna lizards; the topography of the land over which she had a cultural responsibility and the ceremonies in which she participated. Both her subject matter and her approach were innovative for Aboriginal art as she departed from the traditional motifs of circles and animal tracks, producing a wider range of marks and imagery, and applying the paint in a more free and spontaneous way. In around 1993, a shift in style saw the appearance of a series of works on canvas and paper composed almost entirely of parallel stripes in a single colour, and a much-restricted palette. These works have been linked to Awely body-painting designs, but it has also been suggested that her advancing age may have led to these pared-back compositions. This linear phase only lasted for a short time, however, and in her final year she produced several large-scale paintings on the theme of the pencil yam, including *Big Yam Dreaming* (1995, National Gallery of Victoria, Melbourne), an enormous acrylic on canvas measuring around 8 × 3 metres (26 ¼ × 10 ft). Produced in a single, continuous stroke in white on black, the painting represents the meandering vines of the pencil yam as well as its significance for the people of Alhalker. Although it might be tempting to see in this painting similarities with the calligraphic works of the American minimalist Brice Marden or the Infinity Net paintings of Yayoi Kusama, for example, it is important to remember that Kngwarray did not draw on any of the same reference points as these artists. When she began to make art, she had very little contact with the West, having no television and almost no access to print media or books, and although she subsequently travelled occasionally for exhibitions, she continued to live and make art in the Sandover region, close to where she grew up.

By the time she died on 2 September 1996, Kngwarray was one of the most famous artists in Australia. Exhibitions organized by the CAAMA in the 1980s, first of batiks and then of canvases, had generated interest in her work and Aboriginal art in general. In 1981, she and other artists left the Northern Territory to attend the *Floating Forests of Silk* exhibition of their batiks at the Adelaide Festival Centre Gallery. In 1990, Kngwarray was given her first solo exhibition at Utopia Art in Sydney and two years later she was awarded a prestigious Australian Artist Creative Fellowship, the first Aboriginal artist to be recognized in such a way. Her reputation grew internationally when her work began to be purchased by the National Gallery of Australia and other museums, and she is now represented in museums around the world as well as in numerous private collections. The year after she died, her work was exhibited in the Australian Pavilion at the 47th Venice Biennale alongside the art of two other Indigenous artists, Judy Watson (born 1959) and Yvonne Koolmatrie (born 1944). Almost three decades after her death, the National Gallery of Australia held a major retrospective of her work in 2024, which toured to Tate Modern, London, in 2025. Meanwhile in Alhalker and the surrounding area, her legacy lives on among her Anmatyerr descendants.

22

Jacob Lawrence: History Painting

The creative urge to make art can be driven by all manner of things, from a wish to explore form, colour and texture, to the desire to replicate nature or express a specific emotion or sensation, to the pursuit of beauty or calm. Some artists, however, are motivated by a desire to document the world, to record and memorialize a specific experience or a life in an effort to ensure that it can never be forgotten. Between 1910 and 1970, more than six million Black people migrated from America's southern states to towns and cities in the country's North, Midwest and West. The movement was motivated by racial oppression in the South, where segregation laws were still in place until around 1965, as well as by the pursuit of a safer and more prosperous life. Jacob Lawrence was born in Atlantic City in the north-eastern state of New Jersey on 7 September 1917. His parents, Jacob and Rosa Lee Lawrence, were among the many African Americans who had made the journey north, having grown up in South Carolina and Virginia respectively. Known as the Great Migration, Lawrence was to later memorialize this collective experience in a 60-panel series and dedicate his career to documenting the lives of Black heroes and heroines, and the experiences of Black people in America.

Lawrence was 13 in 1930 when he moved with his mother and two siblings to Harlem in New York, the Upper Manhattan neighbourhood that had been home to many African American families from the late nineteenth century onward. After a few years in Pennsylvania, his parents had separated and Lawrence and his siblings were sent to foster homes from 1927 before they were able to rejoin their mother. The American stock market had experienced a catastrophic crash in 1929 and the United States had been plunged into a Great Depression, along with much of the rest of the world. Lawrence's family were not alone in experiencing financial hardship, but despite significant poverty Harlem was a vibrant and supportive community, which Lawrence found to be full of creative opportunities. In addition to attending school, Lawrence spent time at the Utopia Children's House, a centre that provided after-school activities for children including arts and crafts. There, he met the Black painter Charles Alston, who recognized his artistic talents and became a mentor.

Initially, Lawrence painted non-figurative images inspired by patterns he had seen on wallpapers and rugs, but the world around him proved too interesting to ignore and he started to depict scenes of community life, including market stalls, parades and people attending church. It was the time of the Harlem Renaissance, a period spanning the 1920s and '30s during which African American music, poetry, art, dance, fashion and scholarship flourished and had a significant impact on American culture more widely. Lawrence would often visit the theatre, where he would see comedians, big bands and dancers, after which he would find equally stimulating people outside. 'The Harlem scene for me was almost like a theatre,' he later recalled. 'There was tragedy; there was comedy. I would leave the Apollo Theater and go out into the street, and it was almost as if I had never left the theatre.'[88] Among the people he found on the street were orators, who would tell stories about the heroes and heroines of Black history. By his early twenties, Lawrence was telling these stories in his paintings, translating what he had learned from his community into colourful multi-panel narratives. In 1941, he completed his series on the Great Migration, which he viewed as a personal history, a portrait of his family and of many of the families whose stories he had heard growing up in Harlem.

Harlem had a significant oral storytelling culture, and Lawrence's interest in African American history had been piqued by street orators, preachers, teachers and librarians, as well as by personal stories that he had heard in the community. As a teenager, he began to study books on Black history at the library, a pursuit encouraged by the self-taught historian Charles Seifert, whom he had met at the YMCA. By the time he was 23, Lawrence had completed a narrative series on the lives of Toussaint L'Ouverture (1743–1803), leader of the Haitian Revolution, Frederick Douglass (1818–95), an abolitionist and social reformer, and Harriet Tubman (1822–1913), an abolitionist and activist who helped many people escape slavery. He completed the first, *The Life of Toussaint L'Ouverture*, in 1937–8 shortly after seeing W. E. B. Du Bois's play *Haiti: A Drama of the Black Napoleon* at the Lafayette Theater in Harlem. The series comprises 41 panels, now at the Amistad Research Center, New Orleans, each measuring 11 × 19 inches (28 × 48 cm).

Lawrence felt that the story of L'Ouverture, the formerly enslaved revolutionary leader who led Haiti to independence from the French in 1791, was too big to tell in a single painting. Narrative mural painting was prominent in American art at the time, largely due to the programme of public art that provided work for artists as part of President Franklin D. Roosevelt's New Deal, designed to keep people in work during the Depression. But although Lawrence found work as part of this programme when he was 21, he did not receive any mural commissions and so decided to create his narrative as a series. Although figurative, Lawrence's painting style was influenced by Modernist movements including Cubism. His colours were bold and flat, and his images were composed from blocks of geometric shapes in which perspective was slightly skewed and the figures were elongated, angular and simplified. He used a uniform colour palette across the L'Ouverture series of greens, browns, blues, dark reds, yellows and blacks, colours that dominated much of his output throughout his career. Having initially learned to paint with water-based poster paints on cheap paper, Lawrence continued to work with inexpensive materials, preferring water-based tempera, a fast-drying paint with a matte finish, to oils. From this early series, he gave his individual paintings descriptive titles to help explain the narrative, such as 'The Birth of Toussaint', 'Cruelty of the Planters' and 'L'Ouverture Set for War with Napoleon', which Lawrence had devised based on considerable reading and research.

Lawrence had not set out to be an artist. He left school in his mid-teens in order to earn money, which he did from odd jobs such as delivering newspapers and working in laundries, and in 1936 he had worked temporarily in upstate New York with the Civilian Conservation Corps, a New Deal programme, planting trees and undertaking other environmental work. He had continued to paint throughout, however, and in the late 1930s joined the New Deal-funded Harlem Community Art Center and rented working space in Charles Alston's studio at 306 West 141st Street, a space known as the '306'. Lawrence became part of an artistic community there and would often travel downtown to visit museums and galleries with friends, including artist Gwendolyn Knight, whom he married in 1941. The city's vast Metropolitan Museum was within walking distance of Harlem, where Lawrence was able to study the work of great modern artists, including Picasso and the Cubists, as well as artists from the past whom he admired, such as Giotto. Lawrence received great encouragement from the community at the Harlem art workshop, particularly the director, sculptor Augusta Savage, who helped him to find employment under the New Deal jobs programme. For this he was required to produce two paintings every six weeks in exchange for $23.86 a week, a salary that delighted him at the time.

Having followed his Haiti series with *The Life of Frederick Douglass* and *The Life of Harriet Tubman* in 1938–9 (40 and 31 panels respectively), Lawrence began work on *The Migration of the Negro* in 1940, now known as *The Migration Series*. He was able to create the 60-panel work largely because he had received a grant for $1,500 from the Rosenwald Foundation, an organization that supported African American artists, writers and scholars, which enabled him to rent his own studio. There, he was able to spread out all 60 panels and produce the series as a coherent, unified work. With Gwen's help, he prepared the

18 × 12 inch-hardboard panels (46 × 30 cm) with gesso, a mix of animal glue, chalk and white pigment, on to which he sketched the images in pencil before applying the pure, unmixed colours one at a time across all 60 panels simultaneously. The aim was to create a consistent look that would tie the whole series together. The panels told the stories of the millions of African Americans who had journeyed north through images of families in railway stations, on trains, walking with suitcases, and scenes explaining why they left the South, including references to lynchings, abusive treatment by plantation owners and the scourge of the boll weevil pest, which had ravaged the cotton crop. The series also dealt with the reception of the migrants in the North, including the discrimination that they continued to face. In addition to the images, the paintings had descriptive captions, which were revised in 1993 to remove potentially offensive language, primarily the repeated use of the word 'Negro', which was widely accepted as a neutral term in 1940. Again, Lawrence undertook considerable research to make the series, but worked fast once he began to paint, completing the series in six to eight months. He had been given his first solo exhibition in 1939 at the Young Women's Christian Association in Harlem, where he had shown the Toussaint L'Ouverture works, but it was with the *Migration Series* that he broke through beyond his own community. In 1941, the series was included by the gallerist Edith Halpert at the Downtown Gallery as part of the exhibition *American Negro Art: Nineteenth and Twentieth Centuries*. Halpert also arranged for 26 of the paintings to be reproduced in the mainstream *Fortune* magazine, which brought Lawrence considerable attention. At 24, Lawrence had not only become a professional artist, but a famous and

critically successful one. The following year, he became the first African American artist whose work was collected by the Museum of Modern Art, New York when the museum jointly purchased *The Migration Series*, along with the Phillips Collection in Washington, DC.

Following the *Migration Series*, Lawrence continued to make work about Black history and his own experiences. In 1941, he visited New Orleans with his new wife, his first visit to the South, and produced *The Legend of John Brown*, a series exploring the origins of the Civil War, as well as other paintings depicting life in the southern states. In 1943, as war raged across the world, Lawrence joined the US Coast Guard and served on the USS *Sea Cloud*, the US Navy's first racially integrated ship. He initially worked as a steward's mate but was soon moved to a public relations role, which meant he was able to paint on board. His images of life in the navy were exhibited in a solo exhibition at MoMA in 1944, alongside the *Migration* paintings. In 1946, Lawrence was invited by the German artist Josef Albers, who had left Germany for the United States in 1933, to teach over the summer at the progressive Black Mountain College in North Carolina. Albers was an abstract artist whose ideas about form and colour made an impact on Lawrence but, perhaps more importantly, the experience led Lawrence to devote a significant amount of his time thereafter to teaching. He went on to teach at various institutions in New York, including the Pratt Institute, the New School for Social Research and the Art Students League, and the Skowhegan School of Painting and Sculpture in Maine. In 1971, he moved to Seattle to become a professor at the University of Washington. There is a didactic quality to Lawrence's art and one of his aims was to pass on the stories that he had heard as a child. But his paintings do more than educate; they explore and articulate the Black experience, which had hitherto often been excluded from national narratives. In 1943, Lawrence said: 'I do not look upon the story of the Blacks in America as a separate experience to the American culture but as a part of the American heritage and experience as a whole.'[89] It was his aim to incorporate Black history into American history more generally. Over the course of his career, in addition to his paintings, he also produced several print series and collaborated on four children's books telling the stories of L'Ouverture, Tubman, John Brown and the Great Migration. He continued to make art until several weeks before he died on 9 June 2000 at the age of 82.

23

Andy Warhol: The Same Thing, Over and Over

In the early 1960s, just three decades after the devastating Wall Street Crash that shaped the lives of Jacob Lawrence and his American contemporaries, the United States had entered a period of economic prosperity. Most Americans found themselves with more disposable income than their parents, and the prospect of consuming luxury items including washing machines, shiny new cars and convenience food was presented to them on a daily basis on bright, graphic billboards and in shiny magazines. Meanwhile, beneath the gloss, American society was beset with inequality, violence, political upheaval and war. Based in New York, Andy Warhol recognized this dichotomy, and while the visual language of advertising and the mass media proved to be inspiring, his work also reflected the darker side of mid-twentieth-century American life.

In 1962, Warhol presented a series of 32 paintings on canvas at the Ferus Gallery in Los Angeles, each depicting a can of Campbell's soup in red and white, with a shiny silver top, in one of the brand's 32 varieties. Arranged on shelves like products in a shop, the hand-painted images were uniform and simple. Measuring 20 × 16 inches (51 × 41 cm), each painting depicted a single can, outlined in bold, black lines, against a white background. Each can bore the Campbell's logo in its distinctive home-spun script, which would have been familiar to most Americans from trips to the grocery store, and the name of the flavour: cream of mushroom, black bean, turkey vegetable, beef broth … Graphic in style and seemingly devoid of meaning or emotional resonance, the paintings were a world away from the gestural canvases of the Abstract Expressionists whose work had dominated American art for over a decade. They looked like advertisements, not like the 'fine art' paintings that people were used to seeing in galleries and museums.

Warhol understood the language of commercial art; having gained a degree in Pictorial Design in his hometown of Pittsburgh, he had worked successfully as an illustrator for newspapers, magazines, fashion houses and department stores since 1949, the year he moved to New York City. His clients included Tiffany & Co and the shoe company I. Miller & Sons, and his work had appeared in prestigious publications including *Vogue* and *Harper's Bazaar*. From around 1960, however, Warhol had been moving away from commercial work and had begun to produce art of his own, taking what he knew about graphic design and popular visual culture and translating it into a new style of painting. There was something in the air: Warhol was one of a number of emerging artists making graphic-style work inspired by popular culture. In New York, Roy Lichtenstein had started to produce paintings appropriating comic-book imagery and, on the West Coast, Ed Ruscha was making work that borrowed from billboards, urban design and branded goods. Abstract Expressionism was tired, and America was undergoing an economic boom. The Pop artists, as they came to be known, were both reacting against what had come before and commenting wittily on the world that they now found themselves in. Dominant themes in their work include mass consumption, celebrity, American imperialism and the two sides, light and dark, of the American Dream. Warhol's soup cans, however, were a comment on the everyday, on routine and familiarity. When asked in 1963 why he had started to paint them, he said: 'Because I used to drink it. I used to have the same lunch every day, for 20 years, I guess, the same thing over and over again.'[90] Pop, from 'popular', made no distinction between high and low culture; to them, anything could be art, and anything could be depicted in art.

Andrew Warhola was born on 6 August 1928 to Julia Zavacky and Andrej Warhola, working-class Carpatho-Rusyn immigrants and devout Eastern Catholics from modern-day Slovakia (then part of Czechoslovakia), who settled in Pittsburgh, an industrial city in Pennsylvania. Warhol (who changed his name around the time he moved to New York) was introverted and self-conscious by nature. As a child, he developed a rare neurological disorder that required him to spend several months at home and caused some discolouration to his skin, exacerbating his shyness. While recovering at home, he drew and read comics and magazines, and he later took free art classes at the city's Carnegie Museum before enrolling at the Carnegie Institute of Technology in 1945 and becoming the first of his family to go to college. In the 1950s, when he was working in New York, he developed a distinctive, somewhat whimsical drawing style that suited the shoes and fashion items that he was paid to illustrate. At the same time, he was also making personal drawings in a simple, linear style, many of which depict friends and lovers, but the homoerotic nature of many of these early drawings meant that he struggled to find gallery representation. Warhol's commercial work, for which he won awards, kept him financially stable and in the late 1950s he was able to purchase his own townhouse on the Upper East Side, where he lived with his mother who had followed him to New York in the early 1950s. Despite his shyness, Warhol was sociable and had, by the early 1960s, established a wide circle of friends and associates in the art world and in New York's queer communities. The gay artists Robert Rauschenberg and Jasper Johns, with whom he had become acquainted, were both a major influence on him at this time. Both used found imagery and everyday objects in their work, including consumer goods packaging. In 1960, for example, Johns exhibited a bronze sculpture of two Ballantine-branded ale cans in New York's Castelli Gallery. Like Warhol, Johns was interested in objects that were so familiar that people stopped noticing them, like the US flag, which he used repeatedly across different media, or mundane quotidian items such as lightbulbs and coat hangers. Rauschenberg incorporated photographic imagery into his work, including press photos, a source that Warhol would also go on to mine. Warhol began to find his own Pop style in around 1960. His earliest paintings include *Water Heater* (1961), a painting of a black-and-white advertisement for a 55-dollar water heater (Museum of Modern Art, New York), and a series of works featuring the cartoon character Popeye. In 1961, the director of the Ferus Gallery, Irving Blum, visited Warhol's home-cum-studio on a tip-off from a friend. Finding six of the soup canvases there, he offered him a show. The Ferus was instrumental in championing early Pop art. It had been founded in 1957 by Walter Hopps who, in 1962, organized the first survey exhibition of the movement at the Pasadena Art Museum in Los Angeles County, which included work by Warhol, Lichtenstein and Ruscha. The title of the show was 'New Painting of Common Objects'.

Warhol's 32 soup canvases were his boldest statement to date of his Pop art style and were also among his last hand-painted works in the 1960s. Repetition was a key part of Warhol's imagery and he began to explore ways of reproducing images 'that gave more of an assembly-line effect'.[91] In stark contrast to the intensely personal work of the Abstract Expressionists, he wanted to remove any signs of his own hand at work. To begin with, he used rubber stamps and stencils, but in August 1962, he found a better way of creating the assembly-line effect: silkscreen printing. Up to that point, screenprinting was generally used for commercial purposes, but Warhol and other Pop artists found it to be not only a cheap and effective way of reproducing images but also perfect for producing the flat colours and hard edges that they sought to achieve. August 1962 was also the month in which the iconic film actor Marilyn Monroe died by suicide, aged 26. The world was shocked by her death and Marilyn became one of Warhol's first screenprinted subjects. Using a publicity photograph taken for her 1953 film *Niagara*, which he cropped around her head, Warhol produced *Marilyn Diptych*, a monumental canvas in which the filmstar's face is repeated over and over in a grid, like a photographic contact sheet. On the left side, against a bright orange background, her face is a lurid pink, her hair yellow and her eye shadow blue-green and her white teeth shine out between 25 sets of red lips. On the right, her image is monochrome and grainy, like a newspaper reproduction, obscured by dark smudges in areas and fading almost completely at the upper right. Over the following two years, Warhol made a series of single-head portraits of Monroe, silkscreened in a variety of colours, and in 1967 produced a set of ten colour screenprints on paper in an edition of 250.

Warhol was interested in celebrities, but it was their image and the way they were presented in the media that intrigued him the most. He was fascinated by press photographs and footage, and increasingly borrowed from the media to produce his silkscreened paintings. Over the following years, he made a series of works that explored the dark side of American life through the prism of disturbing, shocking and sometimes grisly press images. Known as his *Death and Disaster* series (1963–4), the works include scenes of car crashes, suicides and the electric chair in New York State's notorious Sing Sing prison. This body of work was motivated by the repetition of these images in the press, as he once explained: '…when you see a gruesome picture over and over again, it doesn't really have any effect'.[92] In November 1963, when President John F. Kennedy was assassinated in Dallas, Texas, Warhol responded not to the shocking event, but to the press coverage of Kennedy's widow, Jacqueline, who he presented as a grieving Madonna, emphasizing the half-tone dots of the newspaper print when he reproduced her image. 'I'd been thrilled having Kennedy as president,' he later explained, 'he was handsome, young, smart – but it didn't bother me that much that he was dead. What bothered me was the way the television and radio were programming everybody to feel so sad.'[93]

From 1962 onward, Warhol's paintings were almost exclusively made with silkscreens. The technique not only allowed him to reproduce photographic imagery and hand-created marks, but it enabled him to delegate the work to assistants, creating a true production line. In 1963, he moved his studio to a loft on East 47th Street, which became known as the Factory. There, surrounded by an entourage of artists, performers, filmmakers, poets, photographers, models, dancers, friends and friends of friends, he worked with assistants to create his work. His principal assistant was Gerard Malanga, who did much of the silkscreen printing. The building itself was crumbling, which led Warhol's friend Billie Name to cover the walls and pipes in silver foil and spray almost all other surfaces with a silver paint, including the toilet bowl. The Factory became a hang-out, a place to relax, take drugs, listen to music and party, but also a hive of productivity. Warhol once said that the artist he most admired in all of history was Picasso because he was so prolific. Warhol had a similar creative drive, a need to keep working and a relentless curiosity to try new ways of making art. In 1963, he purchased his first movie camera and over the next few years made hundreds of experimental films featuring Factory regulars, friends and models. His film *Sleep* (1964), for example, depicts the poet John Giorno, his lover at the time, naked and asleep for over five hours as the camera moves slowly around his body. *Eat* (1964) featured the Pop artist Robert Indiana eating a raw mushroom for 45 minutes and *Empire* (1964) is a black-and-white portrait of the Empire State Building shot over eight hours as the light fades. Film and photography became increasingly important to Warhol. In a foreshadowing of the phone-camera age we now find ourselves in, Warhol was almost never without a Polaroid, or later a compact camera, taking many thousands of images. In 1965, he announced his intention to stop painting and focus on his filmmaking, although he later returned to painting and also, from 1967, began to produce editions on paper under the imprint Factory Additions. His work also expanded into performance art. Between 1966 and 1967, he co-organized a series of events with the film director Paul Morrissey under the name The Exploding Plastic Inevitable, which involved musical performances by the band The Velvet Underground and singer Nico, screenings of Warhol's films and performances from members of his circle. He also began to direct the multimedia performances of The Velvet Underground and produced their first album.

By 1968, Andy Warhol was one of the most famous artists in the world. He had cultivated a highly recognizable image, usually dressing in a striped T-shirt with jeans and wearing a bleached blonde wig to hide his premature baldness, and he and his friends were regulars at celebrity haunts such as Studio 54. His public persona was as consciously managed as his looks. When interviewed in the press, he would answer enigmatically, provocatively or with just a 'yes' or 'no'. On 3 June, however, everything changed when Warhol was shot through the lung by Valerie Solanas, a radical feminist who had founded the Society for Cutting Up Men (SCUM) and who was later diagnosed with paranoid schizophrenia. Solanas had hung around the Factory for a while and had lent Warhol a screenplay that she had written, which she was now demanding back, blaming Warhol for problems she was having in getting it published. Warhol survived, but only just, and the incident affected him profoundly. After the shooting, he not only experienced problems with his health, but also became much more careful about who he spent time with and who was allowed in the Factory. He continued to work, however, concentrating on portrait commissions in the 1970s, which he made from Polaroid photographs, and later returned to hand painting. In the late 1970s, he produced a series of *Oxidation* paintings, which he made by urinating on to a canvas coated with a metallic paint, producing gestural marks in iridescent greens and greys. Between 1984 and 1986, he painted over 100 canvases based on Leonardo da Vinci's *Last Supper*. Warhol had remained committedly Catholic, attending church with his mother who lived with him until 1971. The Leonardo paintings have been interpreted as an exploration of his Catholicism, but also a reflection on the AIDS epidemic that was devastating New York's gay community at the time.

Warhol died unexpectedly, aged 58, on 22 February 1987, following gall-bladder surgery. A memorial service at St Patrick's Cathedral in New York was attended by over 2,000 people, and in 1994 the Andy Warhol Museum was founded in Pittsburgh. During his lifetime, Warhol made many paintings, drawings, sculptures and films, and also left a legacy of written work including a diary he kept from the 1970s. He was a compulsive and prolific creator who expanded what we see as art and encouraged us to see art in everything around us. In 1963, he drove to Los Angeles for his second exhibition at the Ferus Gallery. 'The farther west we drove', he later recalled, 'the more Pop everything looked on the highways … Once you "got" Pop, you could never see a sign the same way again.'[94]

24

Yayoi Kusama: Self-Obliteration

The majority of the artists featured in this book have a singular, easily identifiable style, but more than most, over the course of her career, Yayoi Kusama has created a visual language in her art that is instantly recognizable as hers. Recurring motifs such as polka dots, spotted pumpkins, flowers and net-like formations have dominated her work across a variety of media on both a large and small scale. The aesthetically pleasing nature of these motifs, along with her vibrant colours and immersive installations, have led many to describe her art as joyful, an emotion that she has sought to inspire through her work. This positivity and generosity as an artist, and her commitment to 'spread the joy and love of being human', is especially remarkable given the origins of her art.[95] When she was ten years old, Yayoi Kusama began to experience hallucinations that have continued throughout her life. Accompanied by extreme anxiety, her initial hallucinations manifested as flashing lights, auras and repetitive patterns of flowers or dots that seemed to engulf her. She began to draw and paint as a way of coping with the experience, translating the hallucinations into art and turning what had been a frightening experience for her into an uplifting one for others.

Born on 22 March 1929 in Matsumoto, Nagano Prefecture, Japan, Yayoi was not encouraged to make art by her parents. Her family was relatively wealthy and made their living from cultivating plant seeds among other business ventures. They were socially conservative and wanted Yayoi to follow a traditional path to become a wife and mother. Speaking about her childhood, Yayoi has painted an unhappy picture of a physically abusive mother who destroyed her works of art and a philandering father who was often absent from the family home.[96] Her life was complicated further during the Second World War, when, as a young adolescent, she was forced to spend long days working in a parachute factory. But she continued to draw at home, establishing a practice of working late into the night and managing on very little sleep that she has maintained for much of her career. In her late teens, Kusama began to receive psychiatric treatment for her anxiety and hallucinations. Her repetitive and immersive patterns, particularly the dots that are a feature of much of her work, began as an attempt to overcome a condition that at times has caused her great suffering and fear. But they are also an expression of an intimate experience of the world that is unique to her. Yayoi has described the terror that she felt when she first experienced hallucinations, but she has also spoken about her experiences in a more positive way, describing a feeling of being no longer confined to her physical body and becoming part of an infinite universe. She calls this concept, of her body blending with nature, time and space, 'self-obliteration'. In translating this experience into art and offering viewers a glimpse into her singular vision of human existence, Yayoi creates work that is serious and joyful, profound and uplifting, and utterly unlike the art of anybody else.

Despite her family's resistance to her art, Yayoi persuaded her parents to let her move to Kyoto in 1948 to study a style of Japanese painting called *Nihonga*. She had already begun to develop her singular style, however, and found the teaching to be too conservative, so spent most of her time painting in her dormitory. Within a few years, she had created thousands of works on paper in pastel, gouache and ink, and had begun to exhibit her work in Japan, attracting some critical recognition. Yayoi was aware of American art and keen to make a mark beyond Japan, so in 1955 she initiated a correspondence with the Seattle-based painter Kenneth Callahan, who helped her to secure her first solo exhibition in the USA, at the Zoë Dusanne Gallery in Seattle. She also began to write to the New Mexico-based artist Georgia O'Keeffe, whose paintings she had come across in a book, and the two artists exchanged letters over a number of years. Before making the journey to America, Yayoi destroyed many of the drawings that she had produced in the early 1950s, selecting around 200 to take with her, about 20 works of which she exhibited in Seattle. Both Callahan and O'Keeffe had offered Yayoi advice and helped her to make contacts and sell her work once in the United States. The encouragement that she received gave her the confidence first to move to America and then to forge her way into artistic circles once there.

Following her show in Seattle, Yayoi moved to New York City in 1958, where, in a pre-Pop era, the art scene was still dominated by Abstract Expressionist painters including Rothko, De Kooning and Helen Frankenthaler. Their emotionally expressive style of gestural brush-strokes and large expanses of colour influenced Yayoi, but her own art remained distinct. From the late 1950s, she began to produce large-scale paintings composed of tiny repeating marks known as her *Infinity Nets*. Her first solo exhibition in New York, at the Brata Gallery in Manhattan, comprised a group of wall-sized *Infinity Net* canvases painted entirely in white so that the net-like compositions only came into focus as the viewer moved towards them. The American artist Donald Judd reviewed the show for ARTnews, beginning his piece with the sentence: 'Yayoi Kusama is an original paint-er'.[97] He went on to compare her work with that of the dominant American artists of the time, concluding that although her art owed a debt to Rothko and others, 'it is not at all a synthesis and is thoroughly independent'. Judd was so enthusiastic about her paintings that he purchased one from the exhibition, and the two artists went on to become friends and neighbours, working and living in the same building in the East Village. Yayoi continued to work on her time-consuming *Infinity Net* paintings over the following years, expanding her palette beyond white to include reds, yellows and greens, and often working into the night, obsessively adding to the network of arcs and dots and cell-like systems. The paintings helped Yayoi to process the anxiety and hallucinations that she contin-ued to experience, providing a protective layer between her and the wider world. At the same time, they brought her attention and established her name within the art world in the West.

As Pop began to dominate the New York art scene, Yayoi began to incorporate everyday objects into her work, creating collages using food packaging and postage stickers and, from 1962, creating soft sculptures by covering domestic furniture and household items with clumps of hand-sewn, stuffed phallic shapes. Known as her *Accumulations*, these sculptures were influenced by Freudian theories around sexuality and were a way of confronting her own complex feelings about masculinity and sex, to which she had an aversion. In June 1962, Yayoi's sculptures were exhibited at the Green Gallery in midtown Manhattan alongside work by leading American Pop artists, including Andy Warhol and the Swedish-born sculptor Claes Oldenburg, who began to make his own soft sculptures shortly afterwards. The 1960s was to be a decade of extraordinary creativity for Yayoi Kusama, as she embraced both installation and performance art, taking the ideas that underpinned her *Infinity Net* paintings and extending them into three dimensions and live art. In 1965, she created the breakthrough work *Infinity Mirror Room – Phalli's Field* (also known as *Floor Show*), an installation comprising mirrored walls and a floor filled with red-and-white stuffed, polka-dotted protuberances. Yayoi has gone on to create numerous other mirrored rooms, including *Infinity Mirrored Room – Filled with the Brilliance of Life* (2011), in which viewers move around the installation on a walkway above a shallow pool and are surrounded by tiny globes of coloured light that are endlessly reflected in the mirrors. They are intended to evoke the sensation of complete immersion or, as she would describe it, 'self-obliteration'.

During her time in New York, Yayoi repeatedly documented herself in her studio and alongside her work, hiring professional photographers to take her picture. Her appearance became an important part of her presentation as an artist; when she was photographed alongside her work, she would wear clothes that responded to the piece, such as a red catsuit when photographed in *Infinity Mirror Room – Phalli's Field,* or white clothes when pictured with her all-white *Accumulations.* Conscious of her position as an Asian artist in America, she would often wear a traditional Japanese kimono to public events such as gallery openings to assert her identity. In 1966, she created *Walking Piece,* a performance work that involved her walking through the streets of New York wearing a pink-and-red flowered kimono, traditional Japanese sandals, and holding a parasol. The performance was documented in a series of slides by the photographer Eikoh Hosoe. Further performance pieces followed, which became increasingly radical and avant-garde. From the 1950s, performance artists in New York had been staging theatrical events, often in galleries, known as 'Happenings', a term first used in 1959 to describe the work of Allan Kaprow. From around 1967, Yayoi staged many happenings, or 'body festivals', which often involved naked performers being painted with polka dots. She also held fashion shows featuring her own designs, which she began to sell in her own boutique from 1969. Many of the clothes were see-through and featured her signature motifs of flowers and polka dots. In 1968, she designed a two-person bridal gown to be worn by two men at a wedding ceremony over which she presided as the High Priestess of Polka Dots at the Church of Self-Obliteration.

For Yayoi, the clothes, performances and happenings were a continuation of her ideas about self-obliteration.

'Polka dots were the trademark of the Kusama Happenings,' she explained in her autobiography. 'The red and green and yellow dots might represent the circle of the earth, or of the sun or moon, or whatever you like … What I was asserting was that painting polka-dot patterns on a human body caused that person's self to be obliterated and returned him or her to the natural universe.'[98] In addition, her performances were often politically motivated. From 1968, at the time of the Vietnam War, she began a series of happenings called 'Anatomic Explosions' that included one staged at the New York Board of Elections in which she appeared with four naked performers covered in polka dots and wearing masks bearing the faces of that year's presidential candidates. In an open letter to one of the candidates, Richard Nixon, Yayoi wrote, 'Let's forget ourselves, dearest Richard, and become one with the Absolute, all together in the altogether. As we soar through the heavens, we'll paint each other with polka dots, lose our egos in timeless eternity, and finally discover the naked truth: You can't eradicate violence by using more violence.'[99]

Yayoi Kusama continued to experience mental health challenges during her time in the United States and some discrimination in the mainstream art world as a result of her gender and ethnicity. In 1966, she criticized the consumerist nature of the art world through her work *Narcissus Garden*, an installation of around 1,500 mirrored plastic balls in which visitors could view their reflections, which she presented, uninvited, outside the Italian pavilion at the 33rd Venice Biennale. Wearing a gold kimono, she offered to sell the balls to passing visitors for 1,200 lire each (less than £1) under a sign that read 'Your Narcissism for Sale!'. As Yayoi's art became increasingly focused on performances and installations, and therefore less commercially viable, her success in New York declined and in 1973 she returned to Japan, settling in Tokyo. A few years later, she admitted herself to a psychiatric hospital where she has chosen to live ever since, continuing to make art in a studio nearby. Her status as a leading Japanese artist was cemented in 1993 when, 27 years after she crashed the Venice Biennale with *Narcissus Garden*, she was invited to represent her home country in their official pavilion. The work that she presented is titled *Mirror Room (Pumpkin)* (1991), a room in which the yellow walls, floors and ceilings are covered with black polka dots, which are reflected by a mirrored cube at the centre. A peep hole in the cube provides a view of paper mâché yellow-and-black pumpkins infinitely reflected within the cube. The pumpkin has become a dominant subject in Yayoi's art, having first appeared in her teenage drawings and in her paintings, prints and installations since the 1980s. In 1994 a polka-dotted pumpkin was the subject of her first open-air sculpture, which was installed on Naoshima Island in Japan. Yayoi's use of the pumpkin, an everyday food item in Japan, feels very 'Pop', but for her it symbolizes more than an everyday item. Pumpkins have comforting associations for Yayoi, and she also finds the form both humorous and human-like. Humour and comfort both play an important role in Yayoi's art and help her to achieve the mental balance that she has always sought. Her humour is evident in the numerous books that she has produced, which include semi-autobiographical novels and collections of poetry. Now in her tenth decade, Kusama continues to work. She has received considerable international attention since the 1990s, including retrospective exhibitions at the Museum of Modern Art in New York (1998), Tate Modern, London (2021) and the M+ Gallery in Hong Kong (2022–3). She is now one of the most celebrated and recognizable artists in the world, and she continues to make work that brings joy to many.

25

Marina Abramović: The Audience and I Become One

When Marina Abramović was 14 years old, she asked for a set of oil paints for her birthday. Seeking to encourage her interest, her father asked an artist friend to help them pick the colours, after which the artist gave Abramović her first painting lesson at her home. The artist cut a canvas into an irregular shape and laid it on the floor, then proceeded to throw different coloured paints and various other materials on to it, including sand, bitumen and finally turpentine and petrol. He then lit a match, causing the whole thing to explode and called it a sunset. A few weeks later, Abramović returned home from a vacation with her parents only to find the remnants, which she had dried and hung on the wall, had melted in the sun into a pile on the floor. Years later, she realized how impactful this experience had been. The painting had involved an element of performance, an art form to which she has dedicated her life, but it also contributed to her belief that process is the most important element of art. 'When the performance is finished', she has said of her work, 'the memory is something else, but the process is what is essential.'[100] In this view, Abramović was also influenced by the French artist Yves Klein (1928–62), himself a pioneer of performance art, who repeatedly asserted the primacy of his process, famously insisting, 'My paintings are the ashes of my art.'[101] For Marina Abramović, whose work has often relied on her own bodily experiences, process is central. Her work often depends on her interaction with an audience, unpredictability and the energy in a room during a live performance, elements that exist only in the moment. Videos, photographs and re-enactments are the ashes: not without meaning, but something other than her art.

Marina Abramović was born on 30 November 1946 in Belgrade, now capital of Serbia but then part of the Federal People's Republic of Yugoslavia, a communist state established a year earlier under Josip Broz Tito. Abramović's parents, Danica Rosić and Vojin Abramović, both worked for the government, her father in a military role and her mother as an art historian responsible for historic monuments. Despite her teenage lesson in conceptual art, Abramović initially studied academic painting at the Academy of Fine Arts in Belgrade (1965–70) and then as a postgraduate at the Academy of Fine Arts in Zagreb (1972). But as a student in the 1960s, she became aware of more radical ideas in contemporary art and began to make experimental, conceptual work early on, focusing on performance art from the 1970s. In 1973, she performed *Rhythm 10* at Edinburgh Arts, in which she laid her splayed left hand on a floor covered with white paper and repeatedly stabbed down between her fingers quickly and with a sharp knife. A tape recorder captured the sounds that she made each time she caught her flesh, at which point she would groan and switch to a different knife from the selection of 20 that she had laid out. When she had cut herself ten times, she played the tape recording and tried to repeat the movements that had led to each cut by listening to the different sounds. By the end, the paper was marked with her blood. The concept was based on a traditional drinking game practised in Russia and Yugoslavia, which involves the player taking a drink every time they cut themselves. For Abramović, the performance – like so much of her work since – was about enduring physical and mental discomfort and pain, danger, chance, the tension that comes with not knowing what will happen, and the heightened energy created between herself and the audience. Recalling the experience in her memoir, Abramović wrote, '… a very strange feeling came over me, something I had never dreamed of: it was as if electricity was running through my body, and the audience and I had become one. A single organism. The sense of danger in the room had united the onlookers and me in that moment: the here and now, and nowhere else.'[102] From this point on, the audience has been an essential element in much of her work and her body has been fundamental, both as a subject and a means through which she creates.

Between 1973 and 1974, Abramović continued to explore her physical and mental limits through her *Rhythm* series, which relied heavily on audience interaction and reaction. She was completely committed to every performance, to the point of risking serious injury or even death. In 1974, she performed *Rhythm 2*, which involved taking drugs that were intended to treat schizophrenia, which caused her to pass out, and for *Rhythm 5* she lay at the centre of a wooden structure in the shape of a five-pointed star, which was set alight, causing her to lose consciousness due to smoke inhalation. One of her most extreme works of art from this time was *Rhythm 0*, the last of the series, performed in 1974 at Studio Morra in Naples. For this work, Abramović stood for six hours alongside a table on which she had laid 72 objects. Visitors to the gallery were invited to use the objects on her body in whatever way they wished as she remained motionless, maintaining a neutral expression. The objects included some that could elicit pleasure and some that could cause pain, including a feather, a hairbrush, a whip, scissors, honey, a gun and a single bullet. Over the course of the performance, the predominantly male visitors' actions grew increasingly extreme and violent. She was stripped to the waist so that her naked torso was left exposed and at one point a loaded gun was pressed to her neck. Yet she endured the ordeal without comment, although the video of the performance shows her eyes brimming with tears. Abramović later said that the trauma of the event caused a section of her hair to turn white. The footage of the performance shows some of the audience members laughing and taunting the artist, but there appears to be a nervousness among them, too, maybe even fear. As the performance ended, many of them fled the gallery, perhaps appalled at how they had acted. The performance was illuminating, exposing humans' ready capacity for violence and cruelty. It was about the artist but about the audience as well. Over the years, Abramović has explored themes of war, oppression, violence, sex, life, death, spirituality and the experiences of being a woman. Her 1975 work *Art Must Be Beautiful, Artist Must Be Beautiful*, a filmed performance in which she violently brushes her hair while repeating the titular phrase, challenged ideas about what it means to be feminine and how women are expected to look. In the same year, she performed a piece in Amsterdam, the city she moved to from Belgrade in 1976, called *Role Exchange*, for which she swapped places with a sex worker, sitting in her window in the red-light district for four hours while the sex worker pretended to be Abramović at a gallery opening. In both locations, the women, who had both worked in their respective roles for a decade, were on public display, both selling something intensely personal.

Throughout her career, Abramović has made art that is both specific and universal. She has frequently referenced her Serbian heritage and communist upbringing in her work, but usually as a way to explore broader themes, such as the impact on societies of controlling and oppressive regimes. The five-pointed star in *Rhythm 5* was a reference to communism and in 1975 the symbol appeared again when, during a performance piece called *Lips of Thomas* that involved Abramović testing the limits of her body in various ways, she carved the communist star on to her stomach. Two decades later, at the Venice Biennale in 1997, she presented *Balkan Baroque*, a performance in which she cleaned a pile of bloodied bones for four days and six hours while singing Slavic folk songs against a slideshow in which she is pictured with her parents, telling a folk story and dancing to a Balkan song. The work was produced as a response to the violent conflict in the region during the 1990s: a meditation on the horrors of war, but also a reflection on her own cultural identity and her relationship with her homeland. Four years later, following the death of her father in 2000, she made *The Hero*, a film in which she sits on a white horse holding a large white flag while the national anthem of the former Yugoslavia plays. The film is a memorial to her father, a hero of his country, a reflection on the events of history that shaped their lives and, more universally, on grief. In 2009, she made *The Kitchen*, a series of video performances about Saint Teresa of Avila, a nun who levitated after experiencing visions of Christ. Her interest in spirituality, and Christianity in particular, comes in part from her memories of her childhood, during which she absorbed Orthodox Christian traditions alongside folk beliefs.

In 1975, Abramović met the German artist Frank Uwe Laysiepen (1943–2020), known as Ulay, at the De Appel Gallery in Amsterdam where they were both contributing to a television programme about performance art. It was both of their birthdays and they felt an instant connection, both emotionally and artistically. Abramović collaborated with Ulay on many works of art for over a decade. Their partnership required them to find a way in which two independent-minded artists could live, work and make art together, which accommodated both creative forces. Many of the pieces they produced reflect this tension. *Relation in Time*, performed in 1977, involved them sitting back-to-back with their ponytails tied together for 17 hours. A live audience was brought into the room for the final hour to witness the last stage of their endurance. In the same year, they performed *Breathing In/Breathing Out*, in which they had their noses blocked with cigarette filters so that they had to breathe through their mouths, which were each pressed together so that they breathed each other's carbon dioxide. Microphones amplified the sounds as they became increasingly distressed and uncomfortable. They stopped after 19 minutes when all the oxygen had been consumed and they were close to losing consciousness. But the performance that probably comes closest to reflecting the complex dynamic of their relationship was *Rest Energy*, performed at the National Gallery of Ireland, Dublin in 1980. Lasting for four minutes, the filmed performance shows the artists standing against a blank background facing each other, each wearing a white shirt and dark bottoms. Between them, they hold a large bow and arrow, which is drawn, with the arrowhead pointing directly at Abramović's heart. To maintain the balance and hold the bow steady, they were each required to lean back slightly. If the bow fired, Abramović could be killed. Throughout the performance, the two artists maintain eye contact while their positions become increasingly difficult to hold and their bodies begin to tremble as they are forced to give in to complete and total trust.

Abramović's partnership with Ulay came to an end when their relationship broke down in 1988. Their final work together was *The Lovers – The Great Wall Walk* (1988), for which they each walked half the length of the Great Wall of China, starting at different ends and meeting in the middle. The project was beset with difficulties; it took several years to obtain permission from the Chinese authorities and then the walk itself, which lasted for more than 90 days, was arduous and treacherous in places. When the work was first conceived, the pair had intended to marry on its completion, but by the time they reached that point, the relationship had deteriorated and they instead decided to separate, marking the end of their creative collaboration with the work. Following her separation from Ulay and her experiences walking the wall in China, Abramović became increasingly interested in the physical environment and spiritual beliefs about materials, places and the destructive force of humans on the natural world. The focus of her work shifted from performances involving her own body to the creation of sculptural objects and installations with which viewers interact, which are collectively called *Transitory Objects for Human Use*. Made in 1989, *Red Dragon* comprises a seat made from oxidized copper, which viewers are invited to sit on, and a rose quartz pillow, which they are invited to rest their heads on 'until its energy is transmitted'. In interacting with *Black Dragon*, made the following year from green quartz, snowflake obsidian, hematite, blue quartz and brown agate, viewers are invited to 'Face the wall. Press your head, heart and sex against the mineral pillows. Duration: limitless.'

In 2002, Abramović performed a work that relied entirely on the audience's response. For *The House with the Ocean View*, she lived for 12 days across three rooms that had been constructed about six feet above the floor in the Sean Kelly Gallery, New York. One room had a toilet and shower, the central room had a wooden table and chair with a crystal in its back, and the third had a raised platform on which she could sleep. Ladders leading up to the rooms had large knives for rungs. Day or night, visitors were able to observe her as she remained silent, not eating and looking out at them. A metronome ticked, measuring the passing time. Abramović had moved to New York City the previous year, the year of the 9/11 attacks in which terrorists flew two planes into the twin towers of the World Trade Center in Lower Manhattan, killing nearly 3,000 people. At the end of the performance, she told the audience that the work was a response to the attack and that her intention had been to create a moment in which people could come together: 'In a city that has no time I wanted to create an island of time.'[103] In 2010, during a retrospective of her work at the Museum of Modern Art, New York, titled *The Artist is Present*, the museum's first retrospective of a performance artist, she created a similar island of time. For the duration of the entire exhibition, she re-enacted her 1980s piece, *Nightsea Crossing*, which had involved her sitting silently across a table from Ulay for many days at a time, but this time audience members took turns to sit opposite her for as long as they desired. Over 75 days, 1,545 visitors took the opportunity, many of whom had a profound emotional response. During the run, Ulay appeared unexpectedly, and the ex-lovers sat opposite each other again, having not spoken for 20 years and having undergone an acrimonious legal dispute. The artists' eyes filled with tears and they extended their arms to each other across the table. Moved by the significance of the moment and the energy it created, the audience applauded. Ulay then left and another person sat down.

26

Ai Weiwei: An Artist Must Be an Activist

As we have seen in the chapters on Hogarth, Goya, Kollwitz and Hepworth, politics can be an important motivating factor for artists but artistic responses to politics vary considerably, from commentary and satire to propaganda and activism. Ai Weiwei is an artist whose work is inextricably connected to, and indeed part of, the political activism with which he has been engaged throughout his career. Born in Beijing in 1957, Ai spent his childhood living with his family in exile from China's capital city after his father Ai Qing was accused of being a critic of the communist government known as a 'Rightist'. Ai Qing (born Jiang Haicheng) was a poet and an artist who had previously been jailed for three years by the Nationalist government in the early 1930s after he returned from studying painting in Paris and joined a left-wing artists' association. While incarcerated, Ai Qing was unable to paint and so turned to poetry, through which he made his name. Following his release, he expressed his commitment to the Communist Party under Mao Zedong but after several years in the Party's favour, during which he worked as an official delegate for the government, Ai Qing was accused of dissent and in 1958 was forced to go into exile with his wife, Gao Ying, and their young family. To begin with, the family moved to the north-east of China and then to Xinjiang province in the north-west, where Ai Qing was forced to undertake manual labour, which included cleaning communal toilets, and the family lived in an underground shed. It was not until 1976, with the death of Mao, that the family were able to return to Beijing. The circumstances of his upbringing set Ai Weiwei on a path of activism that has determined his whole life. In 1978, he enrolled at the Beijing Film Academy where he joined a group of artists called the *Stars*, who campaigned for freedom of expression. In 1979, they mounted an unofficial exhibition on the railings outside Beijing's National Art Museum, attracting many visitors and international press attention. In the years since, Ai has continued to make art that carries a political message, often with the aim of highlighting corruption and other injustices. He has also explored his own heritage as a Chinese man who grew up during the Cultural Revolution, the history of his country, and the seemingly opposing forces of communism and capitalism.

Ai Weiwei left China for the United States in 1981, moving to New York City in 1983, initially to study at the Parsons School of Design, where he lived for a decade. There, he was exposed to the work of Marcel Duchamp (1887–1968) who, in 1917, placed a ceramic urinal in an exhibition and called it art. Ai was influenced by Duchamp's use of prefabricated, found objects in his art, known as 'readymades', and his conceptual approach, whereby the idea behind a work of art took precedence over the finished work. He also became familiar with the work of Jasper Johns and Andy Warhol, both of whom used pre-existing imagery in their work, including press photographs and familiar public symbols such as the American flag and commercial logos. Pop art's deadpan commentary on America's materialistic society through references to popular culture and consumer goods resonated with Ai, as he experienced life in a capitalist society for the first time. During his time in New York, he took thousands of photographs of the city, exploring life in America, while living among a circle of expat Chinese artists. His early work incorporated found objects and includes *Hanging Man* (1985), a profile portrait of Duchamp made from a wire coat hanger, and *One-Man Shoe* (1987), a sculpture made from the front halves of two shoes joined together. From the beginning of his career as an artist, Ai was interested in the questions posed by Duchamp and others in the early twentieth century: what is art and when does something become art? Conceptual art had gained momentum in the 1960s and '70s, particularly in America, where artists such as Sol LeWitt (1928–2007) and Joseph Kosuth (born 1945) made art that prioritized idea and process over the end result. Ai's output as an artist is varied, but all of his work is fundamentally conceptual. When he returned to Beijing in 1993, having gained a different perspective on his home country and also finding it had changed in many ways, the ideas behind his art became primarily focused on China.

Much of Ai's work in the 1990s explored China's present through its history. His installation *Still Life* (1993–2000) comprised around 4,000 ancient stone axe-heads from China, laid out neatly in rows. In 1994, he made *Han Dynasty Urn with Coca-Cola Logo*, which comprised a 2,000-year-old Han dynasty pot on to which he painted a Coca-Cola logo. Ai was brought up during Chairman

Mao's Cultural Revolution (1966–76) during which, in an effort to strengthen the People's Republic of China and move forward into a new era, there was a widespread state-sponsored purge of the country's heritage, and many historical artefacts and sites were destroyed. On returning to China in the 1990s, Ai found the country still ruled by an authoritarian communist government, albeit one that had opened the country up to capitalism. Ai's use of found, historical objects interrogated China's attitude to its cultural heritage and the value the country now placed on material goods, as well as its burgeoning role as the world's factory. One of Ai's most famous works of art from this period is *Dropping a Han Dynasty Urn* (1995), a series of three black-and-white photographs that depict him standing full-length against a featureless brick wall, facing the camera with a neutral expression. In the first photograph he holds a ceramic urn in both of his hands, in the second it falls to the ground while he continues to look ahead, and in the third, the urn has hit the ground and smashed, creating debris around his feet. The work relies on the viewers' shock at witnessing an ancient object being destroyed in such a seemingly reckless and casual way, a deliberate echo of the Cultural Revolution, although despite using genuine Han-dynasty ceramics in his work, Ai has hinted that the pot in the photographs is not authentically old. In planting this seed of doubt, he encourages the viewer to consider if the age of the object even matters and how we decide, as societies, what has value and what doesn't. In the same year, Ai also made *Study of Perspective, Tiananmen* (1995), a photograph of his hand with his middle finger raised in an offensive gesture towards Tiananmen Square Gate in Beijing, where pro-democracy protests were violently suppressed in 1989, resulting in many deaths. Ai continued the series until 2003, taking photographs of his hand with his middle finger raised in sites around the world associated with powerful institutions or states, including the White House in Washington DC, St Mark's Square in Venice and the Eiffel Tower in Paris.

From the late 1990s, Ai increasingly worked as an architect, writer and curator. In 1997, he co-founded the China Art Archives and Warehouse (CAAW) on the outskirts of Beijing, which was intended to provide a place for contemporary artists to experiment and exhibit their work. During this period, he also built his own home and studio and a building to house CAAW, and in 2003 founded an architecture company called FAKE Design Ltd. One of the many projects that Ai worked on over the following few years was a collaboration with the architects Herzog & de Meuron to design the Bird's Nest Stadium for the Beijing Summer Olympic Games in 2008. Despite his involvement, however, Ai boycotted the Games as he felt that the event had become propaganda for an undemocratic government that continued to deny its citizens freedom of expression.[104] He closed his architecture firm soon afterwards. In the early 2000s, Ai discovered the potential of the internet to amplify his message and became a prolific blogger and user of social media. His blog was fundamental to the work he created in response to the 2008 earthquake in Sichuan province, south-west China, which killed around 70,000 people. Over 5,000 of the dead were schoolchildren due to the country's badly constructed schools, which Ai attributed in part to corrupt local officials. Working with a large team, Ai gathered the names of the children who were killed, as well as other details including their birthdays and parents' names, and published them on his blog. The project led to his blog being shut down and the arrest of some of his assistants. Undeterred, he created *Straight*, an installation made from around 200 tonnes of twisted steel bars recovered from the buildings damaged in the earthquake, which were painstakingly hammered straight by hand and laid out in a row. The following year, he made *Remembering*, which comprised 9,000 school backpacks in different colours installed on the façade of the Haus der Kunst in Munich, which spelled out in Chinese the words spoken by the mother of one of the victims: 'She lived happily for seven years in this world'. Much of Ai's work during this period involved large-scale installations, which culminated in his commission to create a work for the vast space of the Turbine Hall in London's Tate Modern. *Sunflower Seeds* (2010) comprised 100 million painted porcelain seeds spread out across the floor, each of which had been handmade and painted by specialists in Jingdezhen in China, a historic porcelain centre. Sunflower seeds are widely consumed as a snack in China and Ai remembered almost always having a handful in his pocket as a child. In addition, the sunflower had a symbolic value under Mao, who was often depicted with sunflowers against a rising sun.

In 2011, after years of publicly criticizing the Chinese government, Ai was arrested at Beijing airport and secretly imprisoned for 81 days, ostensibly for tax evasion, although the charges were unclear. During his incarceration, he was kept in a small cell and watched by prison guards for 24 hours a day. Following his release without charge, he was forbidden to discuss his experience and had his passport confiscated, which was only returned to him in 2015. He was placed under constant surveillance and issued with an enormous fine of nearly £1.5 million for non-payment of tax, an amount that around 30,000 supporters helped him raise. The traumatic experience caused him to reflect on his personal history, his father's experience of prison and exile, and the impact that had had on his own life. As ever, he examined, processed and commented upon the experience through art. In 2013, he created the work *S.A.C.R.E.D.*, recreating the conditions in which he was imprisoned through six diorama scenes that included fibreglass figures of himself and his prison guards. Visitors were invited to view the scenes by looking through holes in the iron boxes in which they were enclosed. In 2015, Ai left China, moving first to Germany, then the UK and then to Portugal, where he built a replica of a studio he had completed in Shanghai in 2010, which had been destroyed by the authorities in 2011 for supposedly contravening planning regulations. Since leaving his home country, China has remained an important focus of his art but he has also responded to wider global injustices and crises, including the mass movement of refugees around the world, specifically the treacherous journeys they are forced to take. In 2017, he created *Soleil Levant*, an installation of 6,000 refugee lifejackets that had been collected from the Greek island of Lesbos with which he blocked the windows of the Kunsthal Charlottenborg in Copenhagen. In the same year, he also made the feature-length documentary *Human Flow*, about the international refugee crisis.

In recent years, Ai has continued to explore the concept of the readymade in his art. Over the last 15 years he has recreated functional objects in marble, a luxury material associated with ruling classes in China and elsewhere. The objects include a surveillance camera, recalling those installed outside his studio in Beijing. During the Covid-19 pandemic, he made marble sculptures of toilet paper, which for a time, became a precious commodity. Since his incarceration, Ai has also used Lego bricks in his work, recreating famous works of art by Monet, Hokusai and others using the coloured building blocks. His works in Lego reference pixellation in digital art as well as ancient Greek and Roman mosaics, in which pictures are similarly created through the arrangement of square or rectangular components. But politics remains central to his work, and activism the main goal of his art. 'An artist must also be an activist,' he has said. 'That doesn't mean they have to demonstrate in street protests, but rather deal with these issues through a so-called artistic language. Without that kind of consciousness – to be blind to human struggle – one cannot even be called an artist.'[105]

27

Keith Haring: Art in the City

When Keith Haring moved to New York City from Kutztown, Pennsylvania in 1978, he was struck by the graffiti on the streets, in the subways and on the side of trains. In a city rich with art, it was the spray-painted tags, images and slogans, and pasted handbills, which he saw on journeys to and from museums and galleries, that spoke to him most directly. This was the height of the street art movement in New York, before the authorities' so-called 'war on graffiti' significantly quashed the scene in the 1980s. Haring related to the spontaneous nature of what he saw, the cartoonish style and fluid lines that were a feature of many of the images. It connected to his own early work and the non-street artists that he was influenced by at the time, including Jean Dubuffet (1901–85) and Pierre Alechinsky (born 1927). Haring was 20 when he arrived in New York and still finding his style, but he had already developed a cynicism about the art establishment. This underground movement, therefore, which circumvented the traditional system of galleries, museums, critics and dealers, and was inclusive, both in terms of practitioners and audience, greatly appealed. Before long, Haring had become a part of the city's urban art scene and had developed friendships with many of its key players, including Fab 5 Freddy and Jean-Michel Basquiat. He found his own way of using the city as a gallery and dedicated himself to making art that was for everyone, and that communicated a message of human connectivity and compassion.

Haring became interested in art at a young age. He was born in the city of Reading, Pennsylvania, on 4 May 1958 and brought up in nearby Kutztown, the son of Joan and Allen Haring and the oldest of four siblings. He developed a love of drawing cartoons from his father and was influenced as a child by Dr. Seuss illustrations and Walt Disney cartoons. In his teens, he learned about art through books and magazines such as *Life* and *Look*, as well as on occasional visits to museums, including a church trip to the Hirshhorn Museum in Washington DC, where he first saw work by Andy Warhol, who was later to become a friend and mentor. Haring was an obsessive teenager who threw himself into his latest enthusiasm. For a time, he became intensely involved with an evangelical Christian group, then found drugs and rock and roll, devoting himself to the Californian band the Grateful Dead. For several years, he was looking for something to believe in and feel part of. Soon, however, art became that thing. When he was around 16 and experimenting with hallucinogenic drugs, he began to draw in a spontaneous way, allowing his hand to make images on paper in an immediate and unmediated manner. To begin with, abstract shapes emerged before recognizable figures and objects began to form. By the time he had graduated from high school in 1976, he had decided he wanted to be an artist.

Despite Haring's resolve, he was persuaded by his parents and school advisers to take a commercial art course at the

Ivy School of Professional Art in Pittsburgh. Commercial art, meaning graphic design, was not for him and, foreseeing an unfulfilling and miserable career, he dropped out after two semesters. Over the following year, he continued to draw and read about art, and explored the opportunities open to him by hitchhiking around the country to find out about art programmes. On his return to Pennsylvania, he became involved in the Pittsburgh Arts and Crafts Center and took classes informally at the city's university. His distinctive visual vocabulary was beginning to develop and he was further motivated in this direction when he travelled to the Carnegie Museum of Art in Pittsburgh to see a major Alechinsky retrospective exhibition (1977–8). The Belgian artist's semi-abstract images containing repeating forms suggestive of animals, plants and humans resonated deeply with Haring, as did the writings of Dubuffet, who championed the work of 'outsider' artists (untrained artists working outside of the establishment art world) and whose own work often featured strong outlines and cartoonish shapes. The work of both artists also had a spontaneous element to it, much like his own. Reflecting on his visit to the Alechinsky show, Haring commented: 'I couldn't believe that work! It was so close to what I was doing! ... It was the closest thing I had ever seen to what I was doing with these self-generative little shapes.'[106] In 1978, he was given an exhibition at the Pittsburgh Arts and Crafts Center after another artist cancelled. Aged 19, he had his first solo show and for the first time members of the public were able to see his little, interconnected shapes.

By 1978, Haring had realized that he was gay and had started to have sex with men despite the fact he was in a relationship with a woman. His move to New York was partly motivated by a desire to explore his sexuality but also by the knowledge that the city would offer him more opportunities as an artist. He felt it was the only place to go, both for his art and his personal life. There, he enrolled as a scholarship student at the School of Visual Arts, where he was taught by pioneering contemporary artists including Keith Sonnier and Joseph Kosuth, and experimented with different art forms including installation art, performance and video. Drawing remained central to his practice, however, and he drew obsessively during this period, often displaying the results in the hallways of the school where they could be viewed by others. One day, he bought a roll of cheap brown paper and laid it on the floor. He started to draw in a stream-of-consciousness way, and little humans, animals and flying saucers came out. These motifs and a crawling figure, which evolved into a baby, became central to and emblematic of his art. Haring had been looking for a way of taking his art to the street and this language gave him something to say. In the winter of 1980, he began to draw on the streets with a marker, first a dog and then the crawling figure. In the subway stations, he added his little characters to the blank areas of advertising posters. On one, a poster promoting Johnnie Walker whisky, he drew a row of his babies being zapped by flying saucers. He wanted to show that the babies had been energized by the zapping, so drew rays around them, giving birth to the 'radiant baby', his most famous motif. Before long, Haring spotted an even more enticing opportunity in the subway stations, in the form of the matte black paper that was laid on top of unused billboards across the network. Using chalk, which suited his linear style, Haring began to fill the black paper with his distinctive images, which were highly recognizable and soon became well-known. People stopped to watch him work and the drawing became performative; he enjoyed the interactions with people, and after around a month, he started to make badges featuring his glowing babies to hand out in an effort to deepen by-passers' engagement with his art. He was delighted to see that people wearing the badges soon began to interact with each other as well as his work. Haring made hundreds of these transient, public drawings between 1980 and 1985, becoming more fluent with every line. At one point, he was arrested but because the chalk could be brushed away, the police were unsure how to proceed and so took no action. In general, at least at first, people respected the drawings and left them alone, although as his fame grew, they were increasingly stolen and sold. The subway drawings had made both Haring and his art well known, and he had found a way to share his work with everyone, not just those who went to galleries.

Haring left the School of Visual Arts before completing his course, feeling he had got all he could from it and that his time was better spent making art on the streets. He was by this time part of a thriving artistic community based in the East Village, where artists, musicians, writers and performers of all kinds from diverse backgrounds shared ideas, partied together and took control of their creativity and output. Haring had also found a sense of freedom in his personal life and in 1981, aged 23, met his first serious partner, Juan Dubose. By 1980, he had begun to show in exhibitions and his work had started to attract attention. In addition to his street art, he was also making drawings on paper to sell, as well as prints, paintings and sculptures. As his fame grew, demand increased for his work and despite his aversion to the art world, he agreed to be represented in 1982 by the dealer Tony Shafrazi who had a gallery in SoHo where Haring had previously worked as an assistant, one of numerous jobs he had taken to make a living on first arriving in the city. Shafrazi gave Haring a solo exhibition in 1982 and transformed the gallery into a club-like space to echo the East Village scene. The exhibition attracted attention and opened up further opportunities. As Haring's star rose, he was given exhibitions in the US and around the world and increasingly rubbed shoulders with New York's alternative cultural elite. In 1983, he met Andy Warhol, whose work was a great inspiration to him, particularly the way in which he blurred the lines between art and life and challenged the distinction between high-brow and popular culture. The two artists became close and traded artworks. Around the same time, Haring also met the singer Madonna, whose star was also rising. Both she and Haring attracted fans from lower-income and non-white backgrounds, and both experienced snobbery from more traditional cultural gatekeepers. One criticism of Haring's art was that it was too commercial, but Haring leaned into the commercial aspects of his work, refusing to accept that his art should be rarefied and ring-fenced for an elite and 'art-literate' market. To this end, in 1986 he opened the Pop Shop, a store in SoHo selling all sorts of affordable products featuring his images, including posters, badges, T-shirts, watches and toys. Although the store attracted criticism, Haring was supported by his growing number of fans and friends, including Warhol. In his mind, the shop counterbalanced the high prices that some of his works were selling for and brought his art back to a wider audience.

Throughout his career, Haring was motivated by political causes about which he felt strongly, and a community-minded spirit that made him open to making public art and working in collaboration. Between 1982 and 1989, he created more than 50 public works of art around the world, including many for charities, hospitals and children's homes. Haring loved children and enjoyed collaborating with budding young artists. In 1986, he worked with 1,000 children on a ten-storey-high banner to mark the 100th anniversary of the Statue of Liberty. The project was a collaboration with a charity called CityKids, which aimed to give New York children an alternative to high school and help them to feel empowered in the running of their lives. Haring created the banner's black outlines and the children drew or wrote in the spaces between. The making of the banner was a fun and celebratory affair, involving guest performances from the band New Kids on the Block and the jazz musician Herbie Hancock. When it was completed, it was transported to a building under construction in Battery Park City and it was unveiled on the Fourth of July. In 1989, Haring led a similar project in Chicago in which he worked with around 500 school children to produce a 146-metre (480-foot) mural. Painted in the city's Grant Park, the mural was then broken up to create 122 individual panels that were distributed to schools across the city. The Mayor of Chicago, Richard M. Daley, declared 15–19 May that year 'Keith Haring Week'. Haring also painted on the west side of the Berlin Wall, three years before it fell, and held drawing workshops for children in cities across the world. He also made work that was more overtly political. In 1986, he painted his famous *Crack is Wack* mural on New York's FDR Drive, as an anti-drug message. He felt that crack, unlike the drugs he had experimented with, was designed to make businessmen a lot of money and caused great damage to those who used it.

He also made posters and prints advocating safe sex, supporting the anti-apartheid movement in South Africa and in support of the anti-nuclear movement. He had discovered printmaking as a young man at the Pittsburgh Arts and Crafts Center, where he was able to learn various techniques, and had continued to make prints throughout his career. Editioned works were another way of making his art available to a wider audience, and by using techniques such as screenprint or offset lithography, he was able to create many copies of a single image. He contributed numerous prints and posters as fundraisers to benefit various causes.

In 1988, Keith Haring was diagnosed with AIDS. He had known he was vulnerable to the disease, which had already had a devastating impact in New York, especially among gay men and the art community in the East Village. Despite the stigma with which the disease was regarded, Haring spoke publicly about his illness in an interview he gave to David Sheff for *Rolling Stone* magazine in 1989. In that year, he established the Keith Haring Foundation with the intention of continuing to make his art accessible and to support AIDS organizations and children's charities. Since AIDS had begun to significantly affect his community in the mid-1980s, Haring had been an active supporter of ACT-UP, a campaigning organization that protested against the US government's slow response to the epidemic and lobbied for affordable treatment. He made several artworks to raise awareness of the disease, including his 'safe sex' image featuring two of his cartoonish figures masturbating each other, which he produced as a painting in 1988 and in other formats, including stickers. In 1989, he made a colour screenprint that carried the message

'Ignorance = Fear / Silence = Death', echoing a slogan used by ACT-UP. In the same year, he produced a poster to advertise the New York Department of Health's AIDS hotline, which was put up in bus shelters across the city. Haring's own health worsened rapidly and he developed Kaposi's sarcoma, an AIDS-related skin cancer. He died aged 31 on 16 February 1990. On his deathbed, barely able to move, he asked for a pad and a pen. After several attempts he managed to draw what he was struggling to get down on the paper: his radiant baby, a simple yet profound image that continues to resonate with many.

28

The Guerrilla Girls: Collective and Covert

The Guerrilla Girls are unique in this selection of artists, both for being a collective and for being anonymous. Active since 1984 and owing a debt to the same street art scene that inspired Keith Haring, the group was founded with a specific purpose in mind: to highlight and rectify the lack of representation of women artists in museums and galleries through art. Its purpose has since broadened out, and four decades later the group continues to work collectively and creatively to highlight injustices and inequalities of many different kinds both in America and elsewhere.

On 17 May 1984, the Museum of Modern Art (MoMA) in New York opened an exhibition titled *An International Survey of Recent Painting and Sculpture*, with the aim of providing a thorough and authoritative picture of new trends and important names in contemporary art. The exhibition featured work made over the previous decade by 169 artists from 17 countries, including Australia, Brazil, India, the United States, France and Britain, and included art by some whose names are now well known, such as Gerhard Richter, Frank Auerbach and Jean-Michel Basquiat. The press release issued by the museum promised that the exhibition would emphasize 'the full range of recent artistic achievement' but despite this stated intention, only 13 of the artists in the exhibition were women, representing less than eight per cent of the total number, and none were women of colour.[107] Over the previous decade, the representation of women artists in museums and galleries in the United States had begun to increase, as had the representation of non-white artists. Driven by the civil rights movement and second-wave feminism in the 1960s and '70s, the dominance of white male artists in exhibitions and across the art market had increasingly been questioned by academics such as Linda Nochlin, whose landmark essay 'Why Have There Been No Great Women Artists?' was published in 1971. In the United States, galleries dedicated to showing the work of women artists were beginning to spring up, such as A.I.R. in New York (founded in 1972), and experimental women artists such as Mary Beth Edelson (1933–2021), Carolee Schneeman (1939–2019) and Judy Chicago (born 1939) were making a significant impact with work that high-lighted the art world's biases. By 1985, however, progress seemed to be unravelling. America was experiencing an economic boom, New York in particular, and art collectors were increasingly seeking to purchase work that was a financial investment. At the same time, there was a wide-spread backlash against the feminism movement, which had become increasingly fractured and had experienced a decline in organized activity. The MoMA exhibition seemed to highlight this backward trend and, for some, was too much to bear. As the exhibition opened, a group of women staged a protest outside the museum, their rage having been exacerbated by a comment made by the exhibition's curator, Kynaston McShine, that any artist who had not been included 'should rethink his career'.[108] Some of the women began to work in collaboration, collecting data on representation in the art world and finding creative ways to communicate their findings. Working anonymously, they called themselves the Guerrilla Girls in reference to their guerrilla tactics and their combative mission.

The Guerrilla Girls is an evolving group of women artists, activists, curators and critics. Over the years, their identities and numbers have, for the most part, remained undisclosed and their members have come and gone, but their aims have remained fundamentally the same: to highlight inequality in the art world and beyond. Their work has always involved both direct action in the form of physical protests and the production of images, particularly posters and stickers, as a means to gain attention and spread their messages. Following the protests outside MoMA in 1985, the group mounted a covert poster campaign across New York, particularly targeting lower Manhattan around SoHo and the East Village, where artists lived and dealers traded. Early posters targeted commercial galleries that had a poor record of showing work by women artists and the (male) artists who allowed their work to be exhibited by them. They highlighted the lack of solo exhibitions of women artists at New York museums, the lack of interest shown by art critics in the work of women and the tiny number of commercial galleries representing Black women. Initially, the posters were monochrome and text-based, presenting data that the group had gathered from the arts media and through visiting museums and galleries. Using offset lithography, a commercial printing technique that allowed them to mass produce their images, the women printed, distributed and funded (or fundraised for) the works themselves, which helped in maintaining anonymity and allowed them to work outside the art world networks that they were critiquing. Gradually, more pictorial imagery and colour made its way into their work, and they increasingly used humour, which was usually ironic in tone. As the group has said, they learned early on that 'if you can make someone who disagreed with you laugh, then you have a hook in their brain.'[109] In 1986, for example, they produced a poster titled *Dearest Art Collector, It Has Come to Our Attention…* which is presented in the style of a handwritten letter in a knowingly 'feminine' looping cursive on pink paper, with a doodle of a frowning flower at the top. Written in a submissive and apologetic tone, the text scolds art collectors through a superficially polite request for those whose collections do not contain enough art by women (most, according to their research) to 'rectify the situation immediately'.

The guerrilla tactics of the group have included pasting their posters up at night on any available surface, including walls, the fences around construction sites and kiosks, leaving stickers in museum toilets and bookshops, and the 'counts' that they have carried out incognito in museums and galleries. The group's members have always chosen to remain anonymous, in part to protect their individual careers, as many have continued to practise as independent artists and some were already well-known. They also decided that maintaining anonymity ensured the focus remained on the message of their work. From 1986, by which time they were increasingly appearing in public on panels or to give interviews, their members have each adopted the name of a famous woman artist, writer or activist as a pseudonym. The group has included 'Frida Kahlo', for instance, as well as 'Käthe Kollwitz', 'Lee Krasner', 'Zora Neale Hurston' and 'Harriet Tubman'. The idea came to them when they were about to give an interview on the day that American artist Georgia O'Keeffe died (6 March 1986), 'as though Georgia was speaking to us from the grave'.[110] From the beginning, they have worn gorilla masks in public to hide their faces, a punning nod to their name and a means of attracting attention. The Guerrilla Girls have always utilized the language of the mass media and advertising in their work, creating posters with headline-like titles, using soundbites and slogans, and creating a recognizable visual language. From the beginning, they have been deliberately provocative and have embraced the criticism that they have received, viewing it as a sign that their tactics have been successful. Reflecting on their early years in 1995, the member known as Anaïs Nin recalled: 'We were immediately *the* topic at dinner parties, openings, even on the street. Who were these women? How do they dare say that? … Women artists loved us, almost everyone else hated us, and none of them could stop talking about us.'[111]

Throughout the 1980s, the work of the Guerrilla Girls focused on the art world and it was during this period that they produced some of their most well-known posters. Their 1988 poster *The Advantages of Being a Woman Artist* was particularly impactful and has since been produced in various formats and translated into numerous languages. Among the 13 'advantages' listed are 'Not having to be in shows with men', 'Having an escape from the art world in your 4 free-lance jobs' and 'Not having to undergo the embarrassment of being called a genius'.

The following year, they produced *Do Women Have to be Naked to get into the Met. Museum?*, a colour poster highlighting their statistic that 'Less than 5% of the artists in the Modern Art Sections [of New York's Metropolitan Museum] are women, but 85% of the nudes are female'. The text is accompanied by an image of a reclining female nude based on Jean-Auguste-Dominique Ingres' painting *La Grande Odalisque* (1814), with a gorilla mask superimposed on the woman's head. An exhibition of Ingres' work was held at the Metropolitan Museum from December 1988 to March 1989, at the time this poster was created. The statistic comes from a count of female nudes and women artists that members of the group undertook at the Met one Sunday morning, which one referred to as a 'weenie count'. The image was initially made in response to a commission by the Public Art Fund in New York for a billboard for the city, but the proposal was rejected on the basis that the message was not clear enough. Instead, the group ran it as an advertisement on the city's buses. The design has since been repurposed, adapted, updated and translated many times. During their early years, the group routinely signed their work 'conscience of the art world', which they printed at the bottom of their posters. By gaining attention with their images, actions and appearances, they hoped not only to make a change themselves but appeal to those in positions of power. To this end, they produced another poster in 1989 titled *Guerrilla Girls' Code of Ethics For Art Museums*, in which they set out on a tablet-like background a series of 'commandments' for museums that included 'Thou shalt not be a Museum Trustee and also the Chief Stockholder of a Major Auction House' and 'Thou shalt not give more than 3 retrospectives to any Artist whose Dealer is the brother of the Chief Curator'.

In addition to their posters, the Guerrilla Girls have organized various forms of action. In October 1985, they curated an exhibition of work by 85 women artists at the Palladium, a downtown dance club. In 1987, they produced the *Guerrilla Girls Review the Whitney*, a display timed to coincide with the Whitney Museum of American Art's Biennial exhibition. Held at a non-profit gallery, the display highlighted a decline in the representation of women and people of colour in the Whitney Biennial since 1973 and the low numbers of women artists across the Whitney's programme in general. It received a significant amount of press attention at a time when the group were frequently featured in newspapers and magazines for their eye-catching posters and appearances. When appearing in public, they often wore short skirts, fishnet tights and high heels as accompaniments to their gorilla heads, to maximize their impact. They have also spoken at schools and museums, led letter-writing campaigns and distributed faux awards such as the 'Most Patronizing Art Review', which they gave in 1986 to the *New York Times* critic John Russell for his review of a Dorothy Dehner exhibition in which he referred to the artist as 'Mrs David Smith', the name of the male artist from whom she was divorced. Although perhaps the best-known art collective of their kind, the group took inspiration from various other artists. Their poster campaigns, for example, were part of a wider street art movement in New York in the 1980s that included the work of Keith Haring, Jean-Michel Basquiat and Jenny Holzer (born 1950). In 1977, Holzer began to create posters featuring witty one-liners that she called 'Truisms', such as 'A little knowledge can go a long way' and 'Abuse of power comes as no surprise', which she printed as posters and put up around New York. The Guerrilla Girls were influenced by Holzer's approach but also by the tactics of other collectives, particularly the Art Workers' Coalition, which formed in 1969 and whose aims included lobbying for the inclusion of underrepresented groups in museums, and Women Artists in Revolution, a feminist collective formed the following year. The latter undertook letter-writing campaigns to protest against sexism in museums and several of its members founded exhibition spaces and workshops for women.

Since the 1980s, the Guerrilla Girls have expanded the range of issues that they have protested against. They have made work, for example, that addresses racism more widely, abortion rights, homelessness, censorship and war. More recently, they have protested against figures in the art world who have been exposed as sexual predators as part of the worldwide #MeToo movement. Since 1985, they have appeared at events and been given exhibitions around the world. Many of their posters have been published as limited-edition screenprints and are in numerous museum collections. In 2005, there was an exhibition of their posters at the 51st Venice Biennale, the first time the prestigious art festival was curated by women (María de Corral and Rosa Martínez). Today, the heavy bias of most museum collections in favour of white men is generally acknowledged, and widespread efforts have been made to redress the balance and increase inclusivity. Some museums have gone so far as to sell work by male artists who are already well-represented, in order to raise funds to buy work by women or people of colour. In 2019, for example, the San Francisco Museum of Modern Art sold a painting by Mark Rothko for $50 million for this purpose and the year before, the Baltimore Museum of Art took similar action. The art of the Guerrilla Girls has undoubtedly contributed to this change in culture. As 'Georgia O'Keeffe' put it in 1995: 'We're not going to forget Rembrandt and Michelangelo. We just want to move them over to make room for the rest of us!'[112]

29

Rachel Whiteread: The Spaces In-Between

When I think about the art that made an impression on me as a young person, I mainly think of historical figures whose work I saw in civic museums in the north of England (an abundance of Pre-Raphaelites!), art I saw in churches on family holidays to France or Italy, or early twentieth-century giants like Picasso whose work was frequently referenced on TV and in books. Until I was in my twenties, I rarely saw brand-new, contemporary art, just as I rarely read contemporary novels, somehow not realizing that I could skip ahead without having consumed all of Dickens or Jane Austen. But as a teenager in the 1990s, a decade in which British art became cool, I was aware that something exciting was happening in London. Hip young artists were profiled in music magazines and snapped by the paparazzi, and works of art began to make the headlines. From this distance, I somehow learned about *House*, the conceptual, sculptural work by Rachel Whiteread that caused a stir in 1993. I never saw the work in the flesh – it existed for less than three months – but it made a significant impression on me nonetheless, and black-and-white images of the ghostly concrete structure, at once solid and fleeting, have haunted me ever since.

House was a concrete cast of the interior of an entire terraced house in the East End of London, which was exhibited in the location where the house once stood. The project, which Whiteread made with the support of the art commissioning organization Artangel, took two years to realize and required Whiteread to work with a team of engineers. It involved spraying the inside of the house with liquid concrete and then carefully removing the exterior walls. The resulting structure not only preserved the shape of the house, but also that of its architectural features, including the door, window frames, skirting boards and fireplaces. In some areas, colour transferred from the wallpaper on to the concrete, giving the predominantly Brutalist grey a somewhat organic feel and the sense of something aged and decaying. The house itself had been condemned. It was one of many Victorian terraces that had been built in the nineteenth century for working-class families. The area had sustained damage during the Second World War and the remaining terraces had fallen into disrepair. Gradually, as the city's population continued to grow, rows of terraces were replaced by high-rise tower blocks. Number 193 Grove Road in Bow was the final house left in its row. Its final residents, who were still living there when Whiteread began to plan the project, had held out for years against the council's attempts to move them to a block, only agreeing to leave when an alternative house was found. At the time, Britain was emerging from a recession and questions about housing and the cost of living were at the forefront of public and political discourse. For some, the demolition of these houses signified a lost way of life and the fracturing of a community. Whiteread had been born in London in 1963, in Ilford on the north-eastern outskirts of the city, and was familiar with both houses of this type and the many changes that redevelopment was bringing to the area. As such, the project was political, but also autobiographical. The structure not only preserved the space that 193 Grove Road had once enclosed, in which generations of Londoners had once lived, but it also provided a monument to a disappearing world, a world of which the artist was herself a part.

Between 25 October 1993 and 11 January 1994, *House* attracted thousands of visitors and widespread press attention. It became the focal point of public conversations about housing, urban development, class and contemporary art. Two decades earlier, in 1972, London's Tate Gallery had purchased a sculptural work titled *Equivalent VIII* by the American minimalist artist Carl Andre (1935–2024), which comprised 120 fire bricks arranged on the floor in a rectangular block. A public furore blew up a few years later when a journalist wrote an incendiary story about the acquisition for the tabloid newspaper the *Daily Mirror*, describing Andre's work as 'a load of rubbish'. The ensuing debate around the definition of art and how public money should be spent had continued to smoulder in the years since, occasionally reigniting when a controversial art world story hit the headlines. In 1993, *House* was the catalyst. In addition to extensive media coverage, which spilled into the letter pages, the walls around the work were fly-posted with various messages and the structure itself was famously graffitied with the words 'Wot for?' by one person and 'Why not!' by another. In November of that year, Whiteread became the first woman to be awarded the prestigious Turner Prize, Britain's annual prize for contemporary art established in 1984. But on the very day the jury decided that Whiteread should win for *House*, councillors in East London made the decision to demolish the work. Whiteread had always expected the sculpture to be temporary, but since its unveiling there had been growing calls for it to remain in place as a permanent piece of public art. Following the decision, a motion was brought to the House of Commons by a group of Labour MPs who hoped to delay the destruction to allow for public consultation. In the words of the art magazine *Frieze*, Whiteread had become 'the most famous artist in Britain', much to her bemusement, and her silent memorial to the quiet, private lives of ordinary people had become the most talked about work of art in the country.[113] *House* was demolished in January 1994. 'A part of me would like it to remain for the time it takes to become invisible,' Whiteread said before it was gone. 'I'd like it to remain until the crowds stop flocking, and it's just there.'[114]

Rachel Whiteread began to experiment with casting objects when she was a student at the Slade School of Fine Art in London from 1985 to 1987. She had grown up in a politically engaged family, the daughter of Thomas Whiteread, a teacher, and Patricia Whiteread (née Lancaster), an artist, in a home similar to the house that she cast in 1993. Initially, she was drawn to painting, which she studied at Brighton Polytechnic from 1982, but she soon found working in two dimensions on canvas to be constraining and shifted her focus to sculpture. At the Slade, she was taught by Phyllida Barlow, whose large-scale works and use of found objects inspired her, and took classes given by Richard Wilson, with whom she started to explore casting. Her earliest cast sculptures include *Shallow Breath* (1988), the underside of a single bed cast in plaster and exhibited propped up against a wall, and *Closet* (1988), the interior of a clothes cupboard cast in plaster and covered in black felt.

From the beginning, Whiteread was interested in creating negative casts of objects and in capturing the space within or around an object rather than simply replicating the object itself. These early works were fundamentally auto-biographical – *Closet*, for example, related to Whiteread's memories of hiding in wardrobes as a child – but also had a wider resonance, exploring themes of memory, absence, domesticity and loss. *Shallow Breath* and *Closet* were both included in Whiteread's first solo exhibition, at the Carlisle Gallery, London, in 1988, along with *Torso*, the first of a series of casts of the space inside a hot-water bottle. As the name suggests, *Torso* resembles a headless, limbless body, while at the same time bringing to mind the experience of holding a comforting hot-water bottle against one's own body. Puckers, dips and curves captured in the castings conjure the sensation of a malleable little vessel adapting to a human shape. Other quotidian objects and surfaces that Whiteread has cast include doorknobs, sinks, bathtubs and floorboards. At first glance, Whiteread's sculptures can appear stark and austere, but on closer looking, little scars and scuffs become visible, reminding us that the objects she chooses to cast have been used by humans and carry the imprints of life.

Whiteread made her first large-scale sculpture in 1990, aged just 27. The work, titled *Ghost*, is a plaster cast of a living room in a Victorian house on the Archway Road in north London, which was due to be torn down. Whiteread had wanted to find a room that had basic recognizable features including a window, door, fireplace, cornice, skirting board and light switches. Again, she cast the room from the inside, filling the negative space and turning the room inside out. Using plaster, Whiteread cast the room in sections, which were later assembled on a metal frame. When it was displayed at the Chisenhale Gallery, viewers had to walk around it to take it all in, which added a participatory element to the work. It was an ambitious sculpture that gained Whiteread critical attention. The early 1990s were an exciting time for British art. Whiteread was one of a loose group of creatively ambitious and experimental artists who began to exhibit in the late 1980s and became known as the YBAs, or Young British Artists. Her contemporaries included Sarah Lucas, Tracey Emin, Damien Hirst and Chris Ofili. *Ghost* was purchased by Charles Saatchi, a champion and collector of the YBAs, and was included in *Sensation*, an influential exhibition of his collection at the Royal Academy of Arts in 1997. In 2000, it was lent by Saatchi to the Tate galleries for the opening of Tate Modern and in 2004, it was given to the National Gallery of Art in Washington, DC, where it remains. The *Sensation* exhibition also included Whiteread's work *Untitled (100 Spaces)*, an installation work from 1995 comprising resin casts in a range of colours of the spaces beneath 100 chairs, arranged in 10 parallel rows, filling the space of a large room. Whiteread has continued to work on a monumental scale throughout her career. In 1998, in response to a commission from New York City's Public Art Fund, she produced *Water Tower*, a translucent resin cast of a water tower, initially installed on a rooftop in SoHo in lower Manhattan. On grey days, the ice-like resin became almost invisible, but when the sun shone, it twinkled and sparkled against the sky. In 2001, Whiteread became the third artist to make work for the Fourth Plinth, a project to bring contemporary art to an empty plinth in London's Trafalgar Square. For her contribution she created *Monument*, a translucent resin cast of the plinth itself, placed upside down as a mirror image.

Whiteread's art always takes time to fully see and understand. Her large-scale sculptures, such as *Ghost*, reveal themselves gradually, while her smaller works take slow and close looking before all their details become visible. Her work encourages reflection, and a certain amount of projection, as personal thoughts, associations and memories are jogged. It was no doubt these qualities, and her recurring theme of memorial, that led to her commission in the 1990s to create a monument in Vienna to the 65,000 Austrian Jews who were murdered during the Holocaust. Made for the Judenplatz town square, the historic centre of Jewish life in the city, and unveiled in October 2000, the monument is a cast interior of a library, lined with the impression of book pages side out and punctuated with two large, permanently closed doors. Cast in concrete, the monumental block resembles a bunker, an intentional allusion, and is surrounded by engravings on the ground naming concentration camps at which Austrian Jews were killed. The project took five years to complete and involved a significant amount of research. Whiteread has since said that she never would have made the proposal had she not lived in Berlin for 18 months in 1992–3, where she 'could feel the traces of trauma' and gained a greater understanding of the Holocaust, its aftermath and how it was being remembered and processed in Germany.[115] The Judenplatz Holocaust Memorial is a permanent work of public art where viewers can take time to view, think and remember. The experience of designing and making it, however, was daunting and exhausting. In 1997, Whiteread represented Britain at the Venice Biennale, where she presented a work titled *Untitled (Ten Tables)* (1996), a plaster cast of the spaces beneath ten boardroom tables inspired by the meetings she had attended in Vienna in the initial stages of the project (now in the Yale Center for British Art). More recently, in response to the noise generated around her high-profile and politically charged works, she has produced a series of *Shy Sculptures*, quiet structures that are often hidden away in remote or unexpected locations such as *The Gran Boathouse* (2010), a boathouse cast in concrete on the edge of a fjord in Norway, and *Nissen Hut* (2018) in Dalby Forest, Yorkshire.

In addition to her sculptural work, Whiteread has also made works on paper throughout her career, often producing drawings to think through an idea. During her time in Berlin, for example, when she was undertaking a DAAD residency (German Academic Exchange Service), she was very interested in floors and made many drawings of the parquet floor in the apartment that she had been provided with. The residency resulted in an exhibition of her drawings. In 1996 she made her first portfolio of prints, a series of screenprints titled *Demolished*, depicting photographs she had taken of buildings being demolished in the borough of Hackney, East London. It remains her sculptural work, however, for which she is best known. More recently, her sculptures have moved beyond casting. In 2020–21 she produced *Poltergeist* and *Doppelgänger*, two life-sized sculptures of half-destroyed sheds that appear to have been blown up or possibly pounded by hurricane-strength winds. Painted entirely in a ghostly white, the sculptures are made from corrugated iron and wooden slats. They are messier, more chaotic than her earlier work, inspired by the climate crisis and the extreme and unpredictable weather we are seeing as a result. In the past Whiteread has striven to capture the invisible or what is no longer there: the spaces that we cannot see, the buildings that are no more and the signs of life that might otherwise be forgotten. With these new works, however, she is pointing to something terrifyingly present, albeit through the prism of what might also soon be lost.

30

Wangechi Mutu: Beauty, Bodies and Optimistic Futures

When Wangechi Mutu moved to New York to study fine art and anthropology in the mid-1990s, she began to realize that the notion of 'beauty' in art, and in life, was highly subjective. In contemporary American art 'beauty' had become unfashionable, no longer a quality to aim for or to be admired and in class discussions at the Cooper Union, a private art college in Manhattan that she attended from 1996, the word was taboo. As a Black woman from Nairobi in Kenya, Mutu found this to be problematic. She began to understand that notions of beauty are constructed and controlled by those in power. For those who do not hold this power and whose bodies and lives do not fit the prevailing models, the idea of beauty cannot so easily be rejected. In Western art, the ideal female body has traditionally been presented as white. Black women have been portrayed as exotic, primitive, or excluded altogether. Much of Mutu's work is about the body. About women's bodies, and Black women's bodies in particular. But it is also about the way in which power structures, be they determined by race, gender, class, nationality or other cultural factors, dictate the way information is presented in society, how it is organized and prioritized, and what stories are told. While studying at the Cooper Union, Mutu became fascinated with archaeological and anthropological objects, and how they were used in museums to represent entire histories and cultures. She was particularly interested in how African cultures were reduced in this way, and began to make pseudo-anthropological objects from found materials such as old umbrellas and feathers, as well as wearable 'tribal' jewellery, which she photographed in a style and setting that mimicked traditional ethnographic records. This approach to art, of taking existing objects and materials and disassembling them, rearranging them and splicing them together with other materials to create hybrid forms, has been central to her work ever since. She presents viewers with something that seems familiar, but which turns out to be something quite different. Rather than reject beauty, she has used it to draw viewers in, creating art that can seem appealing and seductive, but on closer looking can shock and repel, raising questions about what we are conditioned to expect.

Over the course of her career, Mutu has worked in a variety of media including sculpture, painting, video and performance art, but she made her name with the collaged works that she began to produce after completing her postgraduate degree in sculpture at Yale University. She began her first major collage series – *Pin-ups* – in 2001. Created using photographic imagery cut from fashion and pornography magazines, which she combined with drawn elements in watercolour, ink and gouache, the series depicts women in sexually suggestive poses, their bodies formed from mismatched elements that jar and confuse. In some ways the figures conform to mainstream beauty standards, with their slim but curvaceous bodies, long hair, lipstick and high heels, but other elements of the images are bizarre and grotesque: claw-like hands, eyes and lips too big for their faces and mottled skin suggestive of disease. Mutu has referred to the figures as 'distorted glamour Frankensteins'.[116] Some of the women are missing limbs, a reference to the civil war in Sierra Leone (1991–2002), in which many people suffered mutilations, and the dangers involved in the illegal mining trade in various African countries. The works explore the objectification and sexualization of women in American visual culture, questioning what it means to be beautiful or desirable, and how we react to bodies that are damaged or different.

By the time she began to make the *Pin-ups* series, Mutu had lived in the USA for half a decade. She had begun to view herself less as a Kenyan woman living in America and more as a fusion between the two cultures. The hybrid forms that she was creating in collage were in some ways an expression of her own feeling of being culturally composite. Born in Nairobi in 1972, less than a decade after Kenya gained independence from British colonial rule, Mutu had attended an international secondary school in Wales, travelling around Europe in the holidays, and now found herself making a life in New York. She felt disconnected to the country in which she had grown up, but in many ways she felt like an outsider in America. Black women were largely absent from the fashion magazines that she mined for materials, for example, and they were still hugely underrepresented in the contemporary art world. Her process of dismantling and reconfiguring visual materials to make collages became for her a method of 'taking apart the images of a world that refused to acknowledge me.'[117] Through collage, Mutu was able not only to explore her own identity and her experiences in America, but to address wider themes about the representation of women, the fashion world, art history, pornography and politics. 'You can tell what American mainstream culture is thinking by looking at a newsstand,' she has argued, suggesting that a country's mass media imagery is essentially its waste: 'If you want to know where the animal has been and whether it's healthy, you sift through its stool.'[118]

Mutu developed an interest in collage and found materials before arriving in the United States. As a child, she drew constantly. For a time, her businessman father ran a paper import company, so paper was in ready supply. When she did run out, however, she continued her drawings on the walls. Mutu's mother was a medical practitioner, who first worked as a nurse then later as a pharmacist. Her medical books with drawn diagrams of bodies and surgical instruments fascinated Mutu. During her childhood, Mutu also had an opportunity to view modern and contemporary art on visits to Europe, including a trip to Spain in 1990. Artists who were to prove an influence include the Swiss sculptor Alberto Giacometti (1901–66), Picasso and Frida Kahlo. Mutu's interest in collage was initially sparked by Picasso, who pioneered the art form during his Cubist period. She was also drawn to the way Picasso presented a subject from multiple viewpoints simultaneously, and she began to experiment with perspective herself by making Picasso-like still-life collages using imagery cut out of *Time* magazine and *Newsweek*. Others who used collage to whom Mutu owes a debt include the German artist Hannah Höch (1889–1978), who explored gender and identity through her collages and photomontages, and the American artist Romare Bearden (1911–88), who used photo-collage to explore the experiences of Black people in Harlem, New York. Despite going on to specialize in sculpture, Mutu made collages for her applications to undergraduate courses and continued to make collages and drawings throughout her time as a student. Drawing helped her to capture her thoughts and to shape them into fully formed ideas, while collage offered her the opportunity to re-present and repurpose existing imagery, juxtaposing it and recontextualizing it with the aim of offering a different viewpoint.

Pin-ups was followed with more collage series, including *Histology of the Different Classes of Uterine Tumors* (2005, National Galleries of Scotland). For the latter, she created collaged images on real pages from a nineteenth-century medical book by J. A. Jeancon, called *Diseases of the Sexual Organs*, which featured carefully drawn anatomical illustrations. Using cut-out imagery, including some from ethnographic publications such as *National Geographic*, as well as other found materials such as packing tape and fur, combined with glitter and ink, she collaged distorted and monstrous female heads on top of these pages. The medical illustrations interact and integrate with the collages, both becoming part of the image and peering out from behind. Vulvas become facial features, a uterus becomes a neck and a surgical instrument is embedded in a skull. As the rational, ordered bodies of the illustrations are disrupted, messy, disordered bodies are formed. With titles like *Ectopic Pregnancy* and *Cancer Of The Uterus*, the series explores the various ways in which women's bodies have been classified by the medical profession, anthropologists and others, as well as the bodily experiences that women are sometimes forced to endure.

Mutu's early interests in science and taxonomy are evident in her approach to her work, while her Catholic upbringing also provides a lens through which she has explored the contemporary world. References to Christianity appear frequently, particularly references to Eve, the biblical first woman who let sin into the world by accepting a forbidden apple from the devil as a snake. As a child, Mutu learned Christian stories at Catholic school, including tales of saints and martyrs and the terrible things that happened to their bodies. As an adult, she became interested in the ways that Christianity had been imposed upon African cultures, and the means by which communities had sought to mask and preserve their traditional beliefs and practices by blending them with their colonizers' religion. This spiritual fusion is also present in Mutu's art, which contains references to different religions and beliefs, and uses Christian motifs to comment on secular themes. In 2003, for example, Mutu used the figure of Eve to pay homage to Funmilayo Anikulapo-Kuti (1900–78), the Nigerian feminist and political leader. In the mixed-media diptych *Yo Mama* (Museum of Modern Art, New York), which appears to be set in a pink outer space, Eve is reimagined as a leotard-wearing woman of colour who has defeated the serpent and is presiding over its headless, phallic body. Eve stands on the snake's neck, which she spears with the heel of her stiletto, turning a restrictive and uncomfortable item of clothing into a powerful weapon. By subverting the story of Eve, Mutu celebrates Anikulapo-Kuti's battles against practices that harm and disadvantage women, including female genital mutilation and other forms of discrimination and patriarchal control.

In 2012, Mutu explored a Kenyan creation myth that she has called 'our Adam and Eve' in a suite of etchings titled *The Original Nine Daughters*. The images reference the legend behind the founding of the Kikuyu tribe, the largest ethnic group in Kenya, from which Mutu herself is descended. According to tradition, the founder of the tribe, Gikuyu, fathered nine daughters, each of whom went on to found one of the tribe's clans. The figures in Mutu's etchings are hybrid, fantastical women with wings, claws and hooves. A number are pierced repeatedly by pins, echoing Christian images of Saint Sebastian, who was martyred by arrows or Voodoo dolls, which are thought to have originated in Africa. In one image, the figure is a headless, limbless body on a plinth and in another, an image of a hirsute woman with curled, withered feet strapped to stilts has been annotated with measurements and labels in the form of a scientific diagram. In recent years, Mutu has explored the East African myth of the Nguva, a kind of female water spirit that is related to real-life marine mammals including the manatee and the much-endangered dugong. The Nguva also has counterparts in other cultural traditions, including the mermaid and the siren. Cross-cultural connections such as this are important to Mutu. For her, art can illuminate the way that humans are similar and also the ways in which different cultures have become estranged: 'I discover by creating art how this entire human family born out of the mother-continent is related and belongs to one another and due to our wandering, nomadic, migratory habits we've moved further apart, forgetting each other and our common predecessors and believing myths about how much dissimilar we are.'[119]

In around 2016, after making her name in America, Mutu returned with her family to Kenya and now divides her time between Nairobi and New York. In addition to her collages, she has made video works, room-sized installations and performance pieces. For her 2016 performance work *Throw*, she repeatedly reached into a bag and threw handfuls of a black viscous material at a white wall while wearing a long black dress and gloves. The material was made from magazine pulp, the waste of society, which she had stewed, fermented and soaked with tea leaves and food dye. Mutu also used this stewed pulp for her sculpture *She's got the whole world in her* (2015, Museum of Fine Arts, Houston), a depiction of a woman half caged, contemplating a suspended globe that hangs before her. The sculpture formed part of an installation at the Venice Biennale in 2015, which incorporated a video work, *The End of Carrying All*, in which a woman is seen moving across a landscape carrying an enormous basket filled with consumer goods, as the environment becomes increasingly barren around her. In the end, the weight of her burden proves too much and her collapse causes the end of the world.

In 2019, Mutu offered a more optimistic vision for the future of the planet through her sculptural series, *The NewOnes will free Us*. Made for a commission to fill four empty niches on the front of the Metropolitan Museum of Art, New York, the series comprises four bronze sculptures of seated women. Each wears a gold disc on her head or face and a heavy draped garment made from bronze coils or thick bronze threads. The discs echo traditional East African lip plates, while the coils were inspired in part by a type of mask worn by Mende women of Sierra Leone. The series references the caryatid, a sculptural form that appears in both Western and African art. Traditionally a female figure, the caryatid acts as a pillar, providing architectural support. Mutu's sculptures, however, do not play this role. Stately and powerful, each figure places her hands firmly on her knees rather than raising her arms to bear a burden. At the time they were installed, debates raged around the world about who should be commemorated in public spaces and whether statues of problematic figures should be removed, questions that in some ways Mutu has been considering for her whole career. Mutu's statues were installed between September 2019 and November 2020, as the world collectively grappled with a global pandemic. Raised on plinths along the neo-classical façade of one of the world's greatest temples of art and history, her figures looked ahead with a quiet but determined resilience. Today, they are part of the museum's collection, one of many collections in America and around the world in which her art is preserved and shown.

CONCLUSIONS

Having considered the 30 artists in this book, it is clear that there is a great diversity of thought among artists. There is also diversity of intention, motivation, approach and in ways of seeing the world. But as I suggested in the introduction, I believe that one quality that all artists have in common is an impulse to respond to and interact with the world in a creative way, with the intention, conscious or not, of communicating an idea. It is debatable whether or not this quality is innate. There are myriad examples of artists who began to make art at an early age, apparently instinctively and naturally. Picasso, Yayoi Kusama, Barbara Hepworth, Rosa Bonheur and Wangechi Mutu, for example, all seem to fall into this category. But of course, circumstances also lead people to art: a parent as an artist might lead some along this path, as in the case of Picasso, Bonheur and Hieronymus Bosch, or perhaps a local tradition or opportunity for employment. There is also the question of talent. While I believe that anyone can make art (I do not subscribe to the view that we divide into *creatives* and *non-creatives*), there is no doubt that some people have a greater capacity for making art that is compelling in some way, that has substance, that is beautiful or interesting or thought-provoking, and that makes viewers want to look or engage. And as art relies on ideas, I believe this talent is as much about how an artist thinks as what they can do with their hands.

In addition to the general impulse to make art, however, there are some common threads that can be pulled from the stories of these diverse artists. It perhaps goes without saying, but most artists work very hard. Creating art not only seems something that they are inclined to do, but something that they are *driven* to do, again and again. Plus, for the most part, it takes time to make a work of art; even rapidly produced creations are often the result of many hours of thought, experimentation or practice. Some works even take years. We are told that Apelles drew every day. The perfect lines that he executed on his visit to the studio of Protogenes were many years in the making. Once he set off on his artistic career, Matisse almost never stopped working. Yayoi Kusama worked through the night. Barbara Hepworth was forever thinking about sculpture. In a letter to his brother written in July 1882, Van Gogh described the need he had to keep working, whatever else was happening in his life: 'People like me aren't really *allowed* to be ill... One must work long and hard to arrive at the truthful... Art demands persistent work, work in spite of everything, and unceasing observation.'[120] The unceasing observation that Van Gogh describes is also an approach that I think is common to all artists. Artists look at the world around them. They observe nature, objects and people. They watch and they see what is going on. This might result in art that closely represents the physical world, or that depicts a sensation, an emotion or feeling, or offers a comment or different way of seeing. As Van Gogh suggests, this constant observation leads to art that feels true, no matter what form the work takes.

There is always an element of art that comes from the imagination. Even artists such as Apelles or Giotto or Rosa

Bonheur, who are celebrated for the lifelike depictions of people, animals and the physical world, allow elements of fantasy and fiction into their work. Art is created in the mind and, as such, is always filtered through the artist's inner world. In some cases, this imaginative element is clearly evident in the finished work: Bosch's weird and wild creations, for example, can only be from his mind, while Mutu's 'distorted glamour Frankensteins' represent a highly personal response to the external material that inspired them, and Keith Haring's singular visual language can only have come from his brain. But in some cases, this is more subtle. Hokusai and Van Gogh both added fictional elements, poetic touches, to their depictions of real places, while the empathy and affection that Bonheur felt for the animals that she depicted infuses her art with a warmth and sense of truth that can only have come from her mind. Artists make their best work, I believe, when they find a subject that truly excites them, inspires them or somehow stirs their imagi-nation. Throughout this book we have seen how different artists are motivated by different things: from people, light, landscape and politics to emotion, form, colour and the self. In some cases, of course, especially in past centuries, artists are given subjects to respond to or are forced to make work that will satisfy a particular patron or market. In these cases, however, the best artists find their own way of relating and responding to the subject. Leonardo's *Virgin of the Rocks* reflected his interest in the natural world, Gentileschi's images of female protagonists portray real experiences, real emotions and real female bodies, and are not just made to delight or to stimulate, and Hogarth found ways to make portraiture and conversation pieces more interesting to himself, as well as to his audiences.

I wrote in the introduction to this book that it is not intended as a timeline of art history, but there are clearly connections between some of the artists and an element of progression as we move through the years. Artists react to one another. They look back and from side to side. They borrow, they pay homage, they develop and they reject. Some artists collaborate, some work entirely alone, but all artists learn from what has come before them, and while the most impactful offer something new, the best artists recognize that their work is part of a chain of human ideas and interactions, an ongoing conversation about the world.

ACKNOWLEDGEMENTS

I am indebted to all the many curators, art historians and artists with whom I have worked over the years, and whose work I have read and seen. I am especially grateful to my colleagues in Prints and Drawings at the British Museum whose dedication, knowledge and indefatigable commitment to sharing their love of art is a daily inspiration. It has been a pleasure and a privilege to write for Bloomsbury and work with their superb team. My thanks in particular go to Octavia Stocker, Tomasz Hoskins and Sarah Jones. For their moral support, I would like to thank Sally and Nick Daunt, the Daunt-Smyths, the Currans, Olenka Horbatsch, Marie Vandenbeusch and my long-term exhibition-going buddy Holly Jennison. In addition, the members of the Super Special Sunday Club have provided motivation in the form of their frequent questions and enthusiasm. They are the best. Finally, I could/would not have written this book without James Curran, who encouraged me from the start and has been endlessly patient over the many evenings and weekends I have spent working. Happily, he loves art too, although I did have to leave him on a bench in the Prado when it all became too much. Thank you all.

Catherine Daunt

ENDNOTES

1   Robert Enright, 'Resonant Surgeries: The Collaged World of Wangechi Mutu', *Border Crossings*, 105 (February 2008). https://bordercrossingsmag.com/article/resonant-surgeries-the-collaged-world-of-wangechi-mutu (accessed 1 June 2025).

2   'Address to Pratt Institute, November 1958', Rothko's papers, in Mark Rothko, *Writings on Art*, ed. by Miguel López-Remiro (New Haven: Yale University Press, 2006), pp. 125–8 (p. 125).

3   Pliny the Elder, *Natural History, Volume IX: Books 33–35*, translated by H. Rackham. *Loeb Classical Library 394* (Cambridge, MA: Harvard University Press, 1952), 35: 36.

4   Ibid.

5   Ibid.

6   Ibid.

7   Ibid.

8   Giorgio Vasari, *The Lives of the Artists*, translated by Julia Conaway Bondanella and Peter Bondanella, first published 1991 (Oxford: Oxford University Press, 2009), pp. 15–16.

9   Dante Alighieri, 'Purgatory, XI, 94–96, *Divine Comedy*, translated by Allen Mandelbaum, 1980–84. https://digitaldante.columbia.edu/dante/divine-comedy (accessed 24 April 2025).

10 Vasari, p. 35.

11 Giovanni Boccaccio, *Decameron*, translated by J. M. Rigg (London, 1921, first printed 1903), Sixth Day, Novel V. www.brown.edu/Departments/Italian_Studies/dweb/texts (accessed 24 April 2025).

12 Martin Kemp, ed., *Leonardo: On Painting* (New Haven and London: Yale University Press, 1989), p. 193.

13 Leo Jansen, Hans Luijten and Nienke Bakker, eds, *Vincent van Gogh – The Letters* (Amsterdam and The Hague: Van Gogh Museum and Huygens ING, 2009) www.vangoghletters.org, letter 683 (accessed 1 May 2025).

14 Henri Matisse, 'Notes d'un peintre', *La Grande Revue*, II, 24 (25 December 1908), pp. 731–45, published in English as 'Notes of a Painter, 1908' Flam, Jack, ed., *Matisse on Art*, revised edition (Berkeley, Los Angeles and London: University of California Press, 1997), pp. 30–43 (pp. 41–2).

15 E. H. Gombrich, 'The Earliest Description of Bosch's Garden of Delight', *Journal of the Warburg and Courtauld Institues*, vol. 30 (1967), pp. 403–6.

16 Martin Kemp, ed., *Leonardo: On Painting*, selected and translated by Martin Kemp and Margaret Walker (New Haven and London: Yale University Press, 1989, Nota Bene ed. 2001), p. 16.

17 Mary D. Garrard, *Artemisia Gentileschi: the image of the female hero in Italian Baroque art* (Princeton, N.J.: Princeton University Press, 1989), Appendix B: 'Testimony of the Rape Trial of 1612', pp. 403–87 (p. 462).

18 Quoted in Patrizia Cavazzini, 'Orazio and Artemisia: From "such an ugly deed" to "honours and favours at the English court"' in Letizia Treves et al, *Artemisia* (London: National Gallery, distributed by Yale University Press, 2020), pp. 32–45 (p. 32); quoted in Letizia Treves, 'Artemisia portraying her self', in Treves et al, pp. 64–77 (p. 66).

19 Jansen et al, letter 534 (accessed 14 April 2025).

20 William Hogarth and Martin Myrone, *Anecdotes of William Hogarth: Written by Himself* (London: Pallas Athene, 2024), p. 31.

21 Jonathan Jones, '"Cultural appropriation is a two-way thing": Yinka Shonibare on Picasso, masks and the fashion for black artists', *Guardian*, 14 June 2021. www.theguardian.com/artanddesign/2021/jun/14/masks-monsters-masterpieces-yinka-shonibare-picasso-africa (accessed 18 September 2025).

22 Sarah Symmons, ed., *Goya: A Life in Letters*, with translations by Philip Troutman (London: Pimlico, 2004), p. 237.

23 Ibid, p. 241.

24 Ibid, p. 258.

25 Timothy Clark, 'Late Hokusai, backwards', in *Hokusai: Beyond the Great Wave*, ed. by Timothy Clark (Thames & Hudson in collaboration with the British Museum, 2017), pp. 12–27 (p. 17).

26 Henry D. Smith II, *Hokusai: One Hundred Views of Mount Fuji* (London: Thames & Hudson; New York: George Braziller, 1988), p. 7 (translation Henry D. Smith II).

27 *True Briton*, 4 May 1799, quoted in Sam Smiles, *The Turner Book* (London: Tate, 2006), p. 70.

28 'The Royal Academy Exhibition', *The Times*, 4 May 1841, p. 4.

29 *The Spectator*, 11 February 1837, quoted in Smiles, pp. 88–9.

30 Charles Robert Leslie, *Autobiographical Recollections* (London: J. Murray, 1860), vol. 1, p. 202.

31 British Library, Add. MS 46151, K, f. 22v, quoted in Smiles, p. 182.

32 Quoted in Catherine Hewitt, *Art is a Tyrant: The Unconventional Life of Rosa Bonheur* (London: Icon Books, 2020), p. 101.

33 Anna Klumpke, *Rosa Bonheur: The Artist's (Auto)Biography*, translated by Gretchen van Slyke (University of Michigan Press, 2001), p. 204.

34 Quoted in Klumpke, p. xviii.

35 Quoted in Daniel Wildenstein, *Monet or The Triumph of Impressionism* (Taschen, 1999), p. 69.

36 André Masson, 'Monet le fondateur', *Verve* 7, no. 27–8 (1952), p. 68.

37 Jansen et al, letter 249 (accessed 13 March 2025).

38 Ibid, letter 249 (accessed 13 March 2025).

39 Judy Sund, 'Van Gogh's Lovers' in *Van Gogh: Poets and Lovers*, ed. by Cornelia Homburg with Christopher Riopelle (London: National Gallery; New Haven, Connecticut: Yale University Press, 2024), pp. 81–97 (p. 88).

40 Jansen et al, letter 628 (accessed 13 March 2025).

41 Ibid, letter 698 (accessed 13 March 2025).

42 Jansen et al, letter 712 (accessed 13 March 2025).

43 Hans Kollwitz, ed., *The Diary and letters of Kaethe Kollwitz*, translated by Richard and Clara Winston (Evanston, Ill: Northwestern University Press, 1988), p. 96.

44 Ibid, p. 43.

45 Ibid, p. 42.

46 Wilhelm II, 'True Art' (18 December 1901), translated by Angela A. Kurtz, reproduced online at www.germanhistorydocs.ghi-dc.org/sub_document.cfm?document_id=720 (accessed 20 April 2025).

47 Kollwitz, p. 72.

48 Ibid, p. 72.

49 Ibid, p. 96.

50 Ibid, p. 89.

51 É. Tériade, 'Matisse Speaks', *Art News Annual*, 21, 1952, pp. 40–71, published as 'Statements to Tériade: Matisse Speaks, 1951' in Jack Flam, ed., *Matisse on Art*, revised edition (Berkeley and Los Angeles, California and London: University of California Press), pp. 199–207 (p. 200).

52 Henri Matisse, 'Notes d'un peintre', *La Grande Revue*, II, 24 (25 December 1908), pp. 731–45, published in English as 'Notes of a Painter, 1908' in Flam, pp. 30–43 (p. 42).

53 Tériade, p. 201.

54 Claudine Grammont, *Matisse in the Barnes Foundation*, vol. 2 (New York: Thames & Hudson, 2015), pp. 46–60.

55 Tériade, p. 202.

56 Henri Matisse, cit. in André Verdet, 'A propos du dessin et des odalisques', in *Entretiens, notes et écrits sur la peinture: Braque, Léger, Matisse, Picasso* (Paris, 1978), pp. 121–8 (p. 124), English translation by John Elderfield, in Stephanie D'Alessandro and John Elderfield, *Matisse: Radical Invention 1913–1917* (New Haven and London: Yale University Press, 2010), p. 310.

57 Henri Matisse with Pierre Courthion, *Chatting with Henri Matisse: The Lost 1941 Interview*, ed. Serge Guilbaut (Los Angeles, 2013), p. 107 quoted in Raphaël Bouvier, ed., *Matisse: Invitation to the Voyage*, pp. 12–22 (p. 20).

58 Russell Warren Howe, 'Half-an-Hour With Matisse', *Apollo,*

XLIX (February 1949), p. 29, published as 'Interview with R. W. Howe, 1949' in Flam, pp. 184–7 (p. 185).

59   Henri Matisse, *Jazz*, Paris, 1947, text published in English in Flam, pp. 169–74 (p. 172).

60   Henri Matisse, 'Océanie, tentre murale', *Labyrinthe* 2, no. 3 (December 1946), pp. 22–3, published in English as 'Oceania, 1946', in Flam, p. 169.

61   Herbert Read, letter to *The Times*, 26 October 1956, quoted in Roland Penrose, *Picasso, his life and work* (Berkeley: University of California Press, 1981), p. 307.

62   Michael C. FitzGerald, *Picasso and American Art* (New York: Whitney Museum of American Art; New Haven: in association with Yale University Press, 2006), p. 196.

63   B. H. Friedman, 'An Interview with Lee Krasner Pollock' in *Jackson Pollock: Black and White* (New York: Marlborough-Gerson Gallery, 1969, pp. 7–10 (p. 36).

64   'Picasso Speaks: A Statement by the Artist', *The Arts*, New York (May 1923), pp. 315–26, reprinted in Alfred H. Barr, Jr, ed, *Picasso: Forty Years of His Art* (New York: Museum of Modern Art, 1939), pp. 9–12 (p. 11).

65   Kazimir Malevich, 'From Cubism and Futurism to Suprematism: The New Realism in Painting', translation from T. Anderson, ed., *K.S. Malevich: Essays on Art 1915–1933*, vol. I (Copenhagen, 1969), reproduced in Charles Harrison and Paul Wood, *Art in Theory 1900–1990* (London: Blackwell, 1992), pp. 166–76 (pp. 168, 175).

66   Kazimir Malevich, *The Non-Objective World*, translated from German by Howard Deartsyne (Chicago: Paul Theobald & Co., 1959), p.68.

67   Kazimir Malevich, 'From Cubism and Futurism to Suprematism: The New Realism in Painting', in Charles Harrison and Paul Wood, *Art in Theory 1900–1990* (London: Blackwell, 1992), pp. 166–76 (p. 166).

68   Selden Rodman, *Conversations with Artists* (New York: Devin-Adair Co., 1957), p. 93.

69 Ibid, pp. 93–94.

70 See for example 'Letter to the Whitechapel Gallery', 1961, reproduced in Mark Rothko, *Writings on Art*, ed. by Miguel López-Remiro (New Haven: Yale University Press, 2006), pp. 145–6.

71 'Notes from an interview by William Seitz, January 22 1952' in Rothko, pp. 75–79 (p. 75).

72 John Fischer, 'The Easy Chair: Mark Rothko, Portrait of the Artist as an Angry Man', 1970, based on an interview in 1959 and published in *Harper's* (July 1970), pp. 16–23, reproduced in Rothko, pp. 130–8 (p. 131).

73 'A Talk with Mark Rothko', 1961, *Yorkshire Post*, 11 October 1961, p. 8, reproduced in Rothko, p. 147.

74 Barbara Hepworth, 'The excitement of discovering the nature of carving 1903–1930', in *Barbara Hepworth: Carvings and Drawings*, with an introduction by Herbert Read, London, 1952, reproduced in Sophie Bowness, ed., *Barbara Hepworth: Writings and Conversations* (London: Tate, 2015), pp. 58–60 (p. 58).

75 Ibid.

76 'Approach to Sculpture', *Studio*, London, vol. 132, no. 643 (October 1946), reproduced in Bowness, pp. 32–7 (p. 37).

77 Ibid.

78 'Statements by Hepworth in six autobiographical sections in *Barbara Hepworth: Carvings and Drawings*, with an introduction by Herbert Read, London, 1952, reproduced in Bowness, pp. 57–73 (p. 60).

79 Barbara Hepworth, 'Sculpture' in *Circle: International Survey of Constructive Art*, ed. by Leslie Martin, Ben Nicholson and Naum Gabo, first published in 1937 (New York: Praeger Publishers, 1971), pp. 113–16 (p. 116).

80 Speech made at the unveiling of the United Nations *Single Form* on 11 June 1964, reproduced in Bowness, p. 181.

81 'Statements by Hepworth in six autobiographical sections', in Bowness, p. 68.

82 'Art: Mexican Autobiography', *TIME*, 27 April 1953, p. 92.

83 www.moma.org/collection/works/78333 [accessed 20 June 2025].

84 Frida Kahlo, *The Diary of Frida Kahlo: An Intimate Self-Portrait*, introduction by Carlos Fuentes, essay and commentaries by Sarah M. Lowe (New York: Harry N. Abrams, 1995, p. 274.

85 Antonio Rodríguez, 'Una pintura extraordinaria', *Así*, Mexico City, 17 March 1945, quoted in English in Andrea Kettenmann, *Frida Kahlo, 1907–1954: Pain and Passion* (Cologne and Los Angeles: Taschen, 2002), p. 18.

86 Kahlo, pp. 285, 287.

87 Much of the factual information in this chapter relies on the recent exhibition catalogue: Kelli Cole, Jennifer Green and Hetti Perkins, *Emily Kam Kngwarray* (London: Tate, 2025).

88 Jacob Lawrence and Xavier Nicholas, 'Interview with Jacob Lawrence, *Callaloo*, vol. 36, no. 2 (Spring 2013), pp. 260–7 (p. 266).

89 MoMA artist's questionnaire, 1943. www.moma.org/artists/ 3418-jacob-lawrence (accessed 27 May 2025).

90 G. R. Swenson, 'What is Pop Art? Answers from 8 Painters, Part I', *ARTnews*, 62:7 (November 1963), pp. 26, 60–1 (p. 26).

91 Andy Warhol and Pat Hackett, *POPism: The Warhol Sixties* (London: Penguin Books, 2007), p. 28.

92 Swenson, p. 60.

93 Warhol and Hackett, p. 77.

94 Ibid, p. 50.

95 Derek Peck, 'Yayoi Kusama on Life and Art', *AnOther*, 8 November 2013. www.anothermag.com/art-photography/3165/ yayoi-kusama-on-life-and-art (accessed 6 June 2025).

96 Grady Turner and Yayoi Kusama, 'Yayoi Kusama', *BOMB*, No. 66 (Winter, 1999), pp. 62–9 (p. 65).

97 Donald Judd, 'Reviews and previews: New names this month', *ARTnews* (October 1959). www.artnews.com/art-news/ retrospective/from-the-archives-donald-judd-on-yayoi-kusamas-first-new-york-solo-show-in-1959-7823/ (accessed 10 June 2025).

98   Yayoi Kusama, *Infinity Net: The Autobiography of Yayoi Kusama* (London: Tate, 2013), p. 108.

99   Ibid, pp. 130–2.

100 Janet A. Kaplan, 'Deeper and Deeper: Interview with Marina Abramović', *Art Journal*, vol. 58, no. 2 (Summer, 1999), pp. 6–21 (p. 17).

101 Hannah Weitemeier, *Klein* (Taschen, 2001), p. 81.

102 Marina Abramović, *Walk Through Walls: A Memoir* (London: Penguin Books, 2016), p. 60.

103 Peggy Phelan, 'Marina Abramović: Witnessing Shadows', *Theatre Journal*, vol. 56, no. 4 (Dec 2004), pp. 569–77 (p. 576).

104 Ai Weiwei, 'Why I'll stay away from the opening ceremony of the Olympics', *Guardian*, 7 August 2008. www.theguardian.com/commentisfree/2008/aug/07/olympics2008.china.

105 Tim Lewis, 'Ai Weiwei: "An artist must be an activist"', *Observer*, 22 March 2020. www.theguardian.com/artanddesign/2020/mar/22/ai-weiwei-an-artist-must-be-an-activist (accessed 3 June 2025).

106 John Gruen, *Keith Haring: The Authorized Biography* (New York: Prentice Hall Press, 1991), p.29.

107 https://assets.moma.org/documents/moma_press-release_327369.pdf (accessed 1 June 2025).

108 'Käthe Kollwitz' in Guerrilla Girls and Whitney Chadwick, *Confessions of the Guerrilla Girls* (London: Pandora, 1995), p. 13.

109 Nasher Sculpture Center, 'Guerrilla Girls Guide To Behaving Badly', video 2021. https://www.youtube.com/watch?v=eGflyUXWeso (accessed 15 March 2025).

110 'Rosalba Carriera' in Guerrilla Girls and Chadwick, p. 13.

111 Guerrilla Girls and Chadwick, p. 16.

112 Guerrilla Girls and Chadwick, p. 28.

113 'Rachel Doesn't Live Here Anymore. On Rachel Whiteread's *House* (1993), *Frieze* (6 January 1994). www.frieze.com/article/rachel-doesnt-live-here-anymore (accessed 25 May 2025).

114 Ibid.

115 Alison McDonald, 'Rachel Whiteread: Casting History', *Gagosian Quarterly*, Summer 2025. www.gagosian.com/quarterly/2025/04/30/interview-rachel-whiteread-casting-history/ (accessed 24 May 2025).

116 Robert Enright, 'Resonant Surgeries: The Collaged World of Wangechi Mutu', *Border Crossings*, 105 (February 2008). https://bordercrossingsmag.com/article/resonant-surgeries-the-collaged-world-of-wangechi-mutu (accessed 1 June 2025).

117 Marika Preziuso, 'Is America Really Full? A conversation with Wangechi Mutu', *Transition*, no. 129 (2020), pp. 26–45 (p. 32).

118 Enright.

119 Wangechi Mutu, 'Art, this old medicine, 2021', in Adrienne Edwards et al, *Wangechi Mutu* (Phaidon, 2022), pp. 128–34 (p. 128).

120 Jansen et al, letter 249 (accessed 25 March 2025).

IMAGE PERMISSIONS

Page 1

Hieronymus Bosch (*c.*1450–1516), *The Garden of Earthly Delights*, 1490–1500, oil on oak panel (Museo del Prado, Madrid) © Universal History Archive/Universal Images Group via Getty Images

Page 2

Giotto (1266/7–1337), *Lamentation (The Mourning of Christ)*, about 1305, fresco (Scrovegni Chapel, Padua) © Public domain

Rembrandt van Rijn (1606–69), *Self-Portrait with Two Circles*, about 1666, oil on canvas (Kenwood House, London, English Heritage) © Fine Art Images/Heritage Images/Getty Images

Page 3

Artemisia Gentileschi (1593–1654 or later), *Judith beheading Holofernes*, 1613–14, oil on canvas (Uffizi Galleries, Florence) © Luciano Romano/Electa/Mondadori Portfolio via Getty Images

Francisco de Goya (1746–1828), *Saturn* from the *Black Paintings*, 1820-3, mural transferred to canvas (Museo del Prado, Madrid) © Fine Art Images/Heritage Images/Getty Images

Page 4

Katsushika Hokusai (1760–1849), *Under the Wave off Kanagawa* or *The Great Wave* from *Thirty-six Views of Mount Fuji*, about 1830-2, woodblock print (Metropolitan Museum of Art, New York) © Buyenlarge/Getty Images

Vincent van Gogh (1853–90), *Starry Night over the Rhône*, 1888, oil on canvas (Musée d'Orsay, Paris) © Photo12/Universal Images Group via Getty Images

Page 5

Käthe Kollwitz (1867–1945), *Woman with Dead Child*, 1903, etching and soft ground etching with black chalk, graphite and metallic plates (National Gallery of Art, Washington DC) © Heritage Art/Heritage Images via Getty Images

Page 6

Henri Matisse (1869–1954), *The Joy of Life*, 1905–6, oil on canvas (The Barnes Foundation, Philadelphia) © Heritage Art/Heritage Images via Getty Images

Page 7

Frida Kahlo (1907–54), *The Two Fridas*, 1939, oil on canvas (Museo de Arte Moderno, Mexico City) © Fine Art Images/Heritage Images/ Getty Images

Page 8

Jacob Lawrence (1917–2000), *The Migration Series*, panel no. 1, Casein tempera on hardboard, 1940–41. (Phillips Collection, Washington DC) © 2026 The Jacob and Gwendolyn Knight Lawrence Foundation, Seattle / Artists Rights Society (ARS), New York and DACS, London / © GRANGER Historical Picture Archive/Alamy